# THE DARK & BLOODY

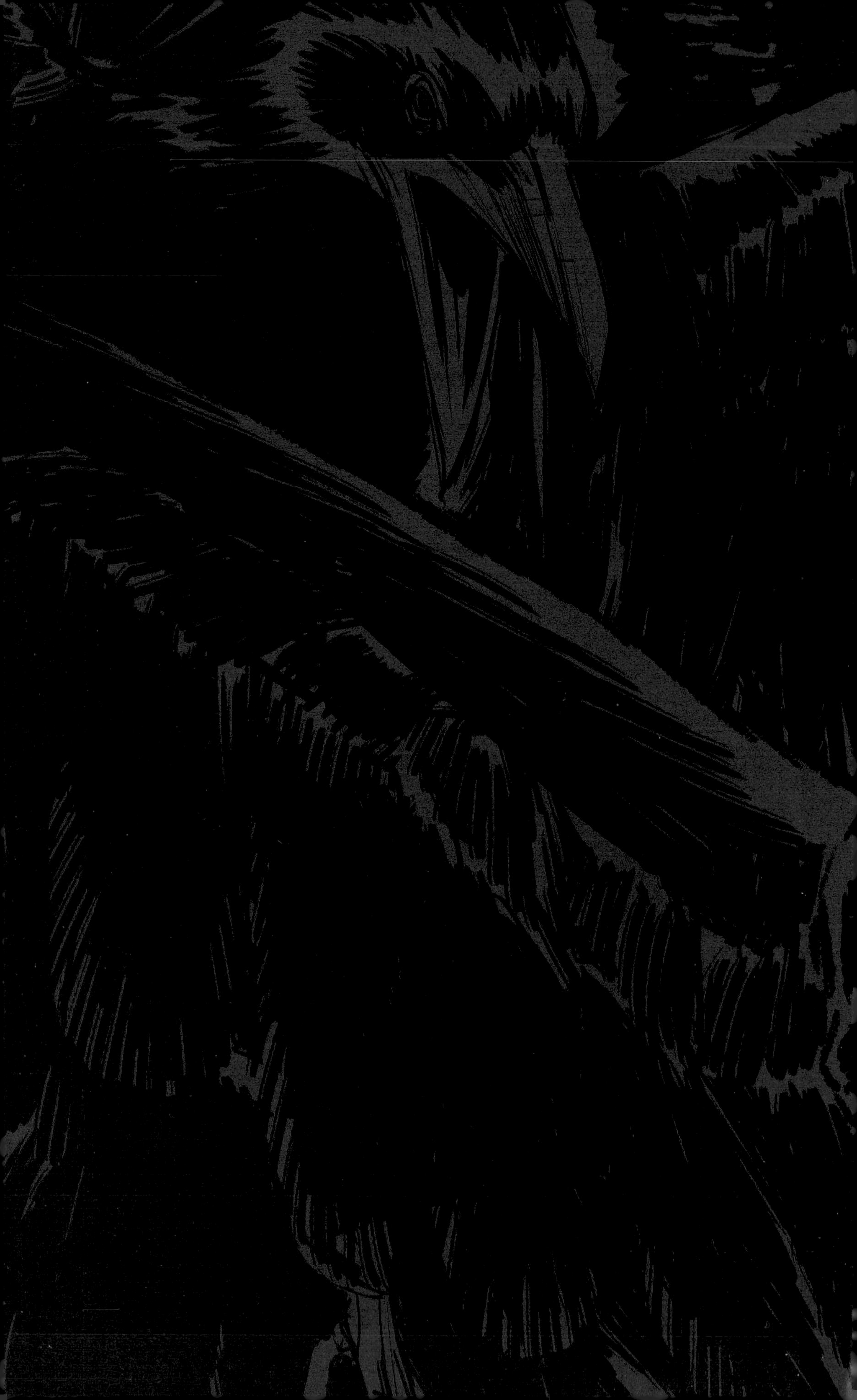

# THE DARK & BLOODY

SHAWN ALDRIDGE
Writer

SCOTT GODLEWSKI
Artist

PATRICIA MULVIHILL
Colorist

CLEM ROBINS
Letterer

TYLER CROOK
Cover Art and Original Series Covers

THE DARK & BLOODY
created by
SHAWN ALDRIDGE and SCOTT GODLEWSKI

**JAMIE S. RICH** Editor – Original Series
**MOLLY MAHAN** Associate Editor – Original Series
**JEB WOODARD** Group Editor – Collected Editions
**SCOTT NYBAKKEN** Editor – Collected Edition
**STEVE COOK** Design Director – Books
**DAMIAN RYLAND** Publication Design

**SHELLY BOND** VP & Executive Editor – Vertigo

**DIANE NELSON** President
**DAN DIDIO** and **JIM LEE** Co-Publishers
**GEOFF JOHNS** Chief Creative Officer
**AMIT DESAI** Senior VP – Marketing & Global Franchise Management
**NAIRI GARDINER** Senior VP – Finance
**SAM ADES** VP – Digital Marketing
**BOBBIE CHASE** VP – Talent Development
**MARK CHIARELLO** Senior VP – Art, Design & Collected Editions
**JOHN CUNNINGHAM** VP – Content Strategy
**ANNE DEPIES** VP – Strategy Planning & Reporting
**DON FALLETTI** VP – Manufacturing Operations
**LAWRENCE GANEM** VP – Editorial Administration & Talent Relations
**ALISON GILL** Senior VP – Manufacturing & Operations
**HANK KANALZ** Senior VP – Editorial Strategy & Administration
**JAY KOGAN** VP – Legal Affairs
**DEREK MADDALENA** Senior VP – Sales & Business Development
**JACK MAHAN** VP – Business Affairs
**DAN MIRON** VP – Sales Planning & Trade Development
**NICK NAPOLITANO** VP – Manufacturing Administration
**CAROL ROEDER** VP – Marketing
**EDDIE SCANNELL** VP – Mass Account & Digital Sales
**COURTNEY SIMMONS** Senior VP – Publicity & Communications
**JIM (SKI) SOKOLOWSKI** VP – Comic Book Specialty & Newsstand Sales
**SANDY YI** Senior VP – Global Franchise Management

Logo design by **RIAN HUGHES**

**THE DARK & BLOODY**



DC Comics
2900 West Alameda Avenue
Burbank, CA 91505
Printed in the USA. First Printing.
ISBN: 978-1-4012-6459-8

Library of Congress Cataloging-in-Publication Data is available.

PEFC Certified
Printed on paper from sustainably managed forests and controlled sources
PEFC
PEFC/29-31-75
www.pefc.org

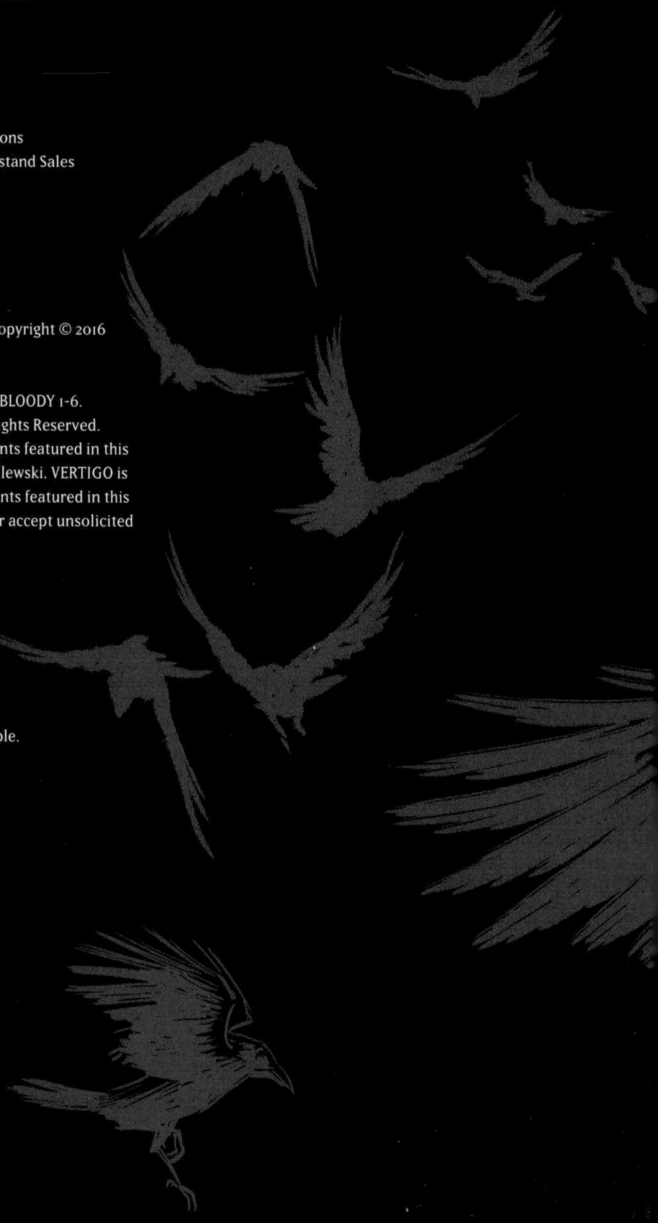

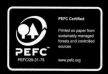

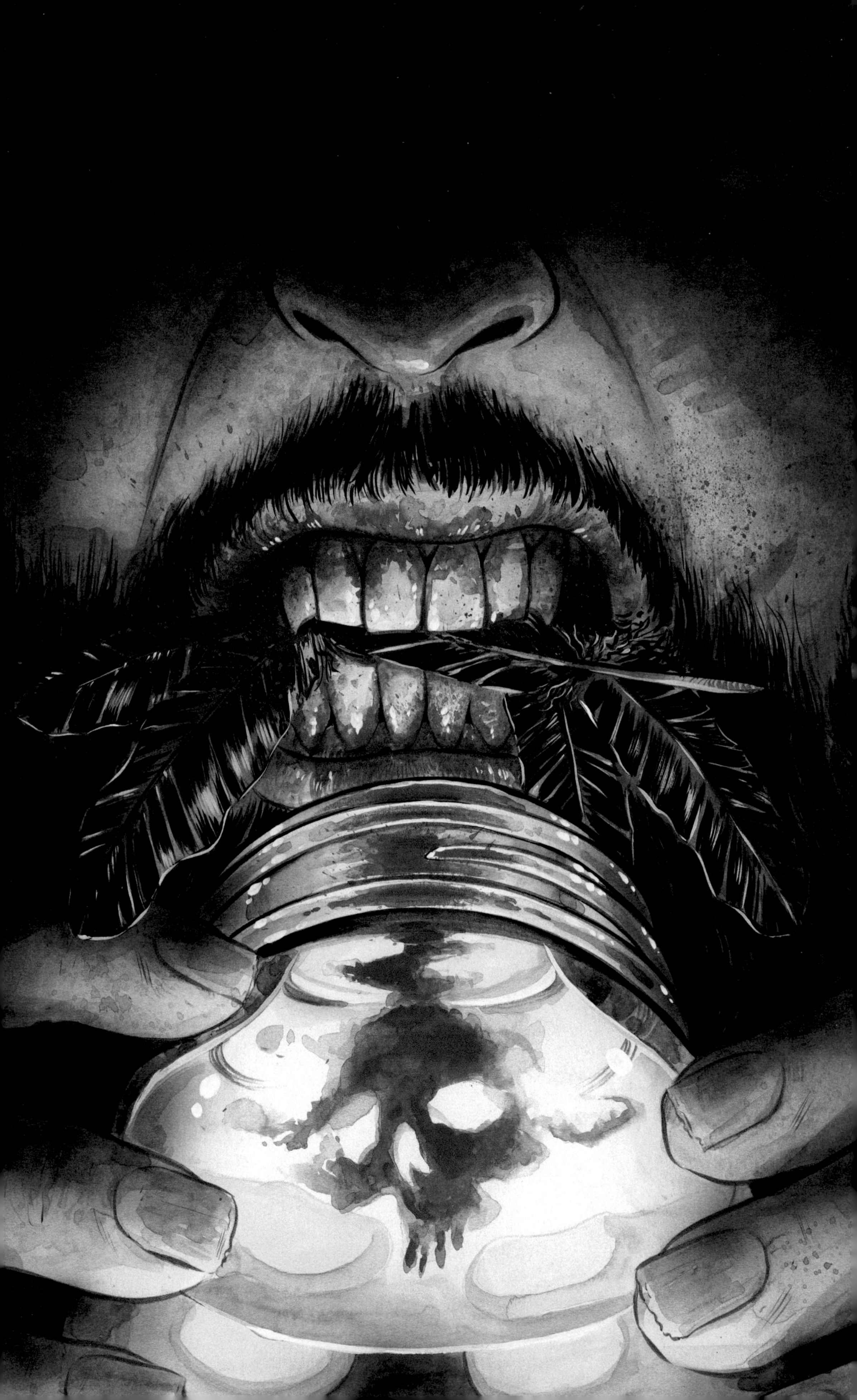

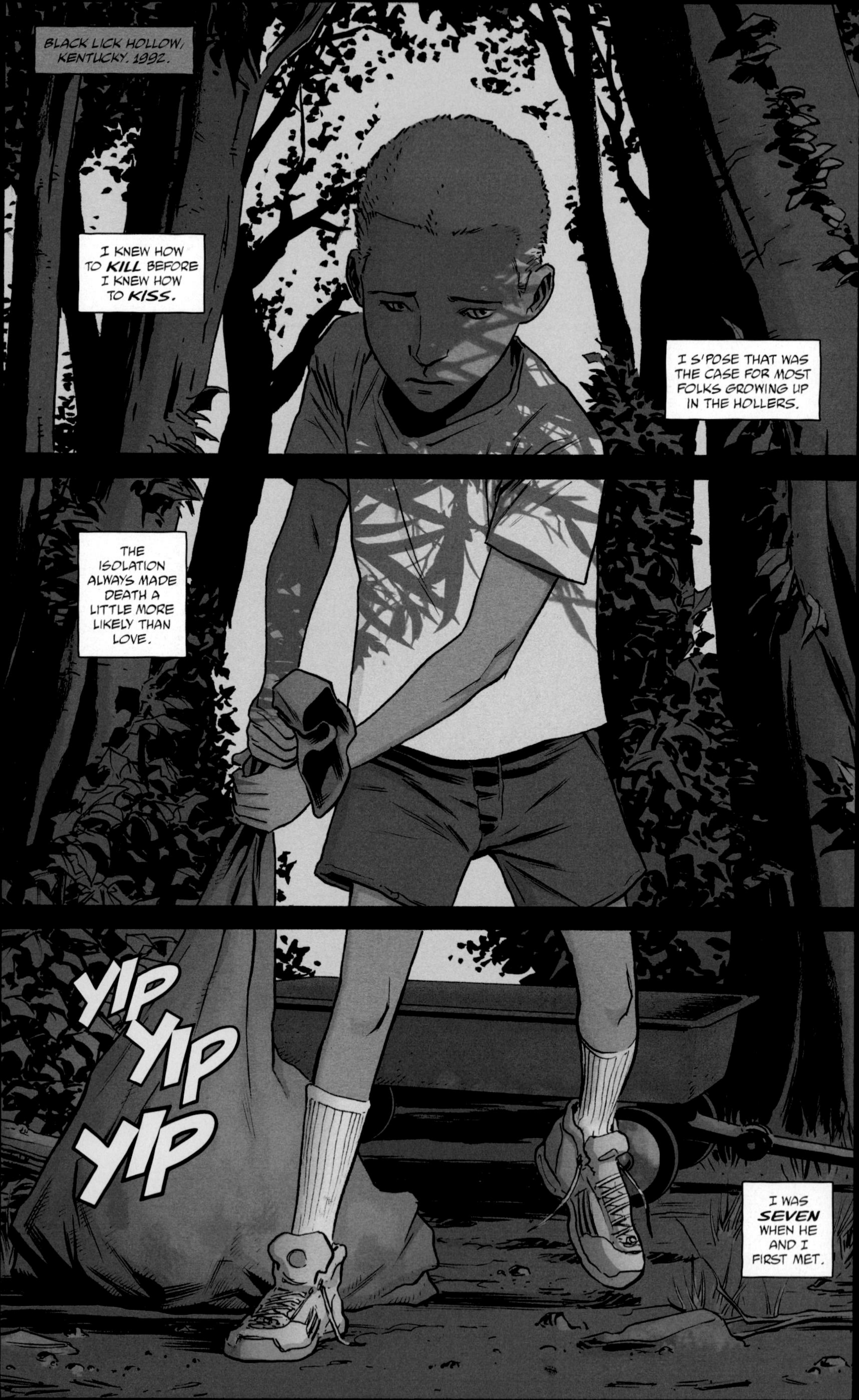
BLACK LICK HOLLOW, KENTUCKY. 1992.
I KNEW HOW TO KILL BEFORE I KNEW HOW TO KISS.
I S'POSE THAT WAS THE CASE FOR MOST FOLKS GROWING UP IN THE HOLLERS.
THE ISOLATION ALWAYS MADE DEATH A LITTLE MORE LIKELY THAN LOVE.
YIP YIP YIP
I WAS SEVEN WHEN HE AND I FIRST MET.

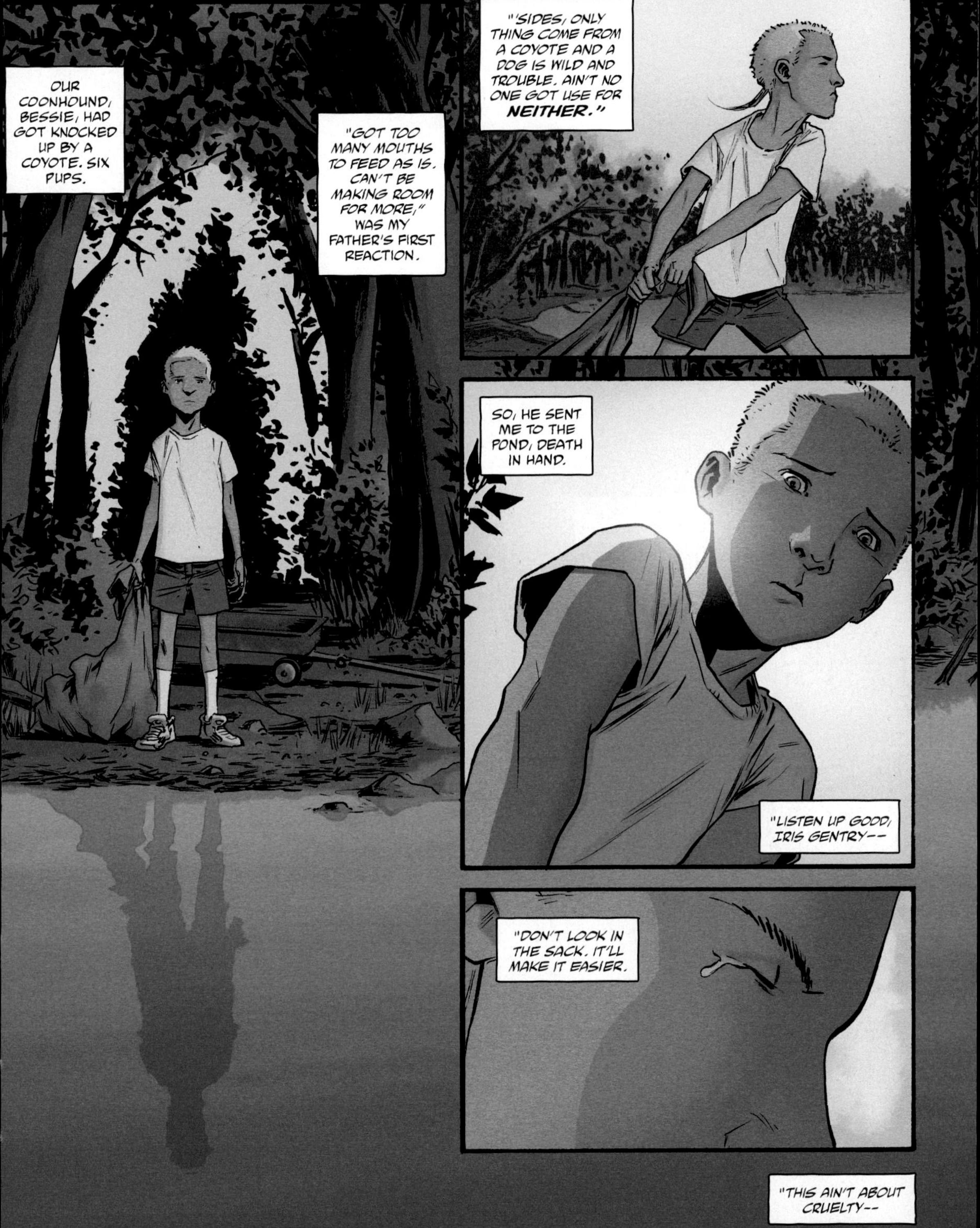
OUR COONHOUND, BESSIE, HAD GOT KNOCKED UP BY A COYOTE. SIX PUPS.
"GOT TOO MANY MOUTHS TO FEED AS IS. CAN'T BE MAKING ROOM FOR MORE," WAS MY FATHER'S FIRST REACTION.
"'SIDES, ONLY THING COME FROM A COYOTE AND A DOG IS WILD AND TROUBLE. AIN'T NO ONE GOT USE FOR NEITHER."
SO, HE SENT ME TO THE POND, DEATH IN HAND.
"LISTEN UP GOOD, IRIS GENTRY--
"DON'T LOOK IN THE SACK. IT'LL MAKE IT EASIER.
"THIS AIN'T ABOUT CRUELTY--

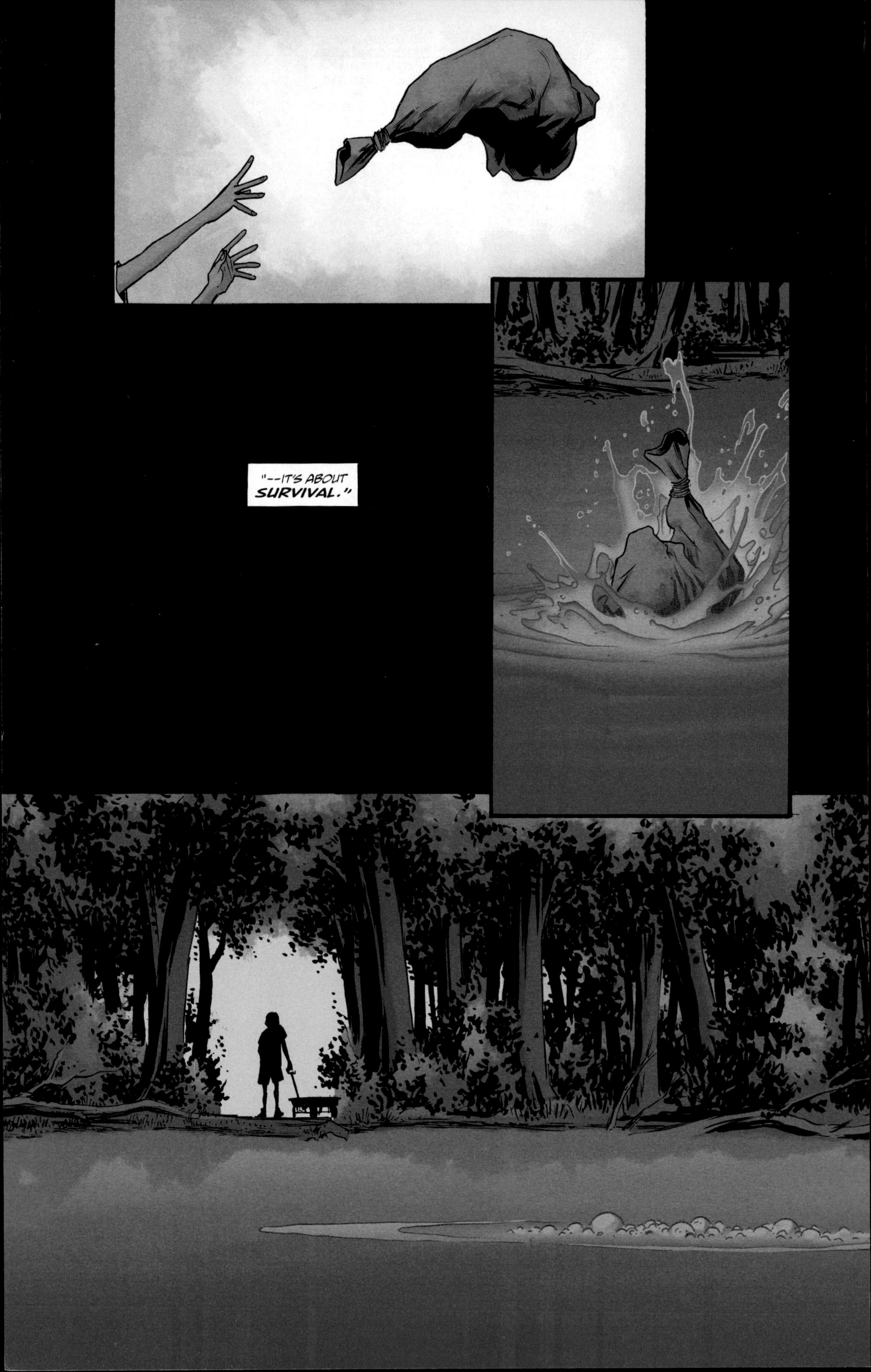
"--IT'S ABOUT SURVIVAL."

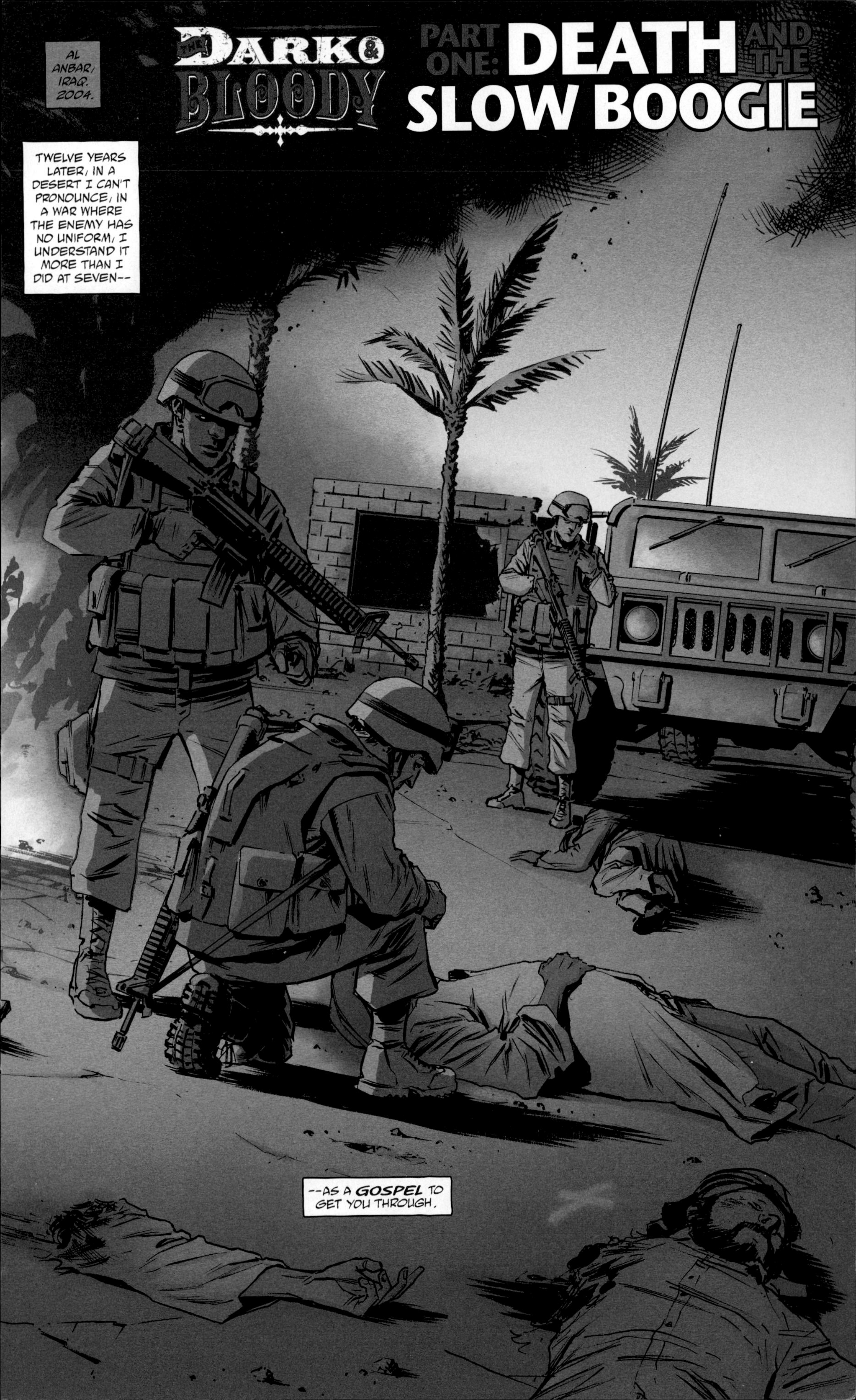

AL ANBAR, IRAQ. 2004.
THE DARK & BLOODY
PART ONE: DEATH AND THE SLOW BOOGIE
TWELVE YEARS LATER, IN A DESERT I CAN'T PRONOUNCE, IN A WAR WHERE THE ENEMY HAS NO UNIFORM, I UNDERSTAND IT MORE THAN I DID AT SEVEN--
--AS A GOSPEL TO GET YOU THROUGH.

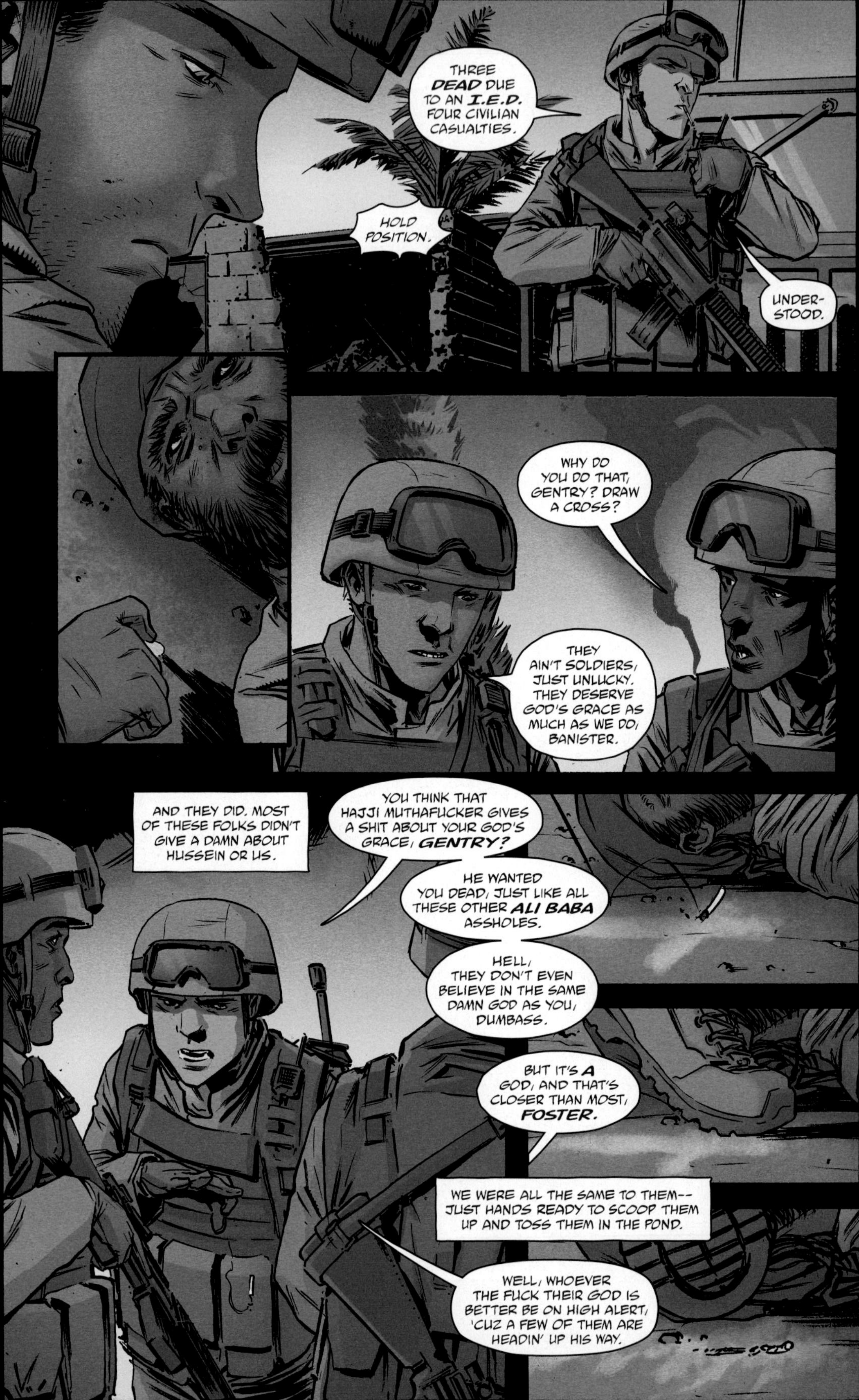
THREE DEAD DUE TO AN I.E.D. FOUR CIVILIAN CASUALTIES.
HOLD POSITION.
UNDER-STOOD.
WHY DO YOU DO THAT, GENTRY? DRAW A CROSS?
THEY AIN'T SOLDIERS, JUST UNLUCKY. THEY DESERVE GOD'S GRACE AS MUCH AS WE DO, BANISTER.
AND THEY DID. MOST OF THESE FOLKS DIDN'T GIVE A DAMN ABOUT HUSSEIN OR US.
YOU THINK THAT HAJJI MUTHAFUCKER GIVES A SHIT ABOUT YOUR GOD'S GRACE, GENTRY?
HE WANTED YOU DEAD, JUST LIKE ALL THESE OTHER ALI BABA ASSHOLES.
HELL, THEY DON'T EVEN BELIEVE IN THE SAME DAMN GOD AS YOU, DUMBASS.
BUT IT'S A GOD, AND THAT'S CLOSER THAN MOST, FOSTER.
WE WERE ALL THE SAME TO THEM-- JUST HANDS READY TO SCOOP THEM UP AND TOSS THEM IN THE POND.
WELL, WHOEVER THE FUCK THEIR GOD IS BETTER BE ON HIGH ALERT, 'CUZ A FEW OF THEM ARE HEADIN' UP HIS WAY.

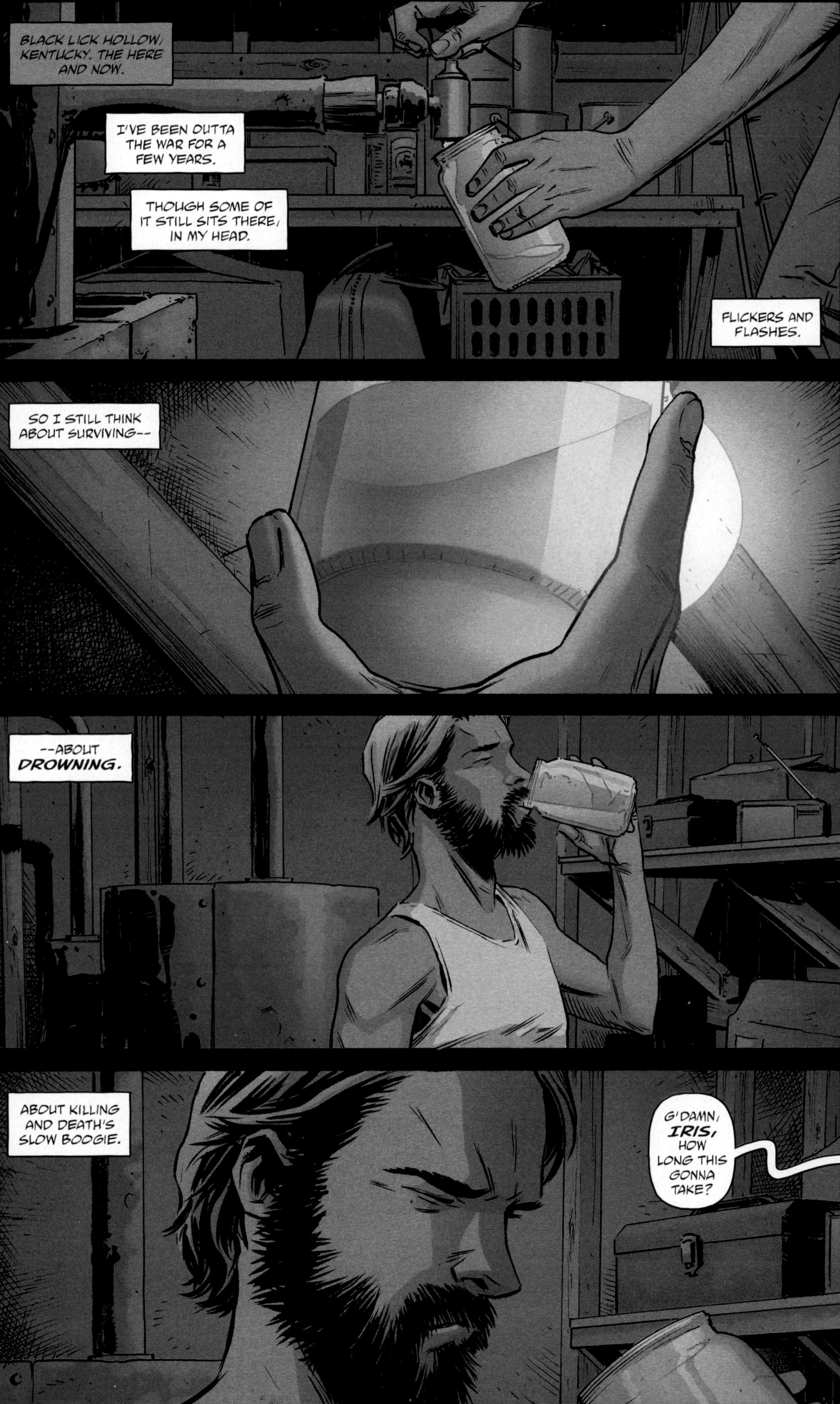
BLACK LICK HOLLOW, KENTUCKY. THE HERE AND NOW.
I'VE BEEN OUTTA THE WAR FOR A FEW YEARS.
THOUGH SOME OF IT STILL SITS THERE, IN MY HEAD.
FLICKERS AND FLASHES.
SO I STILL THINK ABOUT SURVIVING--
--ABOUT DROWNING.
ABOUT KILLING AND DEATH'S SLOW BOOGIE.
G'DAMN, IRIS, HOW LONG THIS GONNA TAKE?

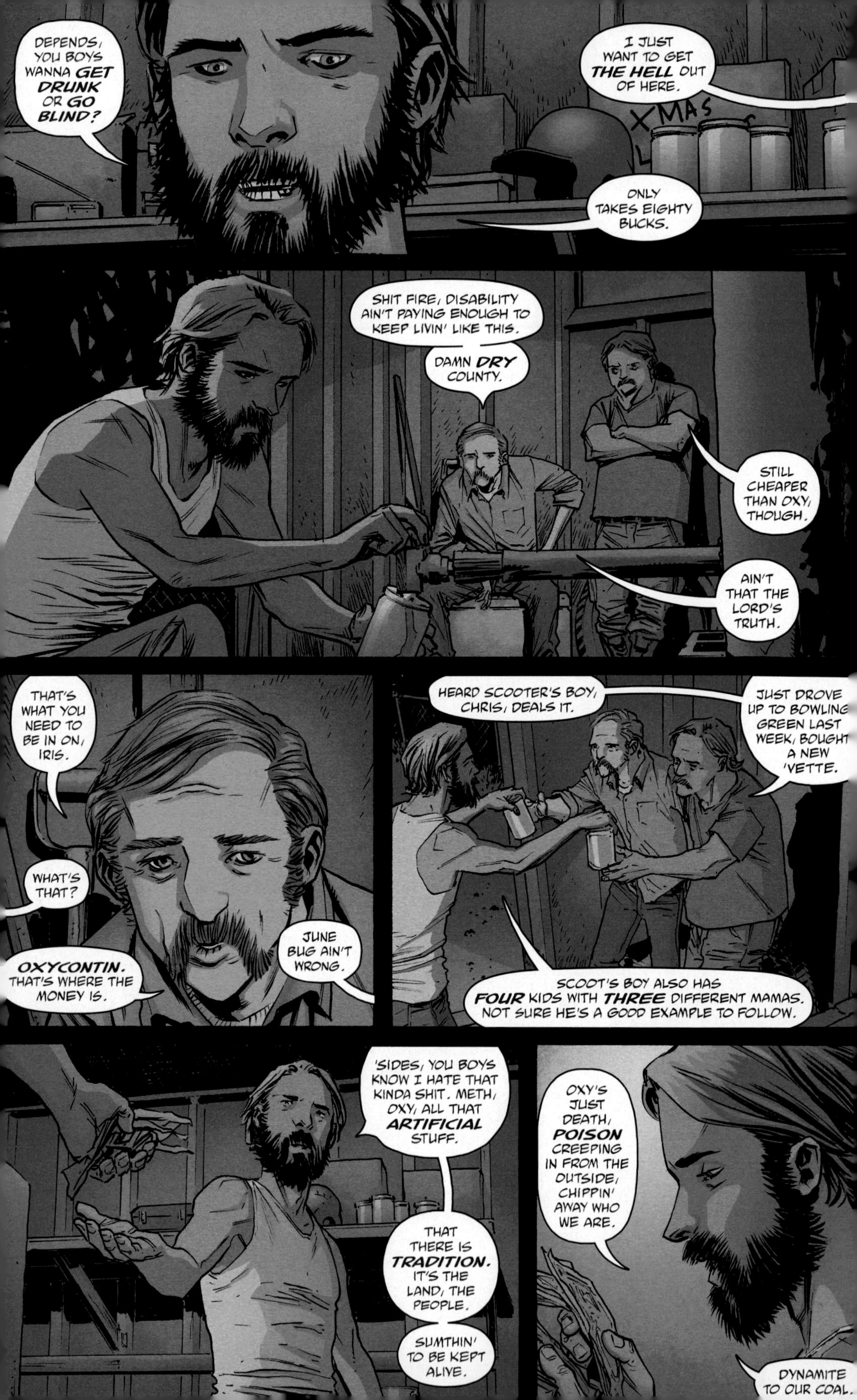
DEPENDS, YOU BOYS WANNA **GET DRUNK** OR **GO BLIND?**
I JUST WANT TO GET **THE HELL** OUT OF HERE.
ONLY TAKES EIGHTY BUCKS.
SHIT FIRE, DISABILITY AIN'T PAYING ENOUGH TO KEEP LIVIN' LIKE THIS.
DAMN **DRY** COUNTY.
STILL CHEAPER THAN OXY, THOUGH.
AIN'T THAT THE LORD'S TRUTH.
THAT'S WHAT YOU NEED TO BE IN ON, IRIS.
WHAT'S THAT?
**OXYCONTIN.** THAT'S WHERE THE MONEY IS.
JUNE BUG AIN'T WRONG.
HEARD SCOOTER'S BOY, CHRIS, DEALS IT.
JUST DROVE UP TO BOWLING GREEN LAST WEEK, BOUGHT A NEW 'VETTE.
SCOOT'S BOY ALSO HAS **FOUR** KIDS WITH **THREE** DIFFERENT MAMAS. NOT SURE HE'S A GOOD EXAMPLE TO FOLLOW.
'SIDES, YOU BOYS KNOW I HATE THAT KINDA SHIT. METH, OXY, ALL THAT **ARTIFICIAL** STUFF.
THAT THERE IS **TRADITION.** IT'S THE LAND, THE PEOPLE.
SUMTHIN' TO BE KEPT ALIVE.
OXY'S JUST DEATH, **POISON** CREEPING IN FROM THE OUTSIDE, CHIPPIN' AWAY WHO WE ARE.
DYNAMITE TO OUR COAL.

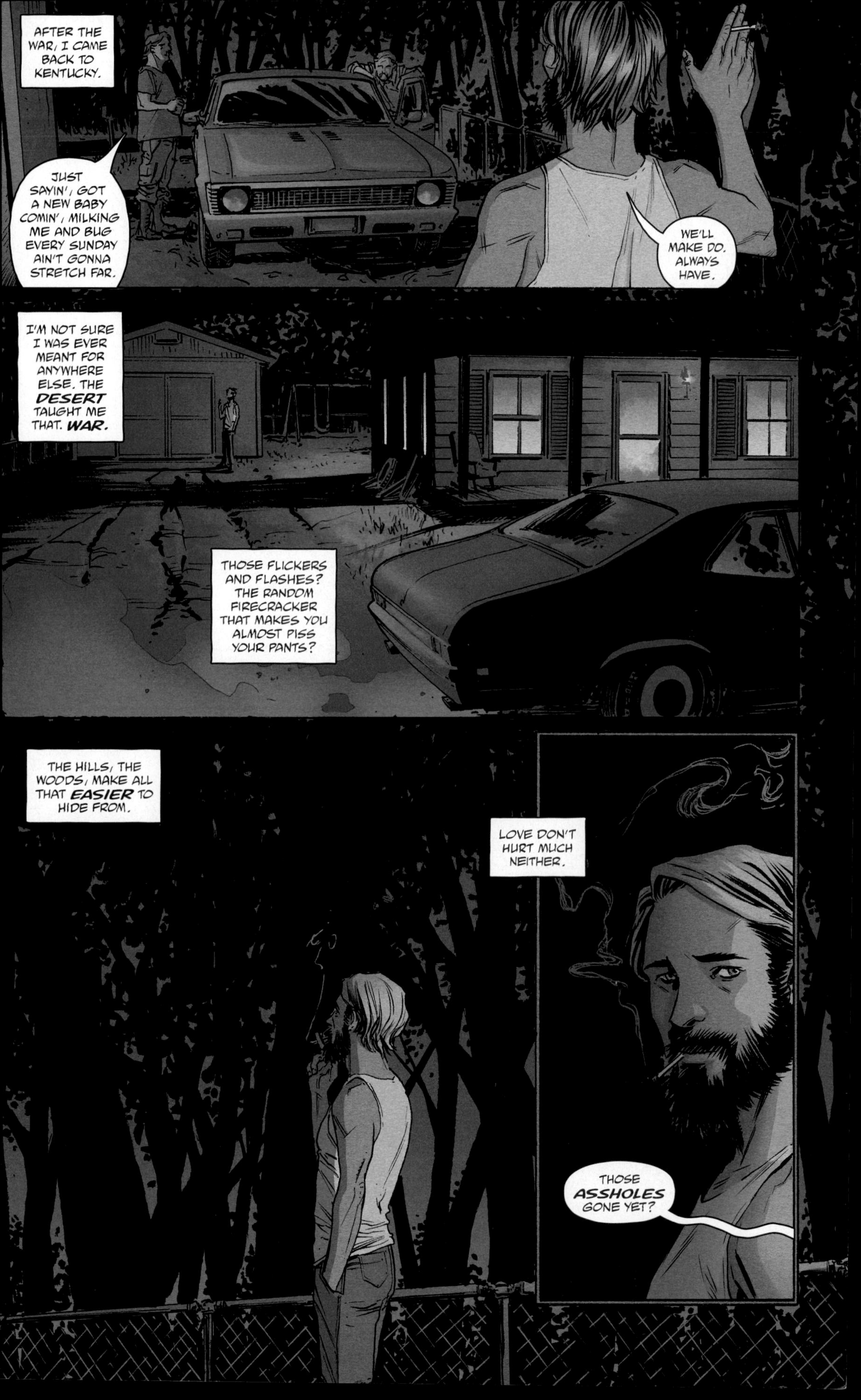
AFTER THE WAR, I CAME BACK TO KENTUCKY.
JUST SAYIN', GOT A NEW BABY COMIN', MILKING ME AND BUG EVERY SUNDAY AIN'T GONNA STRETCH FAR.
WE'LL MAKE DO. ALWAYS HAVE.
I'M NOT SURE I WAS EVER MEANT FOR ANYWHERE ELSE. THE DESERT TAUGHT ME THAT. WAR.
THOSE FLICKERS AND FLASHES? THE RANDOM FIRECRACKER THAT MAKES YOU ALMOST PISS YOUR PANTS?
THE HILLS, THE WOODS, MAKE ALL THAT EASIER TO HIDE FROM.
LOVE DON'T HURT MUCH NEITHER.
THOSE ASSHOLES GONE YET?

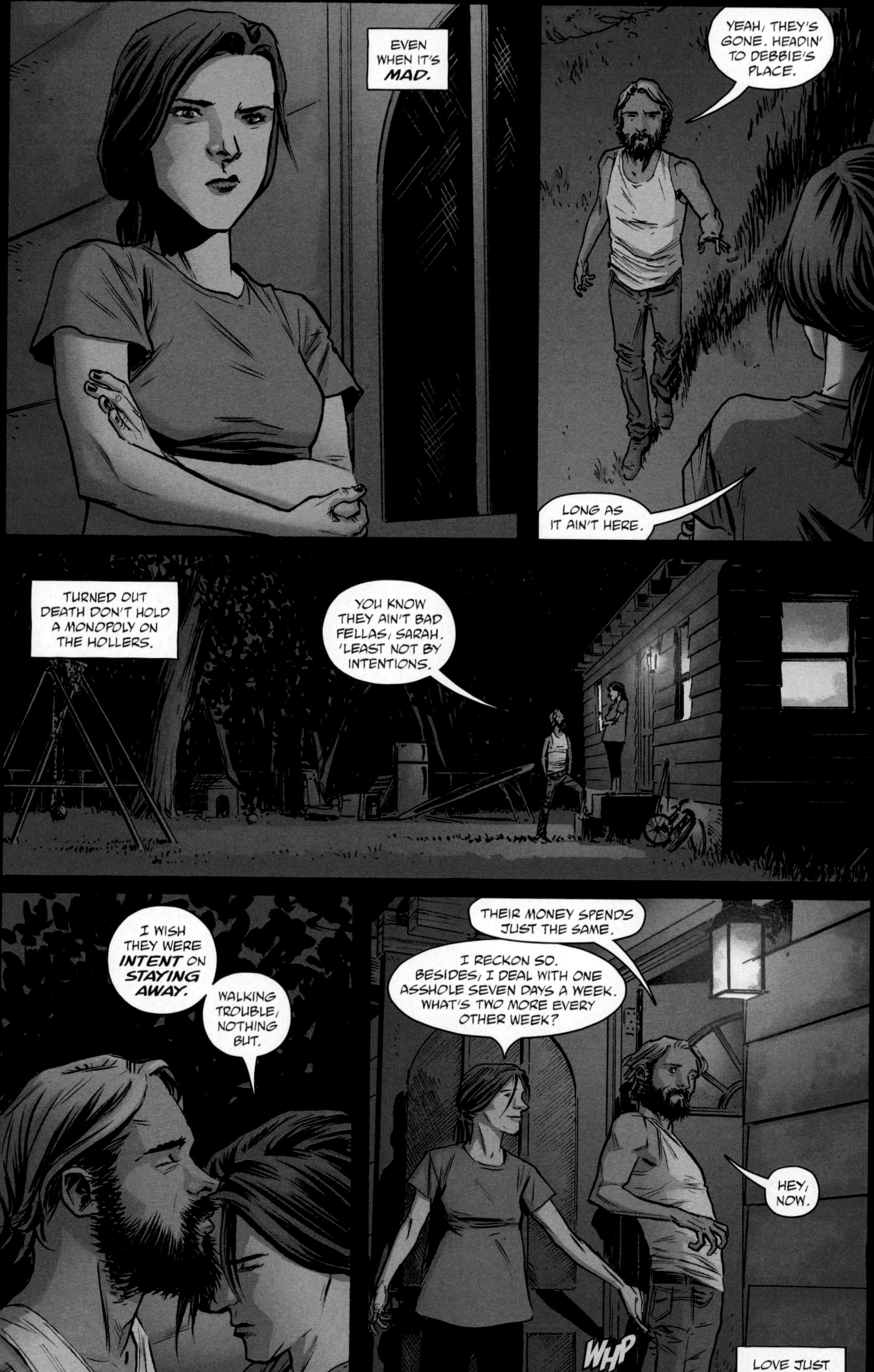
EVEN WHEN IT'S MAD.
YEAH, THEY'S GONE. HEADIN' TO DEBBIE'S PLACE.
LONG AS IT AIN'T HERE.
TURNED OUT DEATH DON'T HOLD A MONOPOLY ON THE HOLLERS.
YOU KNOW THEY AIN'T BAD FELLAS, SARAH. 'LEAST NOT BY INTENTIONS.
I WISH THEY WERE INTENT ON STAYING AWAY.
WALKING TROUBLE, NOTHING BUT.
THEIR MONEY SPENDS JUST THE SAME.
I RECKON SO. BESIDES, I DEAL WITH ONE ASSHOLE SEVEN DAYS A WEEK. WHAT'S TWO MORE EVERY OTHER WEEK?
HEY, NOW.
WHP
LOVE JUST MAKES YOU WORK FOR IT.

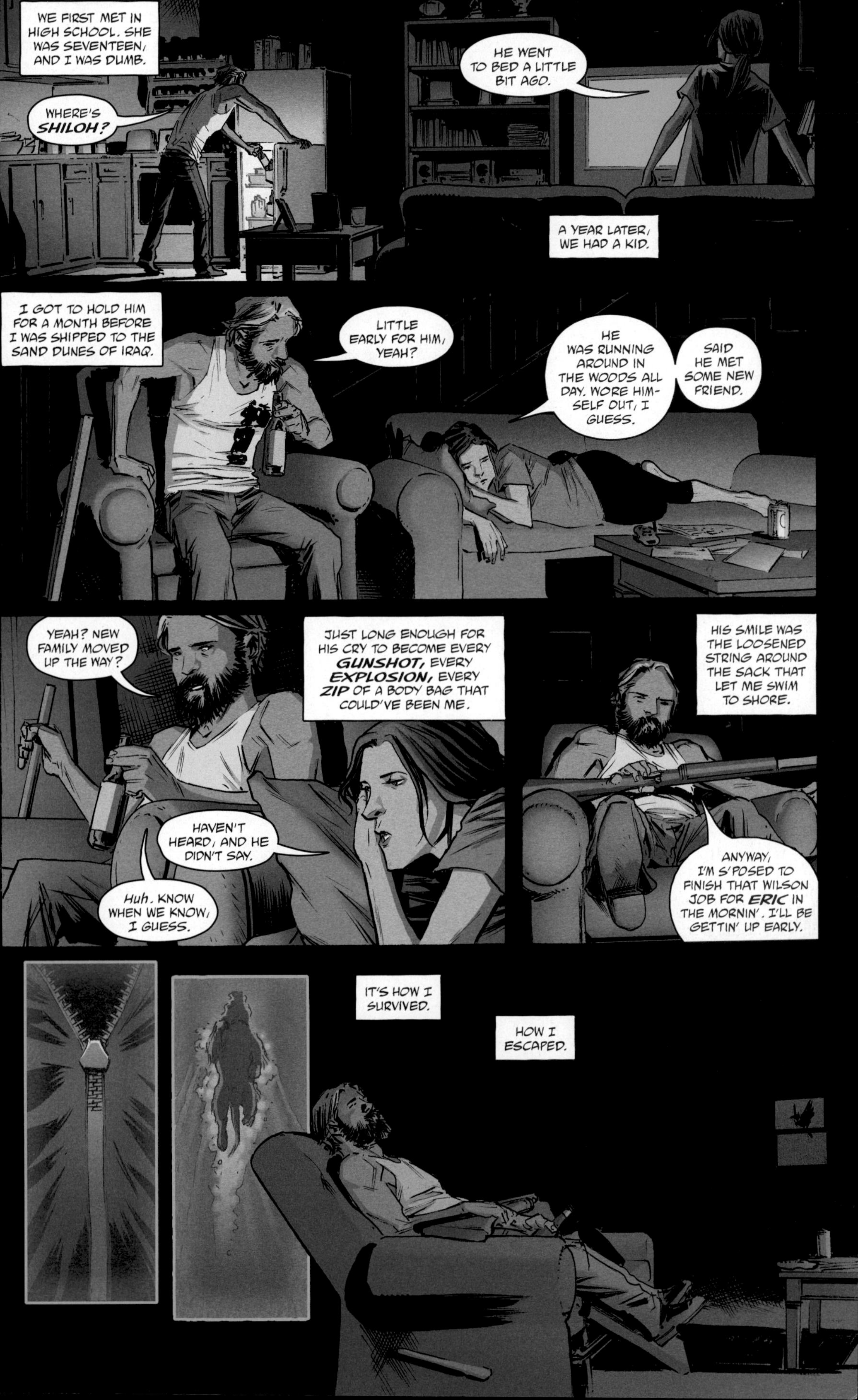
WE FIRST MET IN HIGH SCHOOL. SHE WAS SEVENTEEN, AND I WAS DUMB.
WHERE'S SHILOH?
HE WENT TO BED A LITTLE BIT AGO.
A YEAR LATER, WE HAD A KID.
I GOT TO HOLD HIM FOR A MONTH BEFORE I WAS SHIPPED TO THE SAND DUNES OF IRAQ.
LITTLE EARLY FOR HIM, YEAH?
HE WAS RUNNING AROUND IN THE WOODS ALL DAY. WORE HIM-SELF OUT, I GUESS.
SAID HE MET SOME NEW FRIEND.
YEAH? NEW FAMILY MOVED UP THE WAY?
JUST LONG ENOUGH FOR HIS CRY TO BECOME EVERY GUNSHOT, EVERY EXPLOSION, EVERY ZIP OF A BODY BAG THAT COULD'VE BEEN ME.
HAVEN'T HEARD, AND HE DIDN'T SAY.
Huh. KNOW WHEN WE KNOW, I GUESS.
HIS SMILE WAS THE LOOSENED STRING AROUND THE SACK THAT LET ME SWIM TO SHORE.
ANYWAY, I'M S'POSED TO FINISH THAT WILSON JOB FOR ERIC IN THE MORNIN'. I'LL BE GETTIN' UP EARLY.
IT'S HOW I SURVIVED.
HOW I ESCAPED.

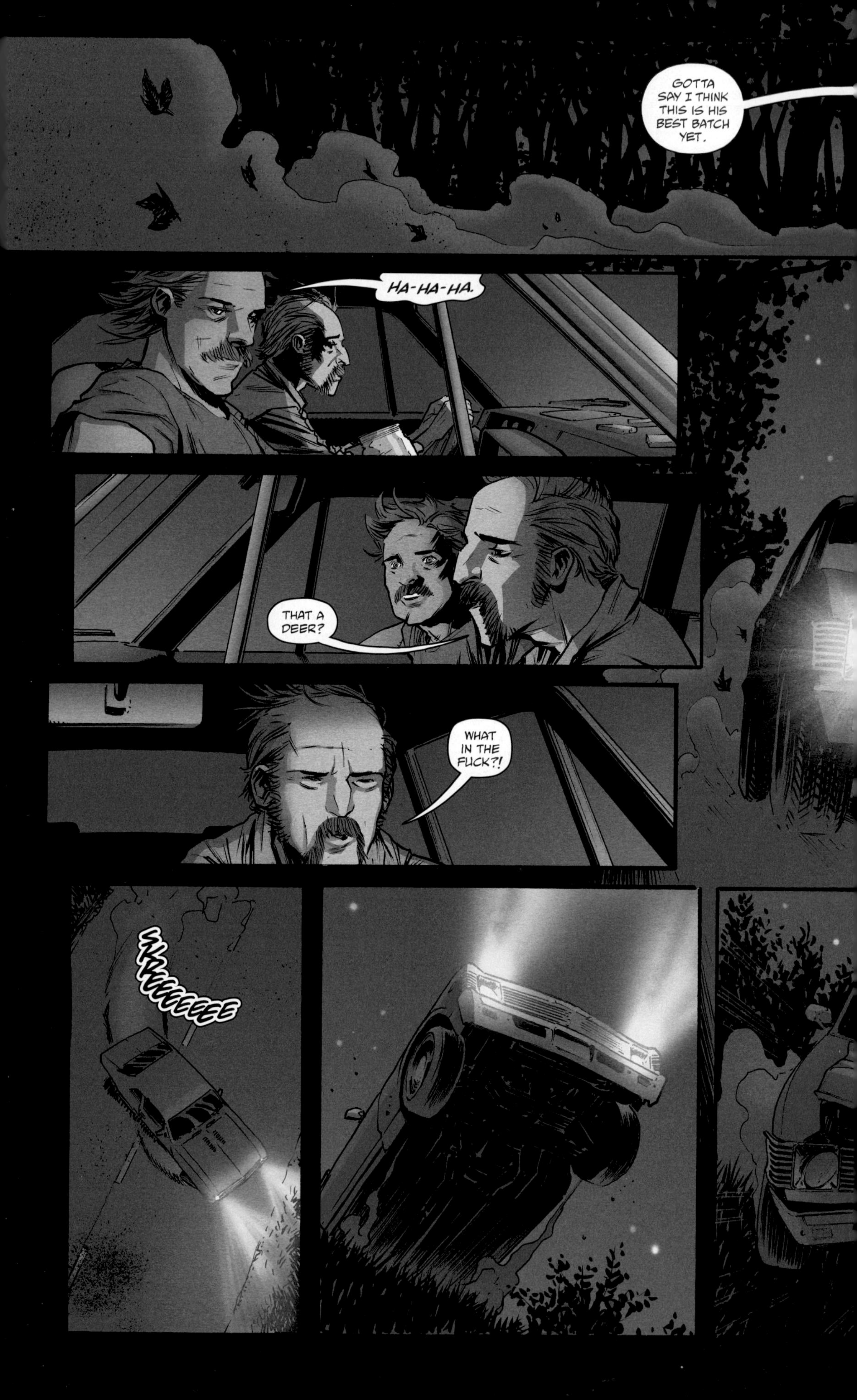
GOTTA SAY I THINK THIS IS HIS BEST BATCH YET.
HA-HA-HA.
THAT A DEER?
WHAT IN THE FUCK?!
SKREEEEEEE

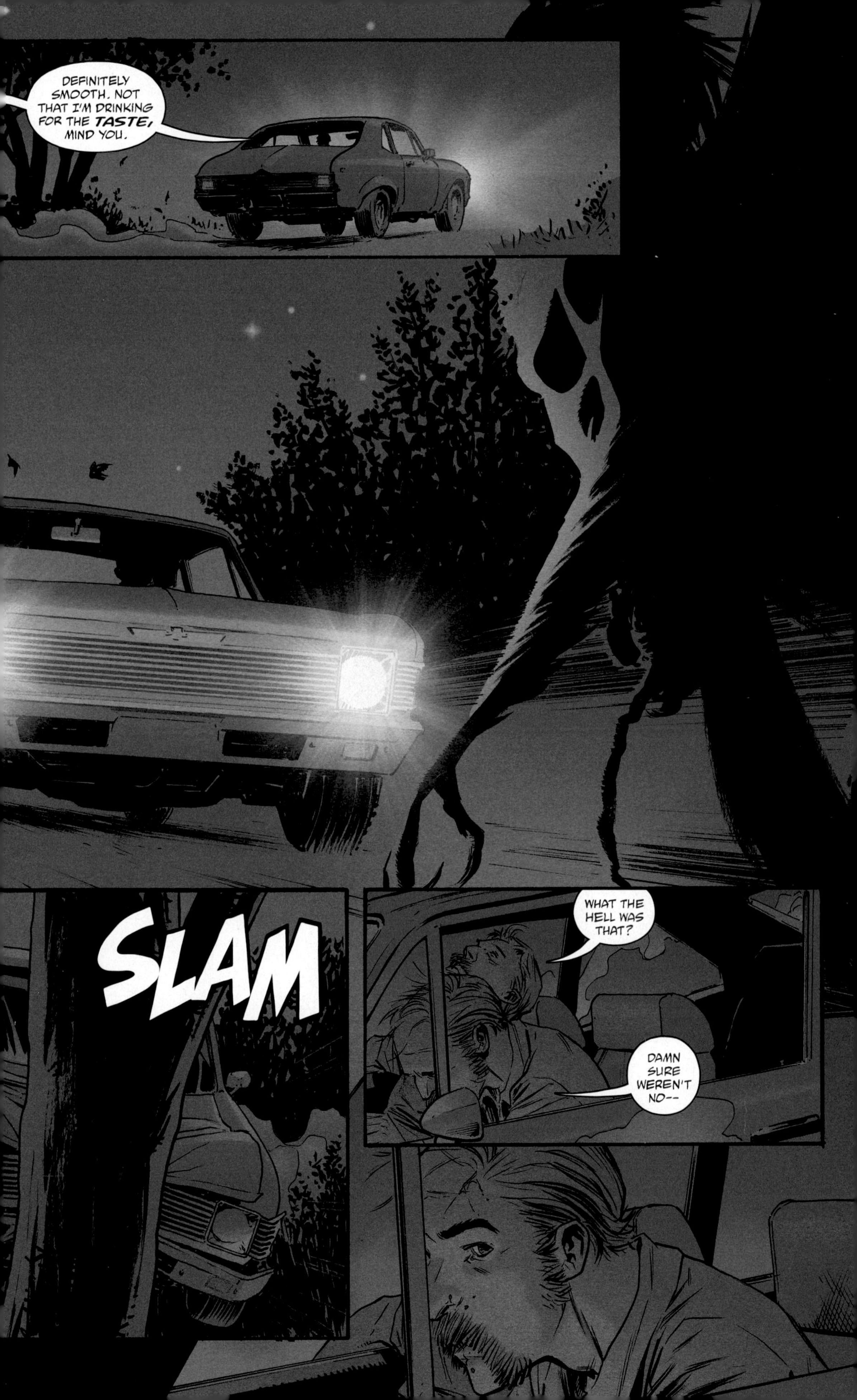
DEFINITELY SMOOTH. NOT THAT I'M DRINKING FOR THE TASTE, MIND YOU.
SLAM
WHAT THE HELL WAS THAT?
DAMN SURE WEREN'T NO--

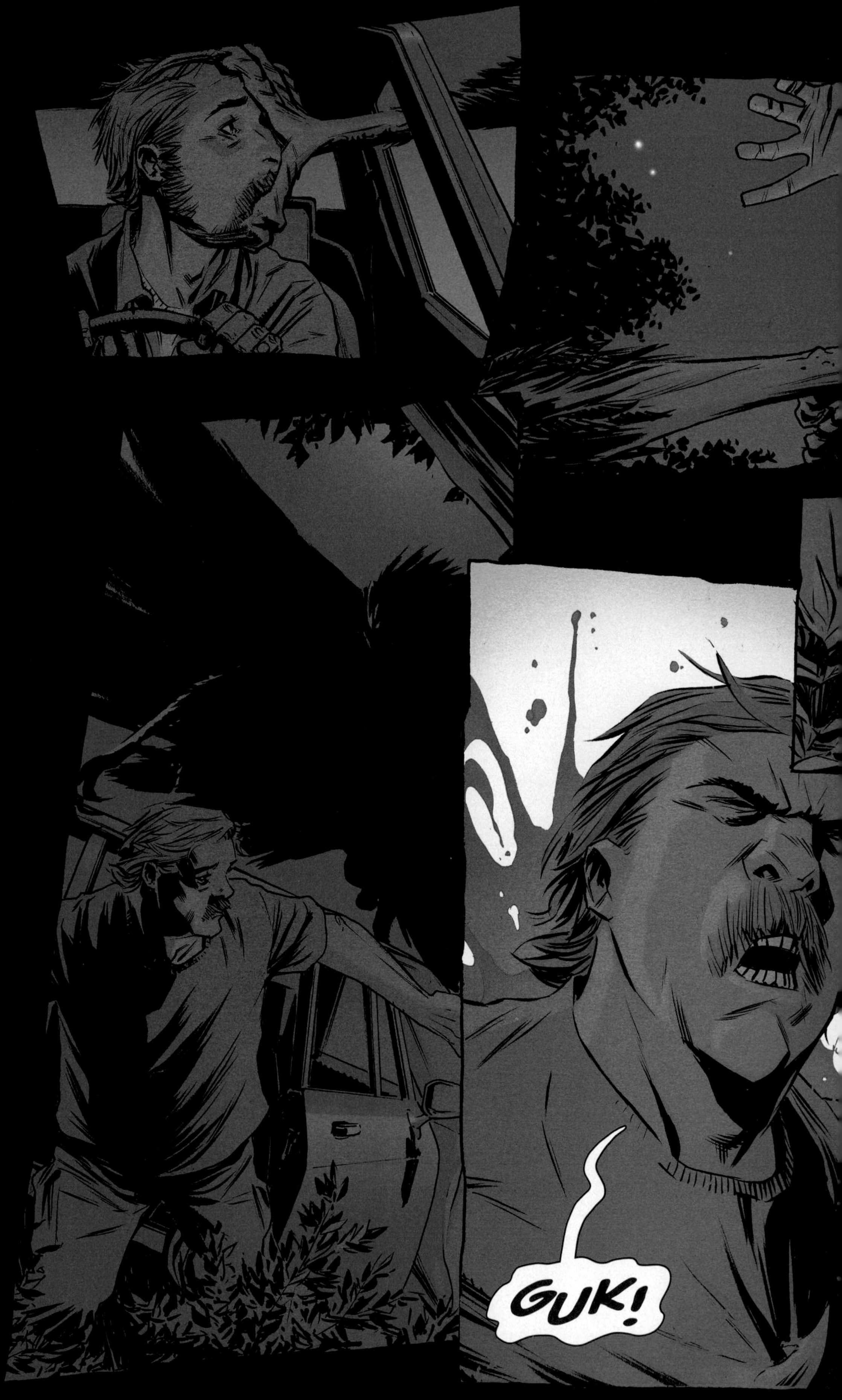
GUK!

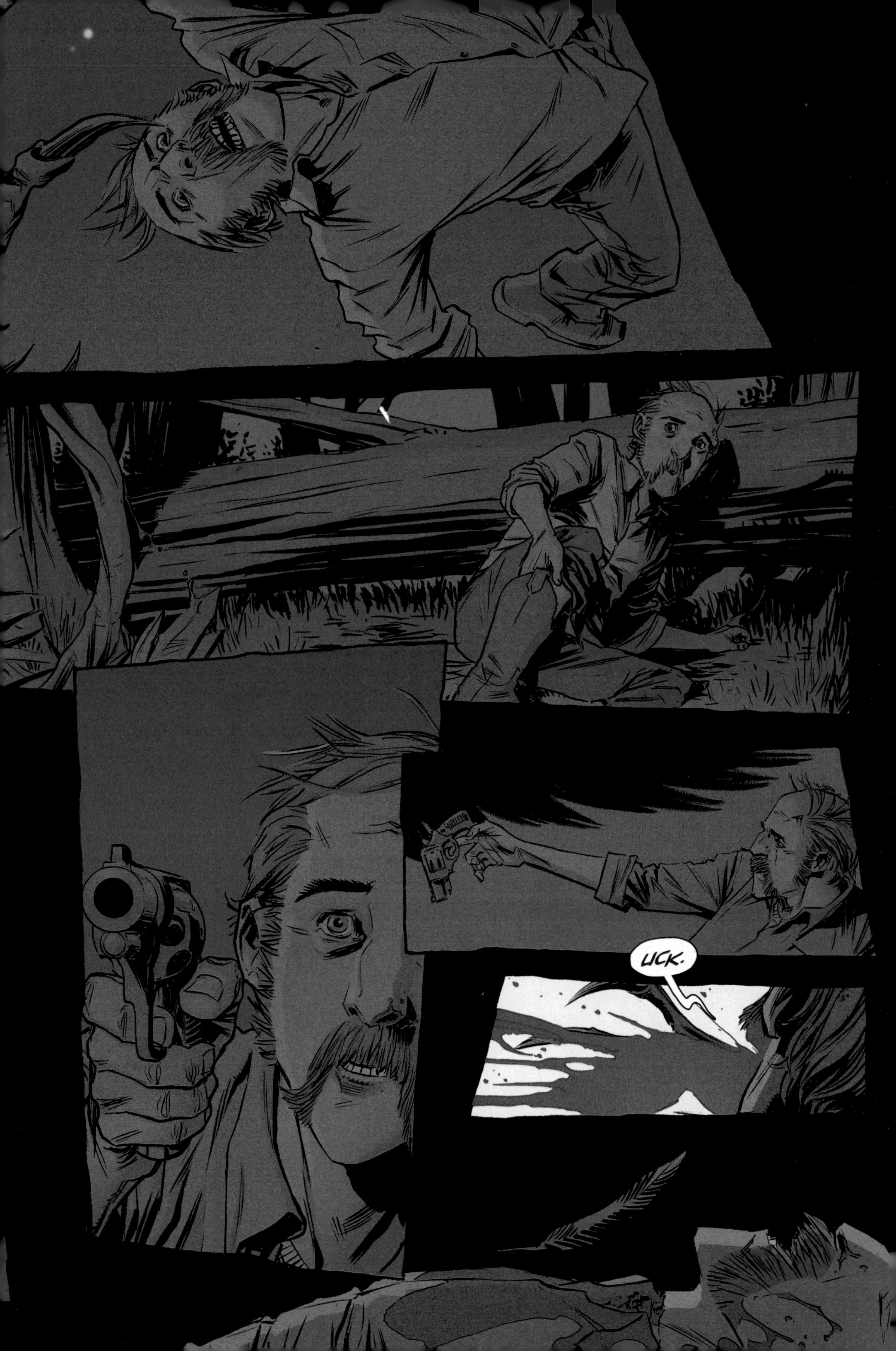
UCK.

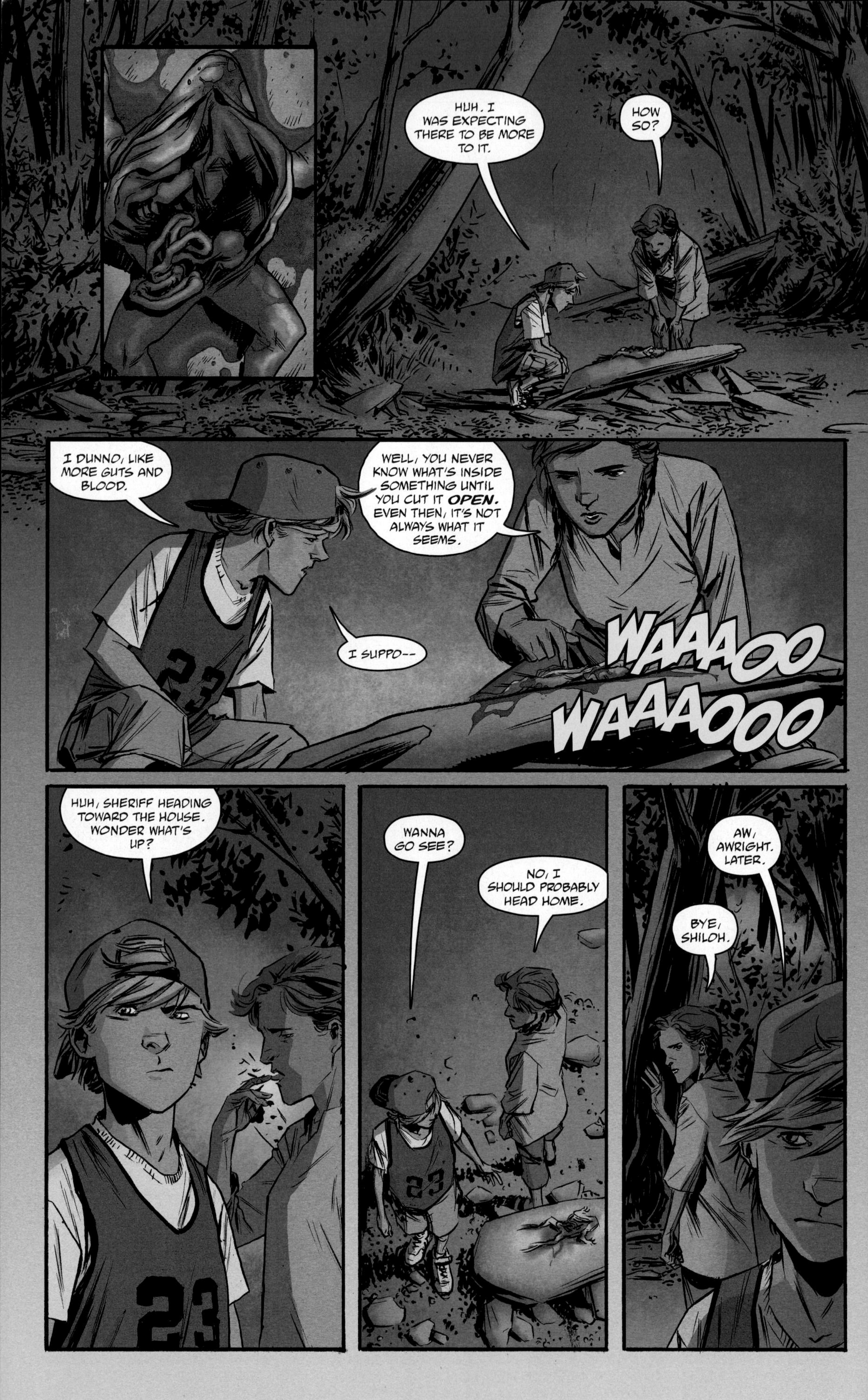

HUH. I WAS EXPECTING THERE TO BE MORE TO IT.
HOW SO?
I DUNNO, LIKE MORE GUTS AND BLOOD.
WELL, YOU NEVER KNOW WHAT'S INSIDE SOMETHING UNTIL YOU CUT IT OPEN. EVEN THEN, IT'S NOT ALWAYS WHAT IT SEEMS.
I SUPPO--
WAAAOO
WAAAOOO
HUH, SHERIFF HEADING TOWARD THE HOUSE. WONDER WHAT'S UP?
WANNA GO SEE?
NO, I SHOULD PROBABLY HEAD HOME.
AW, AWRIGHT. LATER.
BYE, SHILOH.

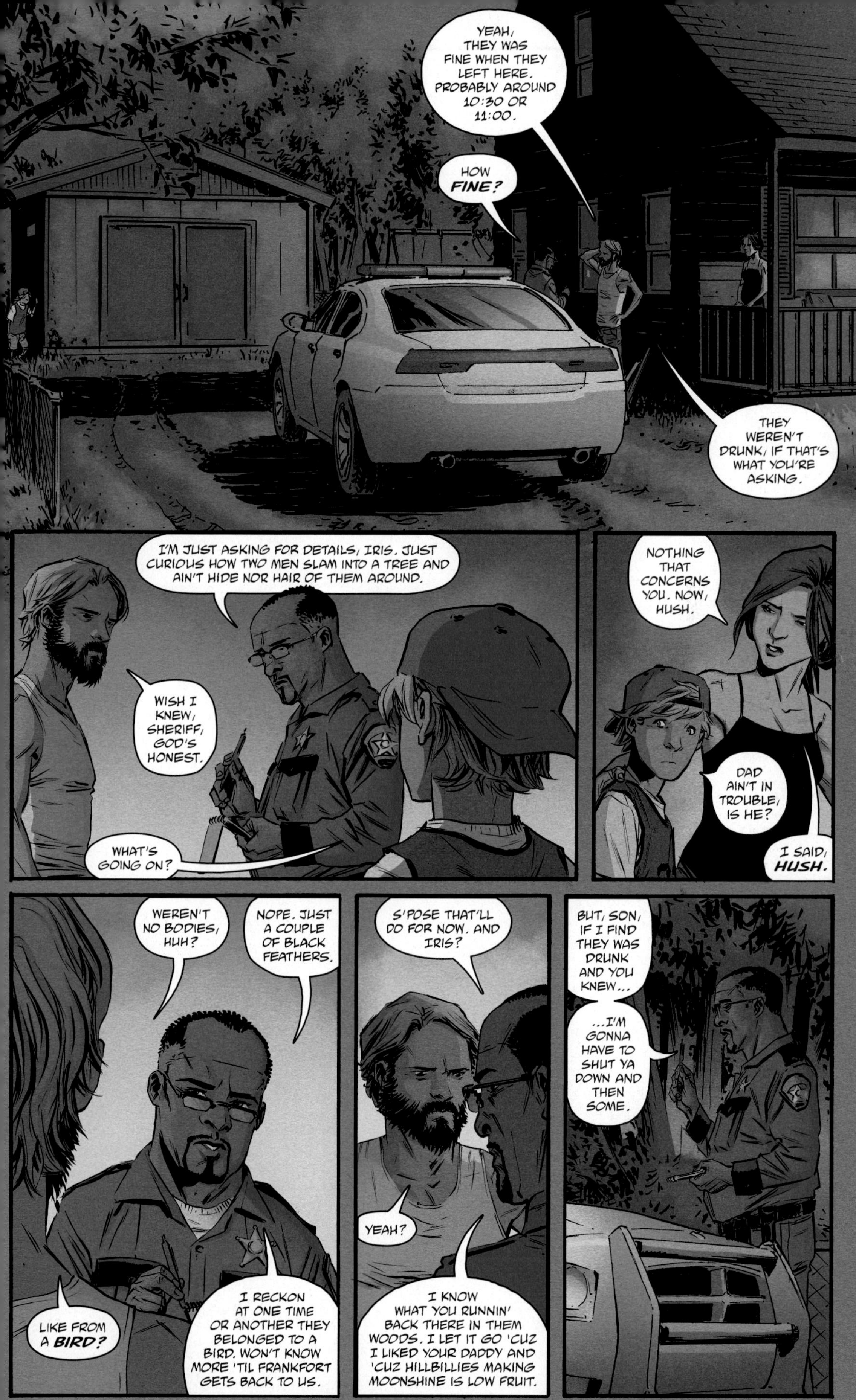
YEAH, THEY WAS FINE WHEN THEY LEFT HERE. PROBABLY AROUND 10:30 OR 11:00.
HOW *FINE?*
THEY WEREN'T DRUNK, IF THAT'S WHAT YOU'RE ASKING.
I'M JUST ASKING FOR DETAILS, IRIS. JUST CURIOUS HOW TWO MEN SLAM INTO A TREE AND AIN'T HIDE NOR HAIR OF THEM AROUND.
WISH I KNEW, SHERIFF, GOD'S HONEST.
WHAT'S GOING ON?
NOTHING THAT CONCERNS YOU. NOW, HUSH.
DAD AIN'T IN TROUBLE, IS HE?
I SAID, *HUSH.*
WEREN'T NO BODIES, HUH?
NOPE. JUST A COUPLE OF BLACK FEATHERS.
LIKE FROM A *BIRD?*
I RECKON AT ONE TIME OR ANOTHER THEY BELONGED TO A BIRD. WON'T KNOW MORE 'TIL FRANKFORT GETS BACK TO US.
S'POSE THAT'LL DO FOR NOW. AND IRIS?
YEAH?
I KNOW WHAT YOU RUNNIN' BACK THERE IN THEM WOODS. I LET IT GO 'CUZ I LIKED YOUR DADDY AND 'CUZ HILLBILLIES MAKING MOONSHINE IS LOW FRUIT.
BUT, SON, IF I FIND THEY WAS DRUNK AND YOU KNEW...
...I'M GONNA HAVE TO SHUT YA DOWN AND THEN SOME.

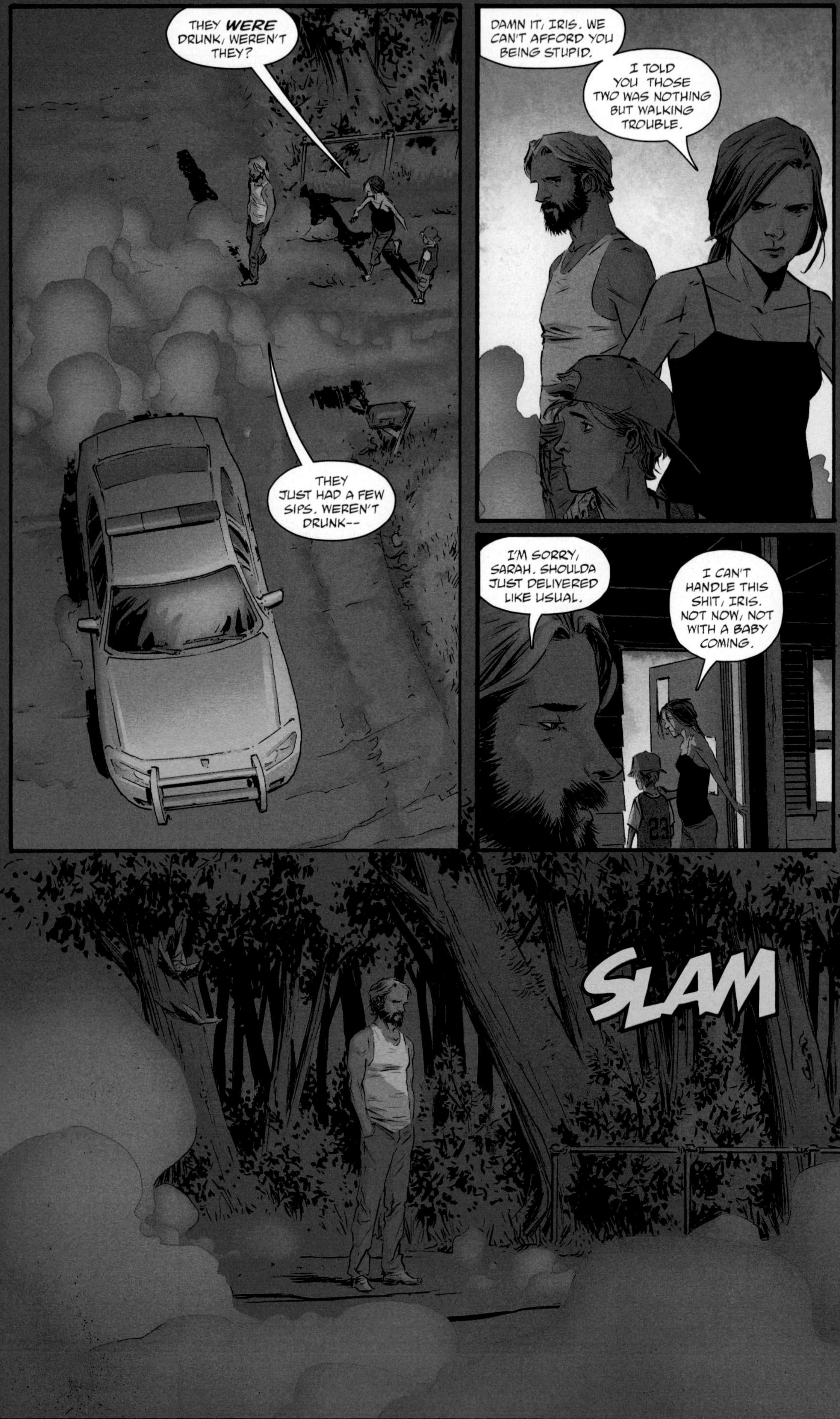
THEY WERE DRUNK, WEREN'T THEY?
THEY JUST HAD A FEW SIPS. WEREN'T DRUNK--
DAMN IT, IRIS. WE CAN'T AFFORD YOU BEING STUPID.
I TOLD YOU THOSE TWO WAS NOTHING BUT WALKING TROUBLE.
I'M SORRY, SARAH. SHOULDA JUST DELIVERED LIKE USUAL.
I CAN'T HANDLE THIS SHIT, IRIS. NOT NOW, NOT WITH A BABY COMING.
SLAM

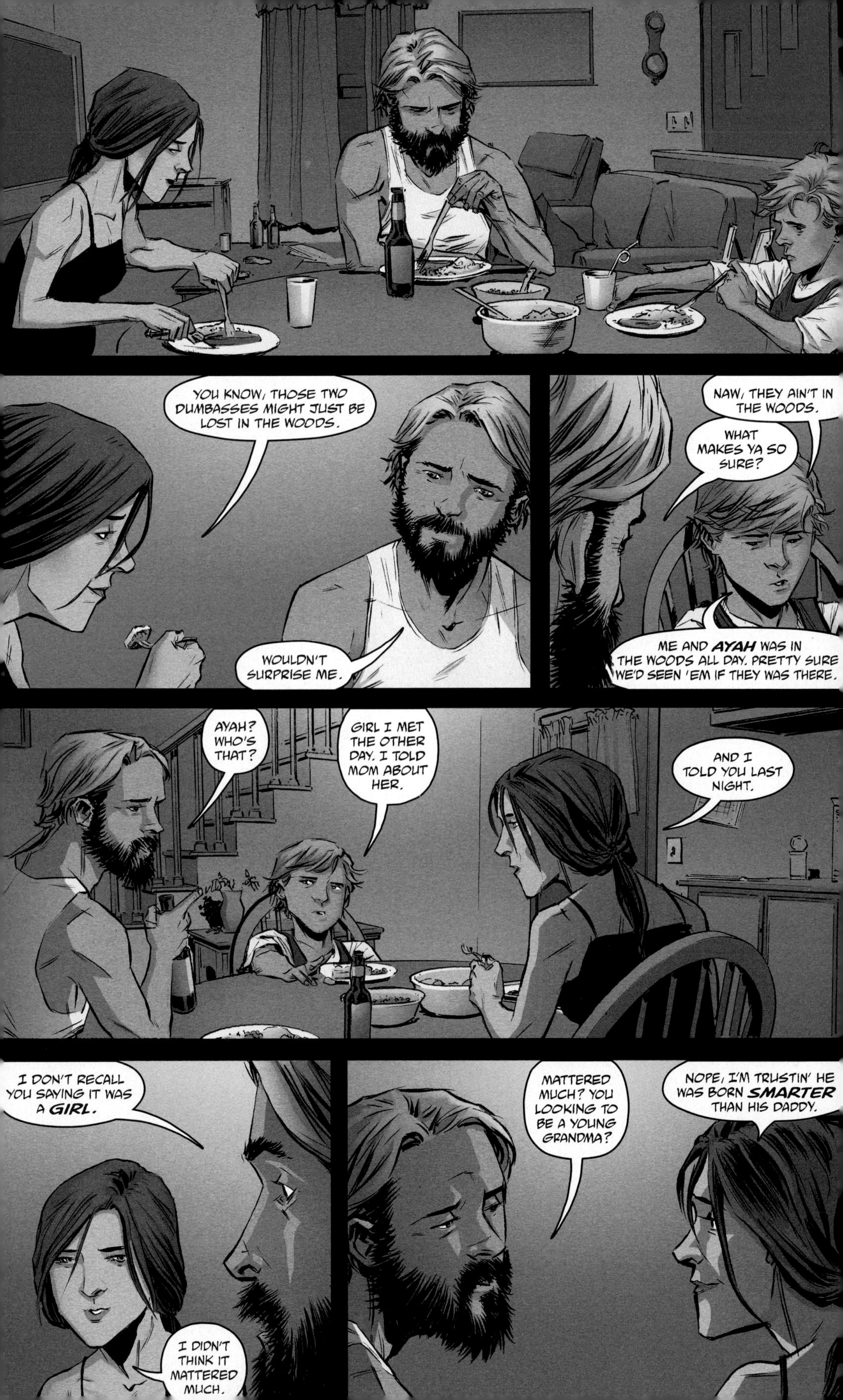
YOU KNOW, THOSE TWO DUMBASSES MIGHT JUST BE LOST IN THE WOODS.
WOULDN'T SURPRISE ME.
NAW, THEY AIN'T IN THE WOODS.
WHAT MAKES YA SO SURE?
ME AND AYAH WAS IN THE WOODS ALL DAY. PRETTY SURE WE'D SEEN 'EM IF THEY WAS THERE.
AYAH? WHO'S THAT?
GIRL I MET THE OTHER DAY. I TOLD MOM ABOUT HER.
AND I TOLD YOU LAST NIGHT.
I DON'T RECALL YOU SAYING IT WAS A GIRL.
I DIDN'T THINK IT MATTERED MUCH.
MATTERED MUCH? YOU LOOKING TO BE A YOUNG GRANDMA?
NOPE, I'M TRUSTIN' HE WAS BORN SMARTER THAN HIS DADDY.

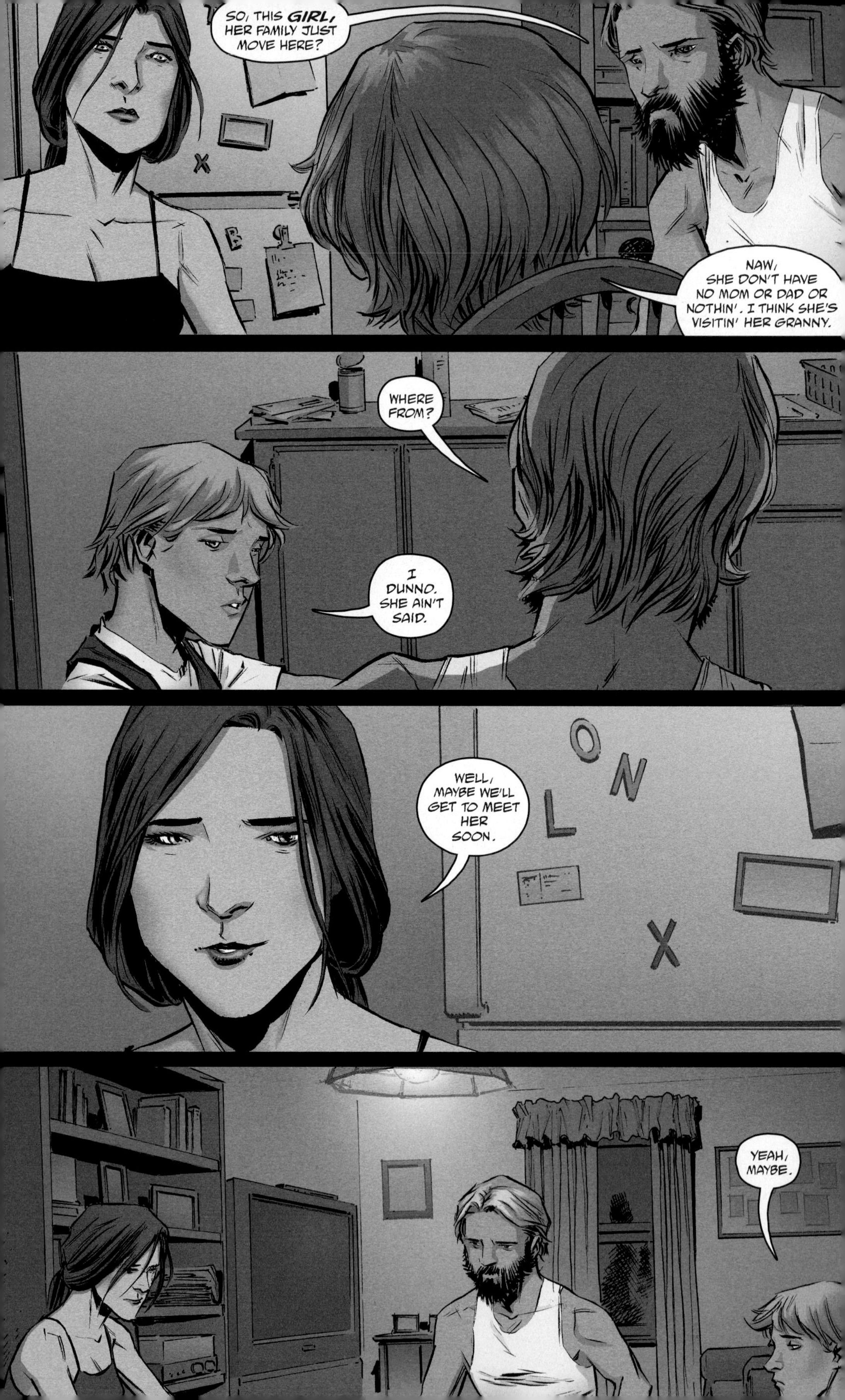
SO, THIS **GIRL**, HER FAMILY JUST MOVE HERE?
NAW, SHE DON'T HAVE NO MOM OR DAD OR NOTHIN'. I THINK SHE'S VISITIN' HER GRANNY.
WHERE FROM?
I DUNNO. SHE AIN'T SAID.
WELL, MAYBE WE'LL GET TO MEET HER SOON.
YEAH, MAYBE.

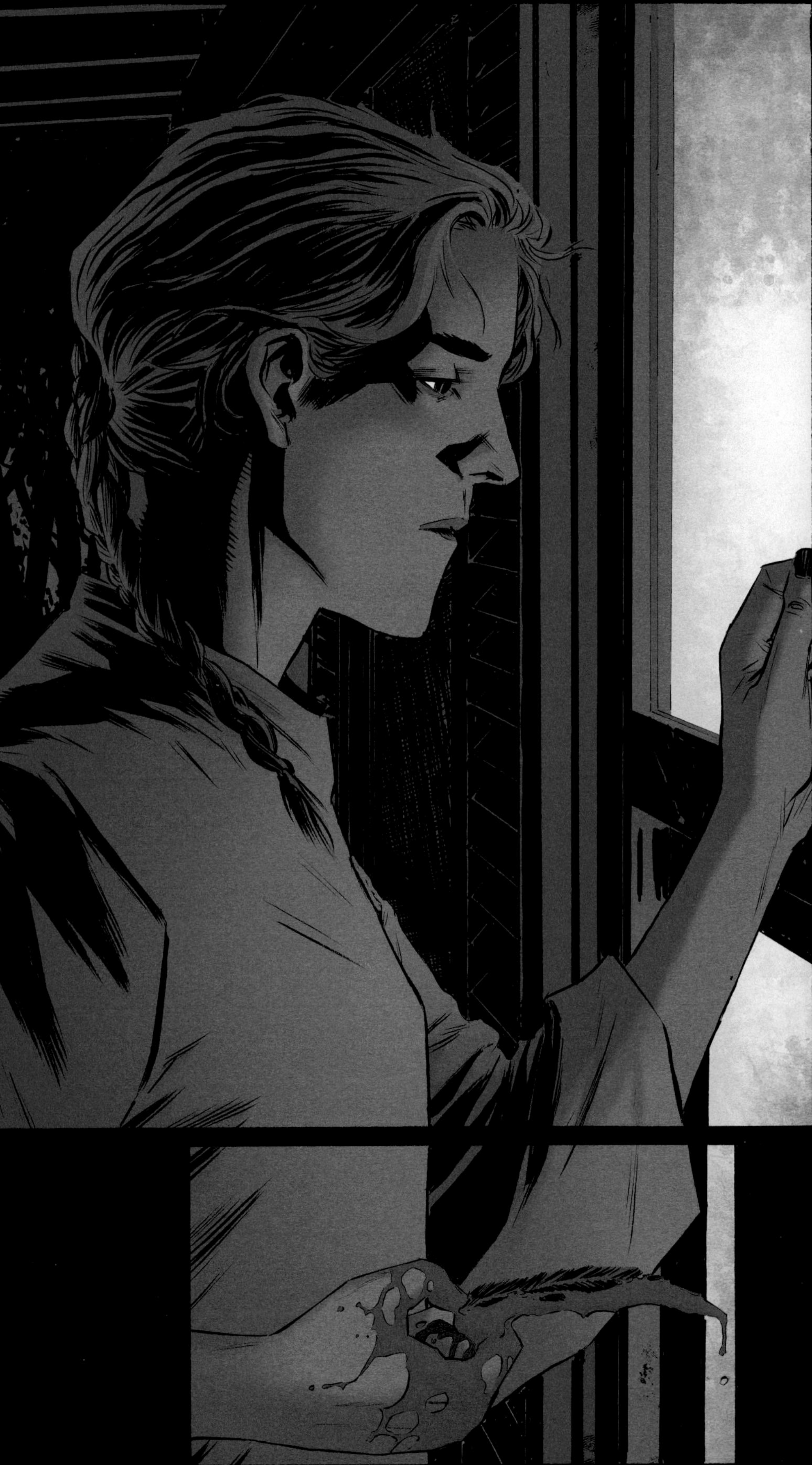

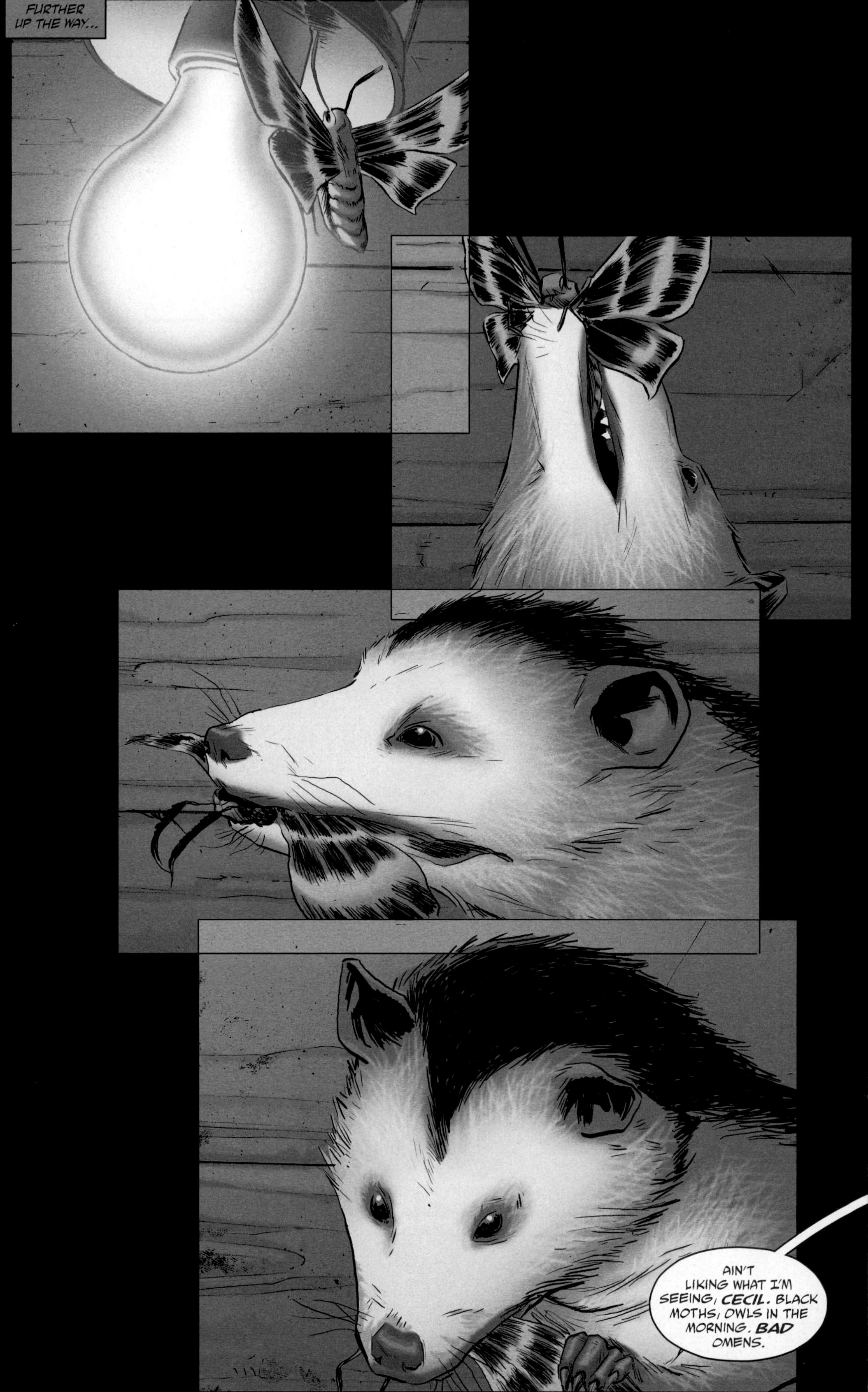
FURTHER UP THE WAY...
AIN'T LIKING WHAT I'M SEEING, **CECIL**. BLACK MOTHS, OWLS IN THE MORNING. **BAD** OMENS.

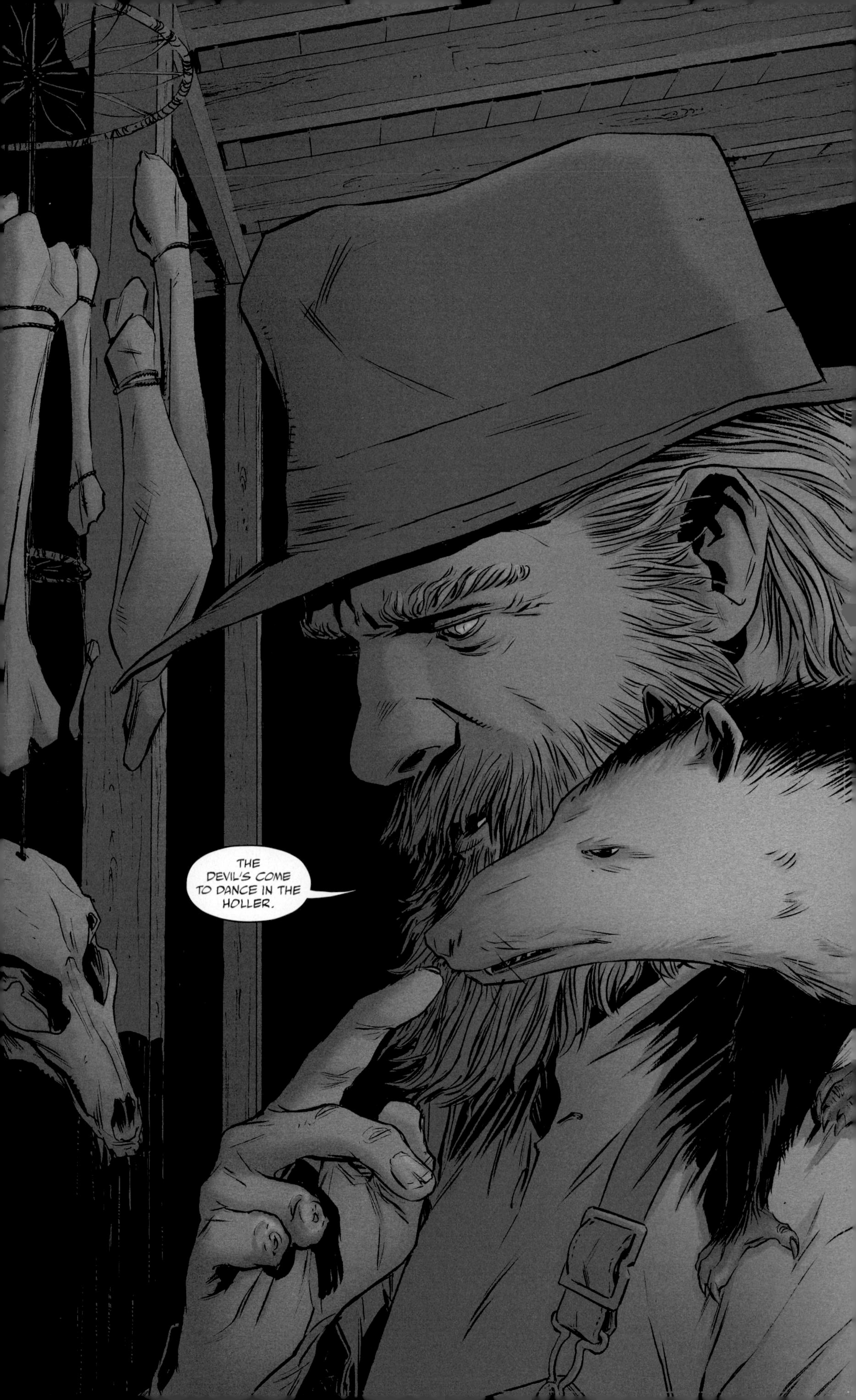
THE DEVIL'S COME TO DANCE IN THE HOLLER.

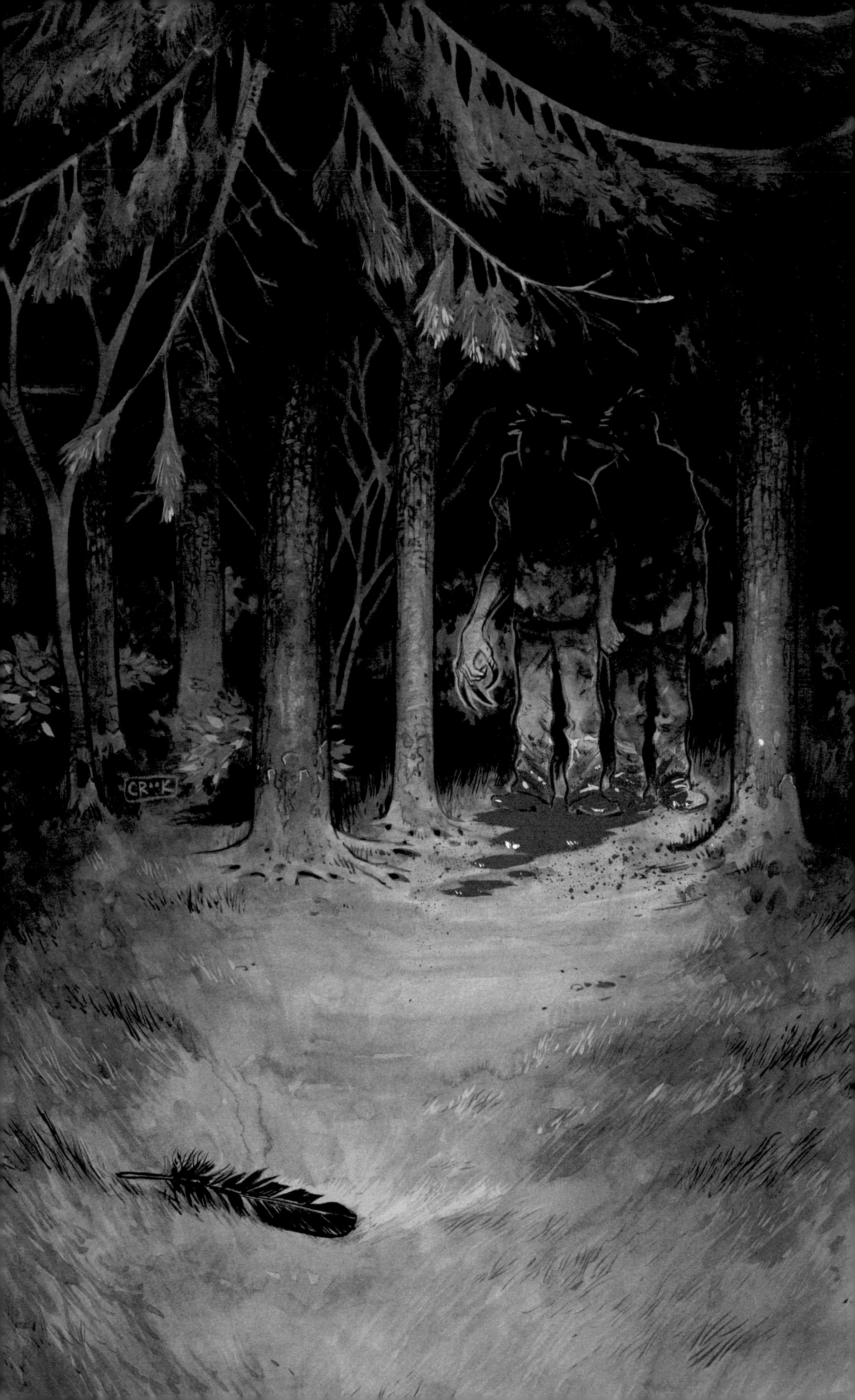

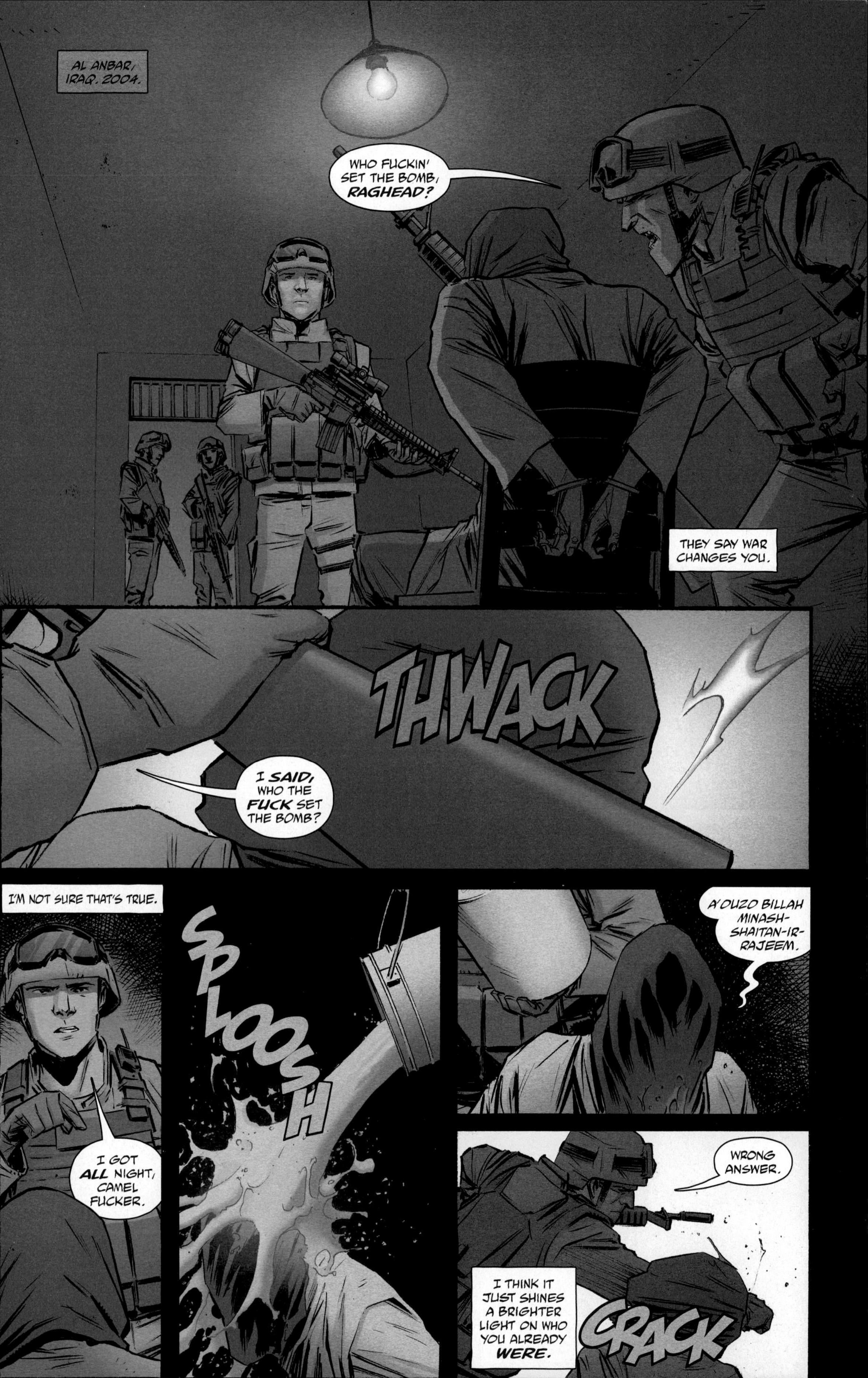
AL ANBAR, IRAQ. 2004.
WHO FUCKIN' SET THE BOMB, RAGHEAD?
THEY SAY WAR CHANGES YOU.
THWACK
I SAID, WHO THE FUCK SET THE BOMB?
I'M NOT SURE THAT'S TRUE.
I GOT ALL NIGHT, CAMEL FUCKER.
SPLOOSH
A'OUZO BILLAH MINASH-SHAITAN-IR-RAJEEM.
WRONG ANSWER.
I THINK IT JUST SHINES A BRIGHTER LIGHT ON WHO YOU ALREADY WERE.
CRACK

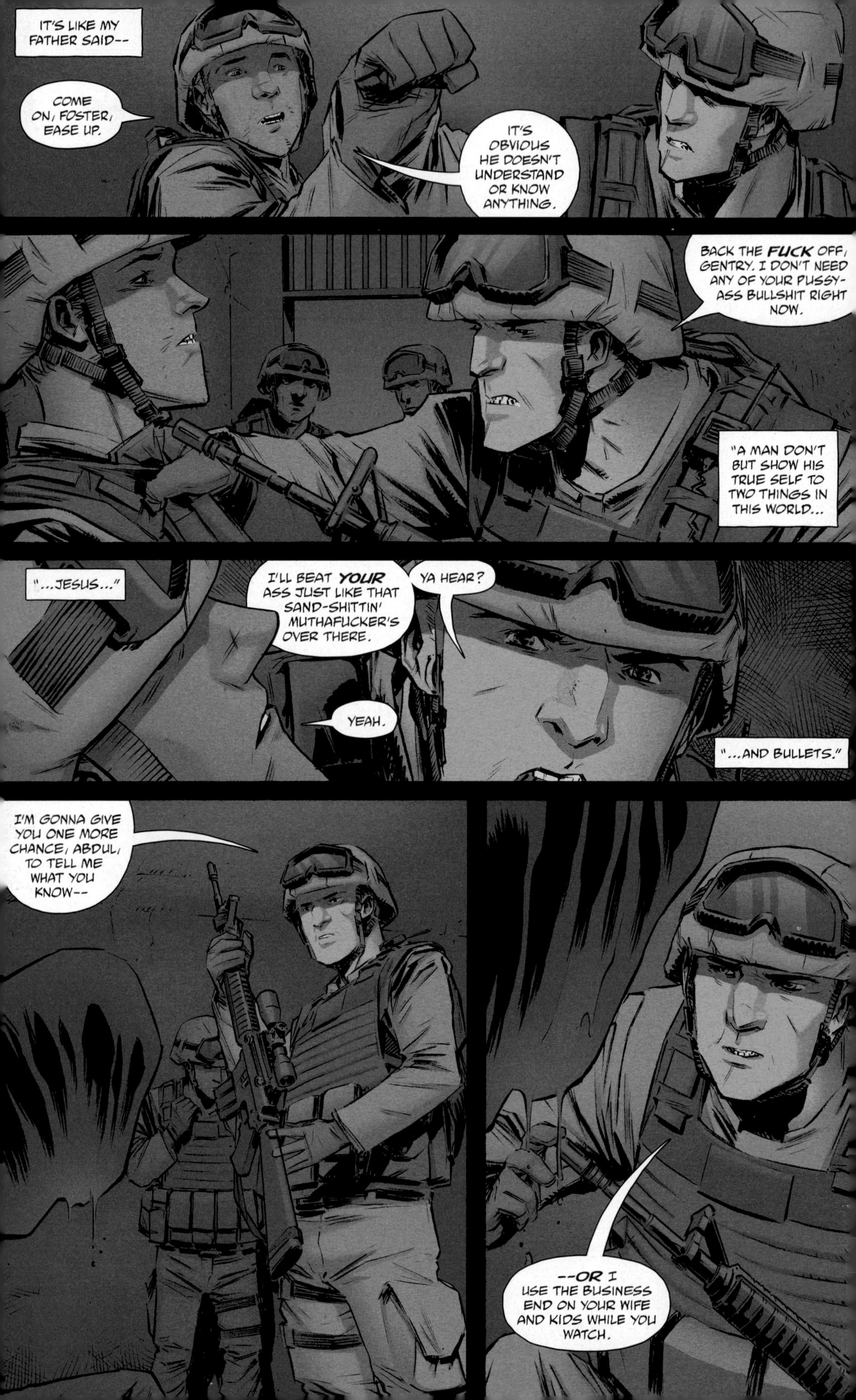
IT'S LIKE MY FATHER SAID--
COME ON, FOSTER, EASE UP.
IT'S OBVIOUS HE DOESN'T UNDERSTAND OR KNOW ANYTHING.
BACK THE **FUCK** OFF, GENTRY. I DON'T NEED ANY OF YOUR PUSSY-ASS BULLSHIT RIGHT NOW.
"A MAN DON'T BUT SHOW HIS TRUE SELF TO TWO THINGS IN THIS WORLD...
"...JESUS..."
I'LL BEAT **YOUR** ASS JUST LIKE THAT SAND-SHITTIN' MUTHAFUCKER'S OVER THERE.
YA HEAR?
YEAH.
"...AND BULLETS."
I'M GONNA GIVE YOU ONE MORE CHANCE, ABDUL, TO TELL ME WHAT YOU KNOW--
**--OR** I USE THE BUSINESS END ON YOUR WIFE AND KIDS WHILE YOU WATCH.

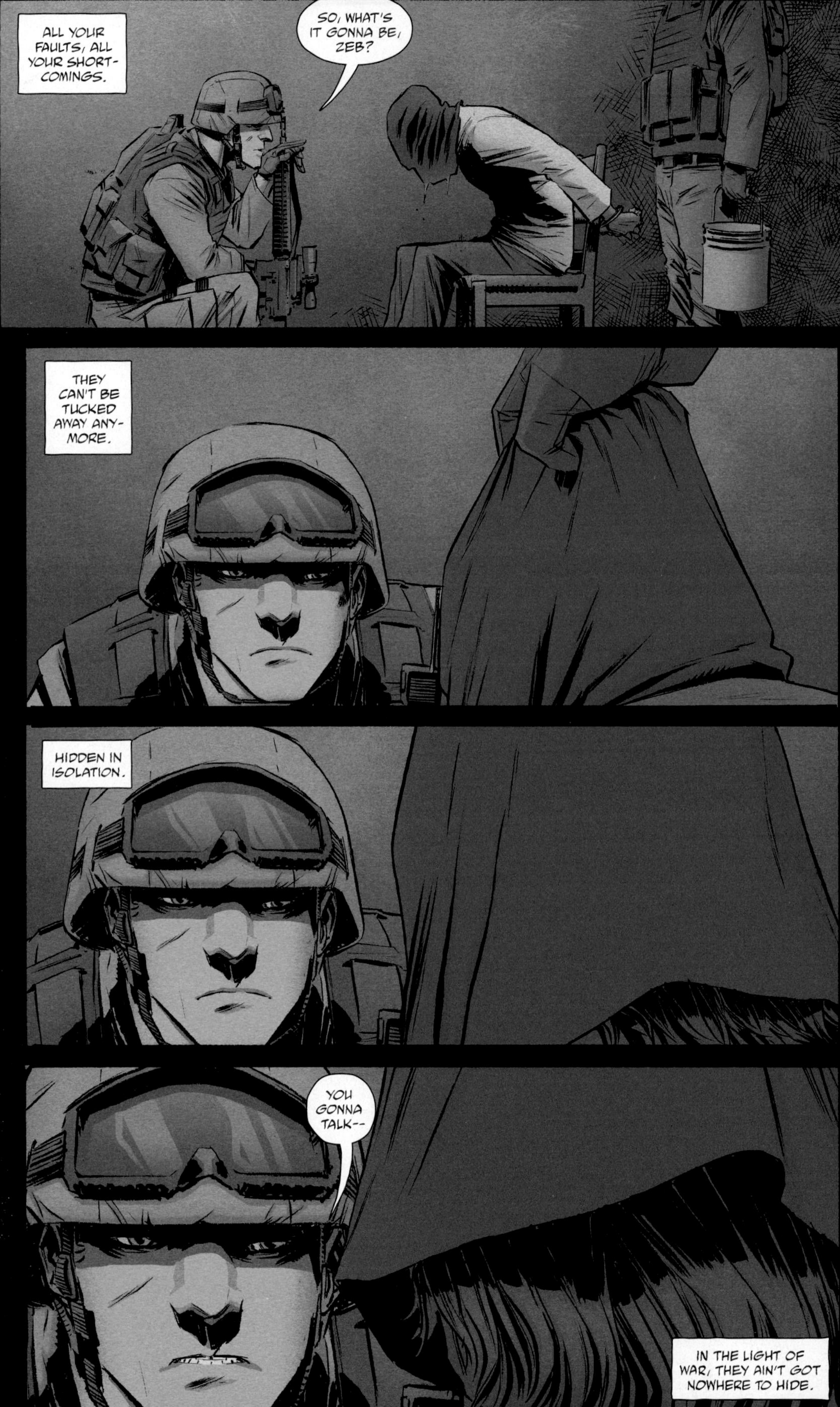
ALL YOUR FAULTS, ALL YOUR SHORT-COMINGS.
SO, WHAT'S IT GONNA BE, ZEB?
THEY CAN'T BE TUCKED AWAY ANY-MORE.
HIDDEN IN ISOLATION.
YOU GONNA TALK--
IN THE LIGHT OF WAR, THEY AIN'T GOT NOWHERE TO HIDE.

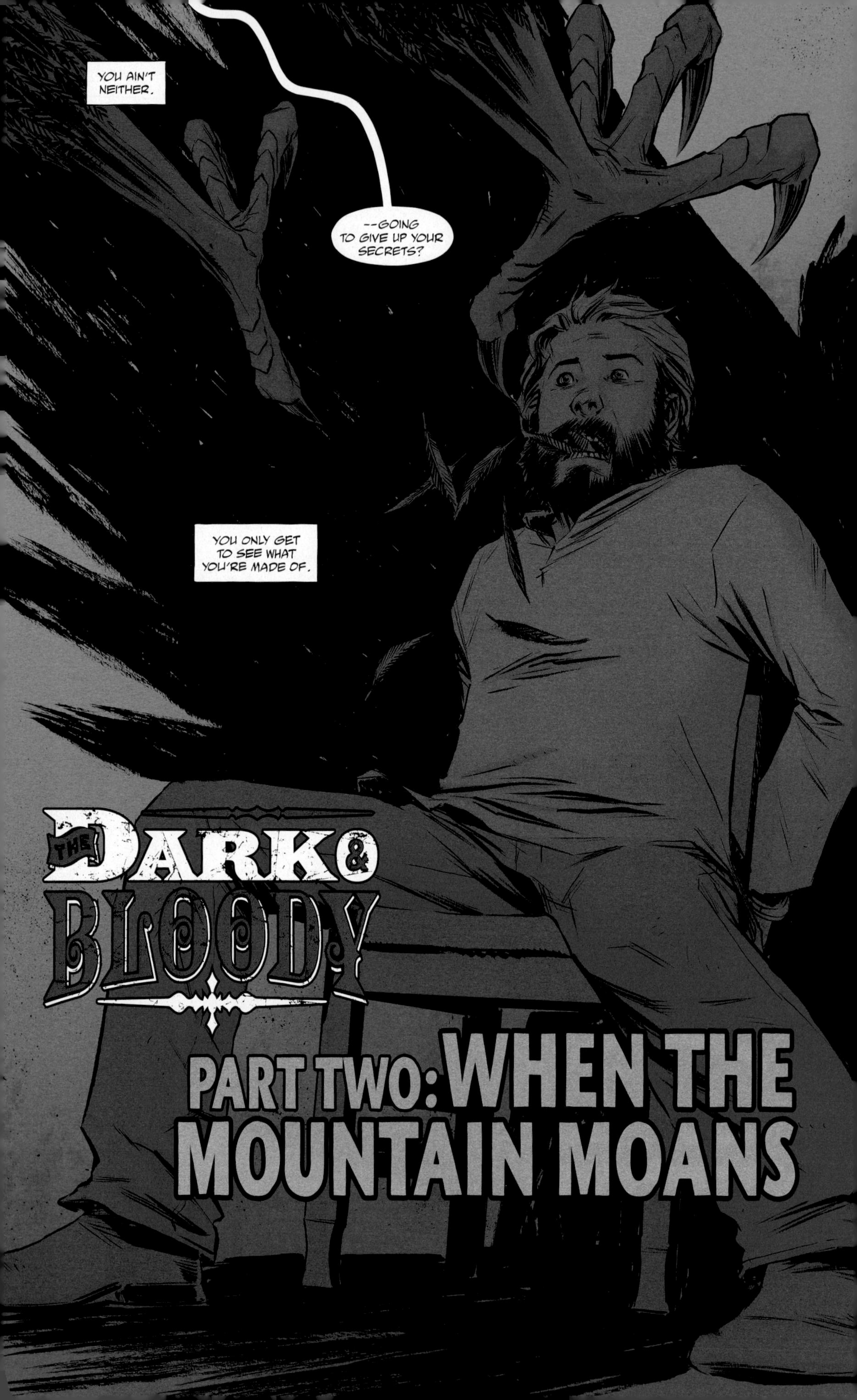
YOU AIN'T NEITHER.
--GOING TO GIVE UP YOUR SECRETS?
YOU ONLY GET TO SEE WHAT YOU'RE MADE OF.
THE DARK & BLOODY
PART TWO: WHEN THE MOUNTAIN MOANS

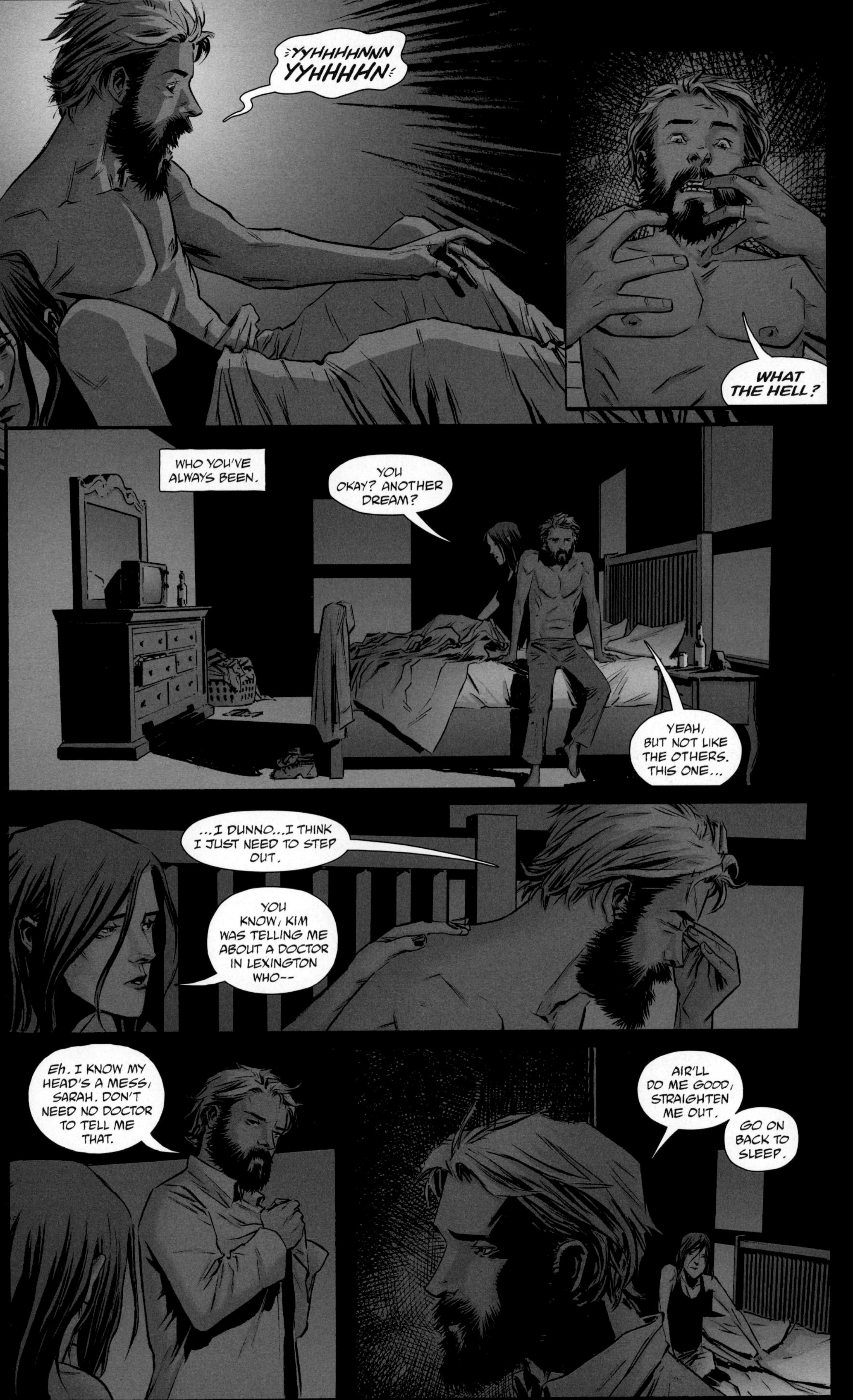

YYHHHHNNN YYHHHHN
WHAT THE HELL?
WHO YOU'VE ALWAYS BEEN.
YOU OKAY? ANOTHER DREAM?
YEAH, BUT NOT LIKE THE OTHERS. THIS ONE...
...I DUNNO...I THINK I JUST NEED TO STEP OUT.
YOU KNOW, KIM WAS TELLING ME ABOUT A DOCTOR IN LEXINGTON WHO--
Eh. I KNOW MY HEAD'S A MESS, SARAH. DON'T NEED NO DOCTOR TO TELL ME THAT.
AIR'LL DO ME GOOD, STRAIGHTEN ME OUT.
GO ON BACK TO SLEEP.

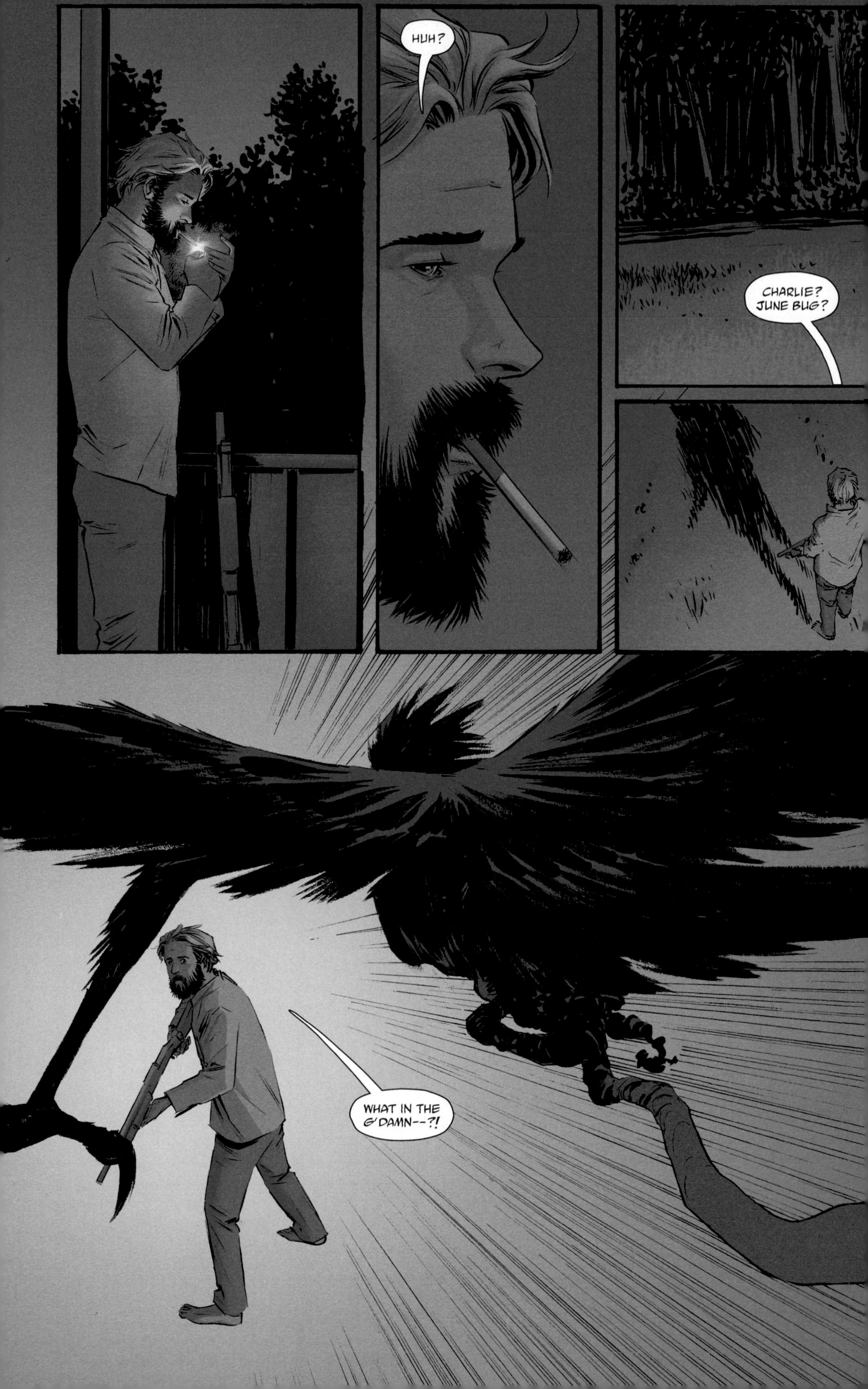
HUH?
CHARLIE? JUNE BUG?
WHAT IN THE G'DAMN--?!

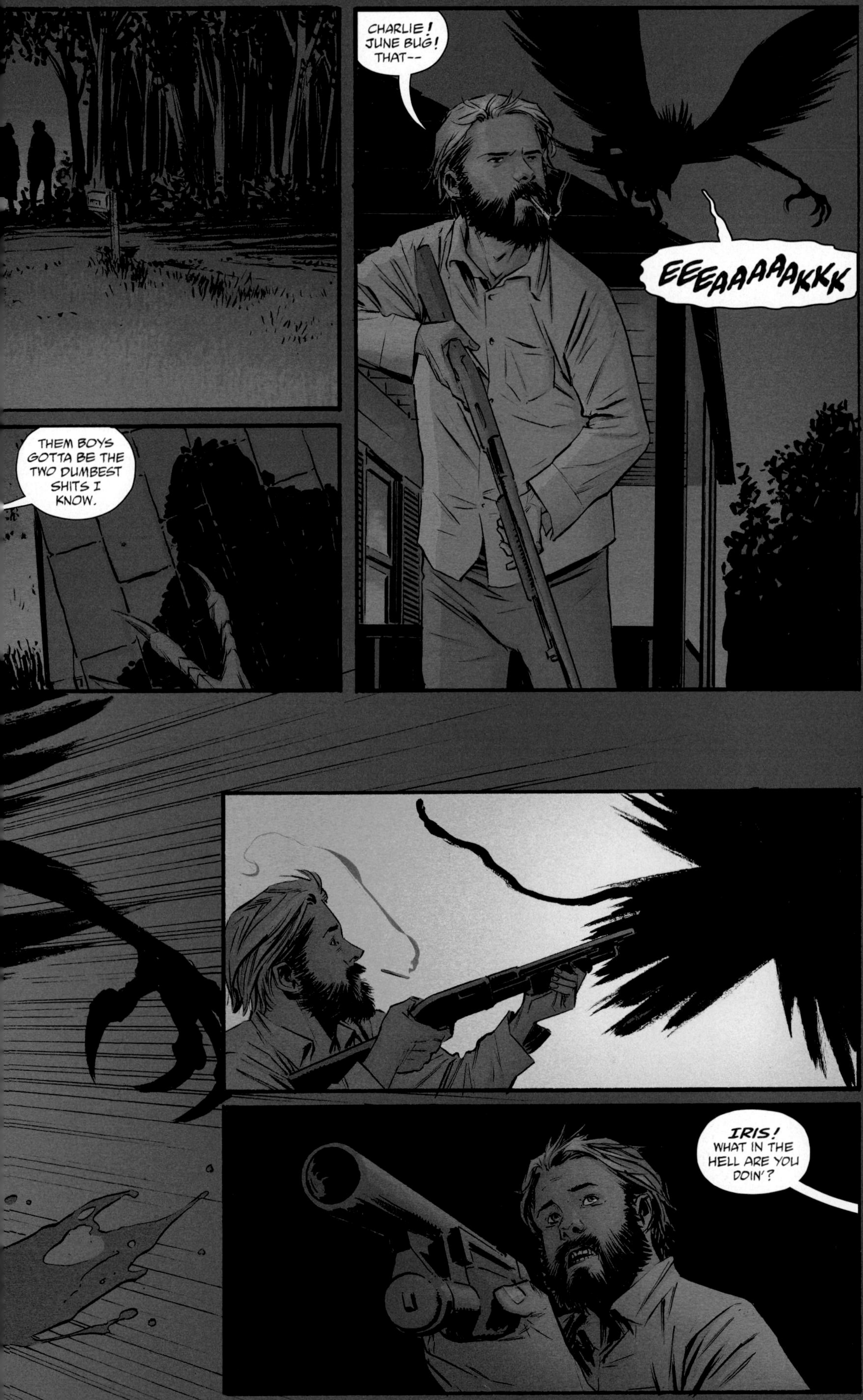
CHARLIE! JUNE BUG! THAT--
EEEAAAAAKKK
THEM BOYS GOTTA BE THE TWO DUMBEST SHITS I KNOW.
IRIS! WHAT IN THE HELL ARE YOU DOIN'?

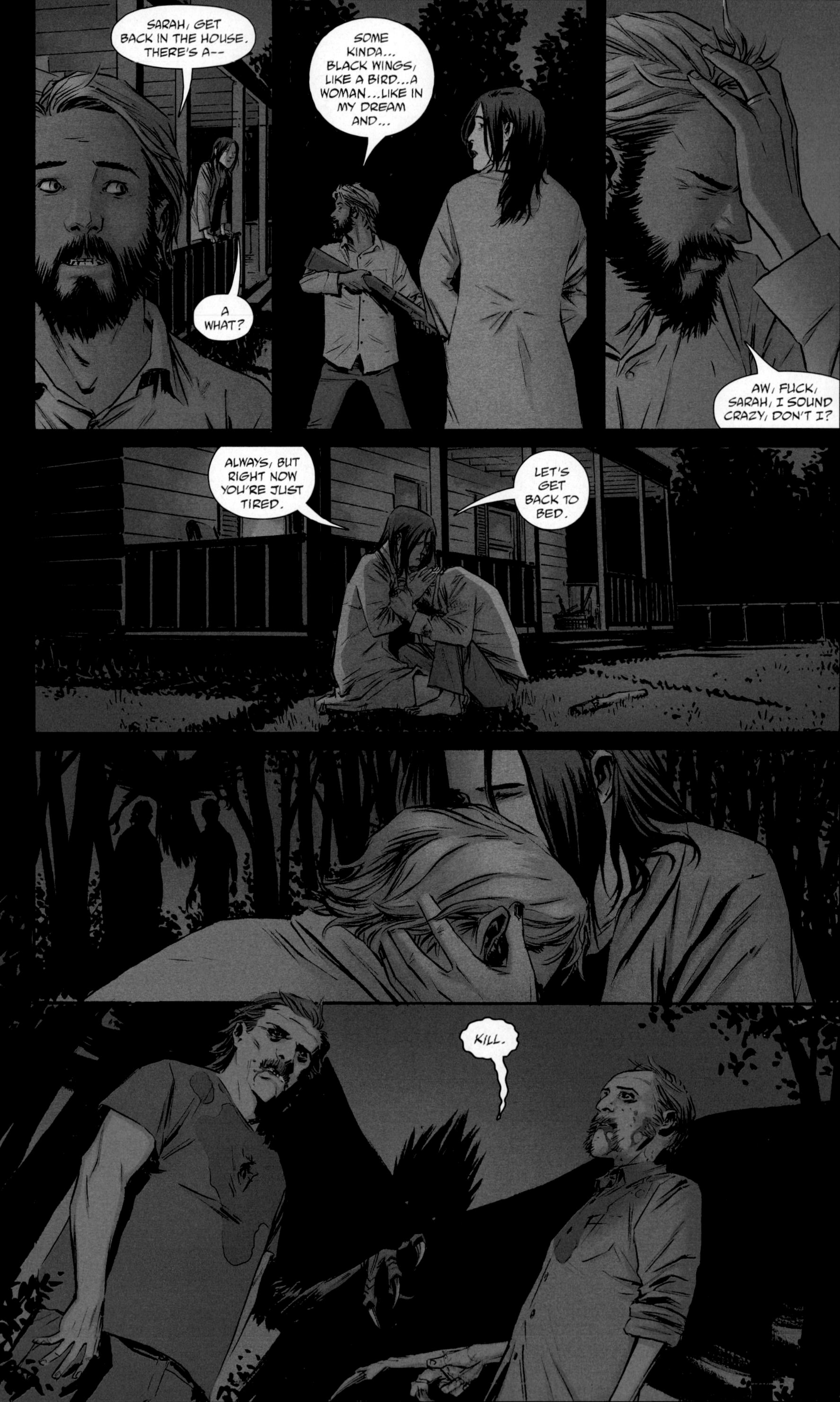
SARAH, GET BACK IN THE HOUSE. THERE'S A--
A WHAT?
SOME KINDA... BLACK WINGS, LIKE A BIRD...A WOMAN...LIKE IN MY DREAM AND...
AW, FUCK, SARAH, I SOUND CRAZY, DON'T I?
ALWAYS, BUT RIGHT NOW YOU'RE JUST TIRED.
LET'S GET BACK TO BED.
KILL.

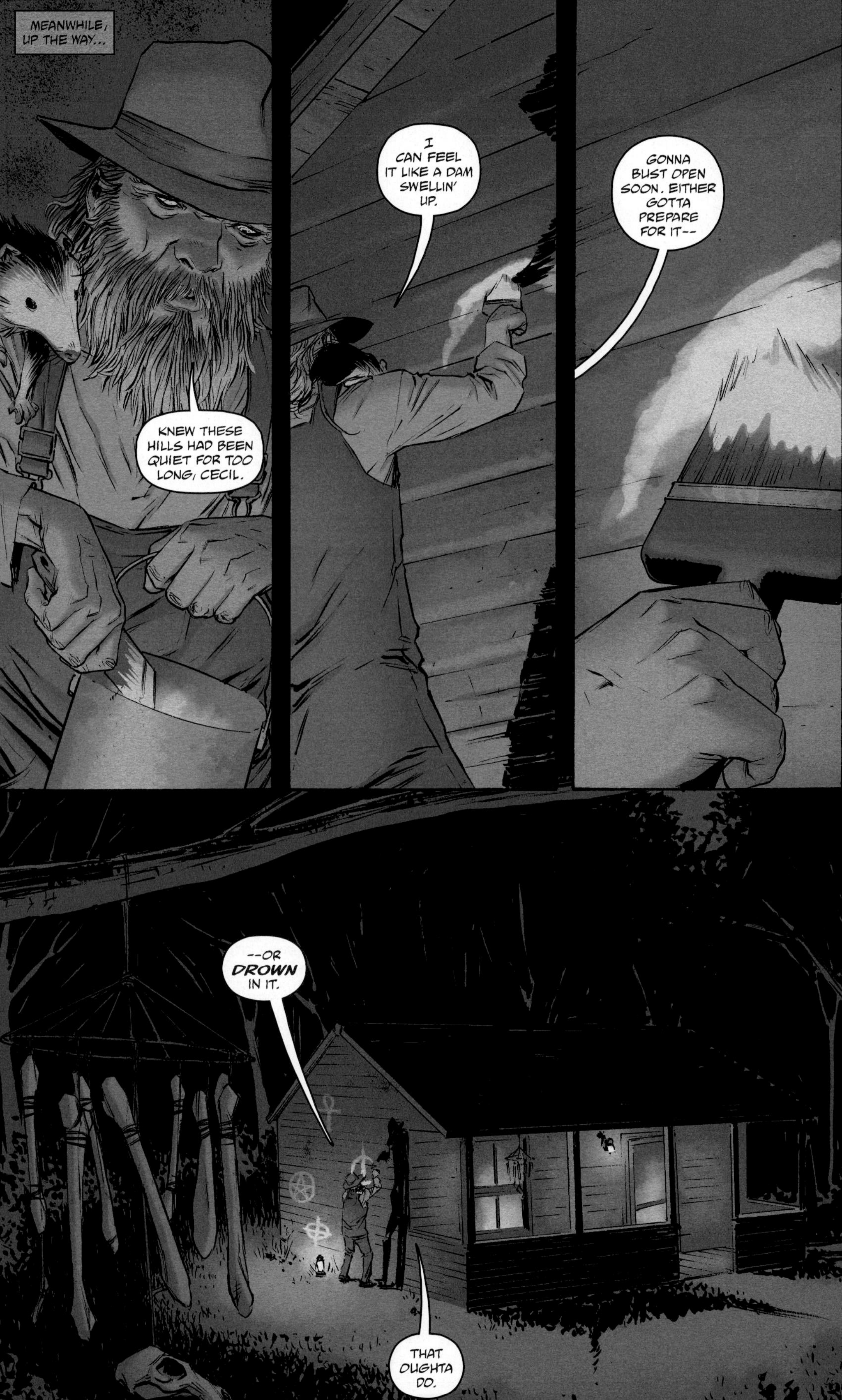
MEANWHILE, UP THE WAY...
KNEW THESE HILLS HAD BEEN QUIET FOR TOO LONG, CECIL.
I CAN FEEL IT LIKE A DAM SWELLIN' UP.
GONNA BUST OPEN SOON. EITHER GOTTA PREPARE FOR IT--
--OR DROWN IN IT.
THAT OUGHTA DO.

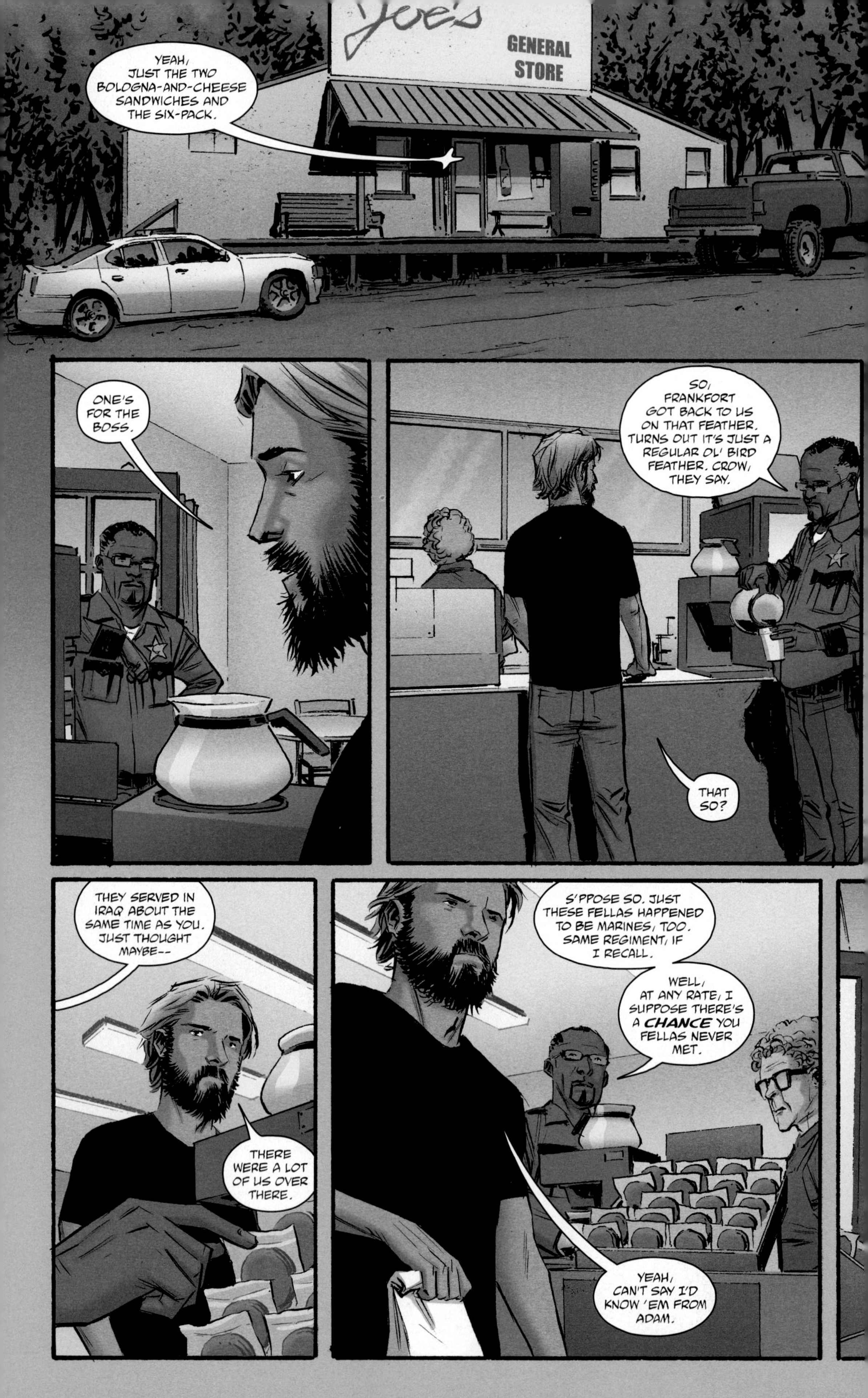
JOE'S
GENERAL STORE
YEAH, JUST THE TWO BOLOGNA-AND-CHEESE SANDWICHES AND THE SIX-PACK.
ONE'S FOR THE BOSS.
SO, FRANKFORT GOT BACK TO US ON THAT FEATHER. TURNS OUT IT'S JUST A REGULAR OL' BIRD FEATHER. CROW, THEY SAY.
THAT SO?
THEY SERVED IN IRAQ ABOUT THE SAME TIME AS YOU. JUST THOUGHT MAYBE--
THERE WERE A LOT OF US OVER THERE.
S'PPOSE SO. JUST THESE FELLAS HAPPENED TO BE MARINES, TOO. SAME REGIMENT, IF I RECALL.
WELL, AT ANY RATE, I SUPPOSE THERE'S A CHANCE YOU FELLAS NEVER MET.
YEAH, CAN'T SAY I'D KNOW 'EM FROM ADAM.

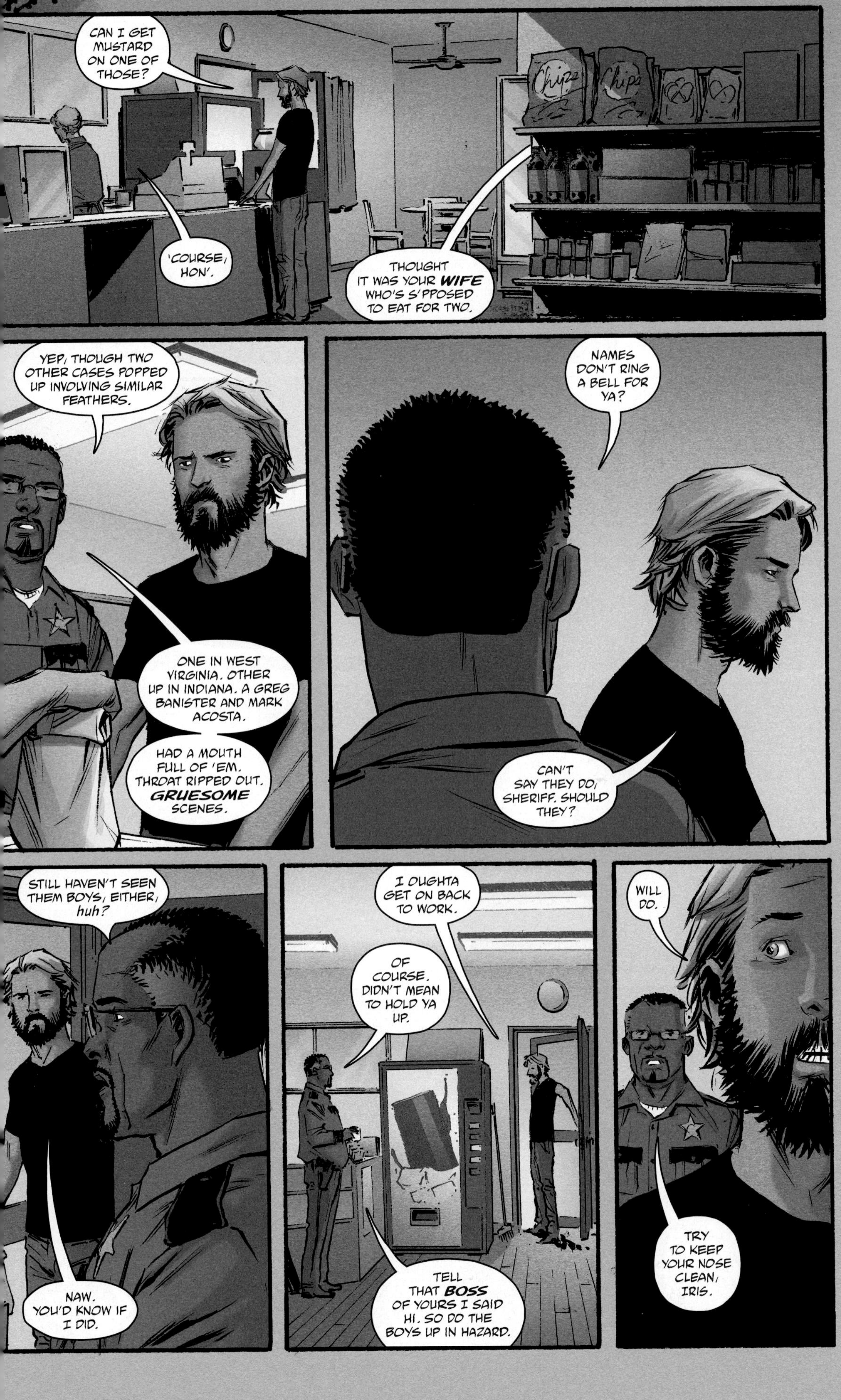
CAN I GET MUSTARD ON ONE OF THOSE?
'COURSE, HON'.
THOUGHT IT WAS YOUR WIFE WHO'S S'PPOSED TO EAT FOR TWO.
YEP, THOUGH TWO OTHER CASES POPPED UP INVOLVING SIMILAR FEATHERS.
ONE IN WEST VIRGINIA. OTHER UP IN INDIANA. A GREG BANISTER AND MARK ACOSTA.
HAD A MOUTH FULL OF 'EM. THROAT RIPPED OUT. GRUESOME SCENES.
NAMES DON'T RING A BELL FOR YA?
CAN'T SAY THEY DO, SHERIFF. SHOULD THEY?
STILL HAVEN'T SEEN THEM BOYS, EITHER, huh?
NAW. YOU'D KNOW IF I DID.
I OUGHTA GET ON BACK TO WORK.
OF COURSE. DIDN'T MEAN TO HOLD YA UP.
TELL THAT BOSS OF YOURS I SAID HI. SO DO THE BOYS UP IN HAZARD.
WILL DO.
TRY TO KEEP YOUR NOSE CLEAN, IRIS.

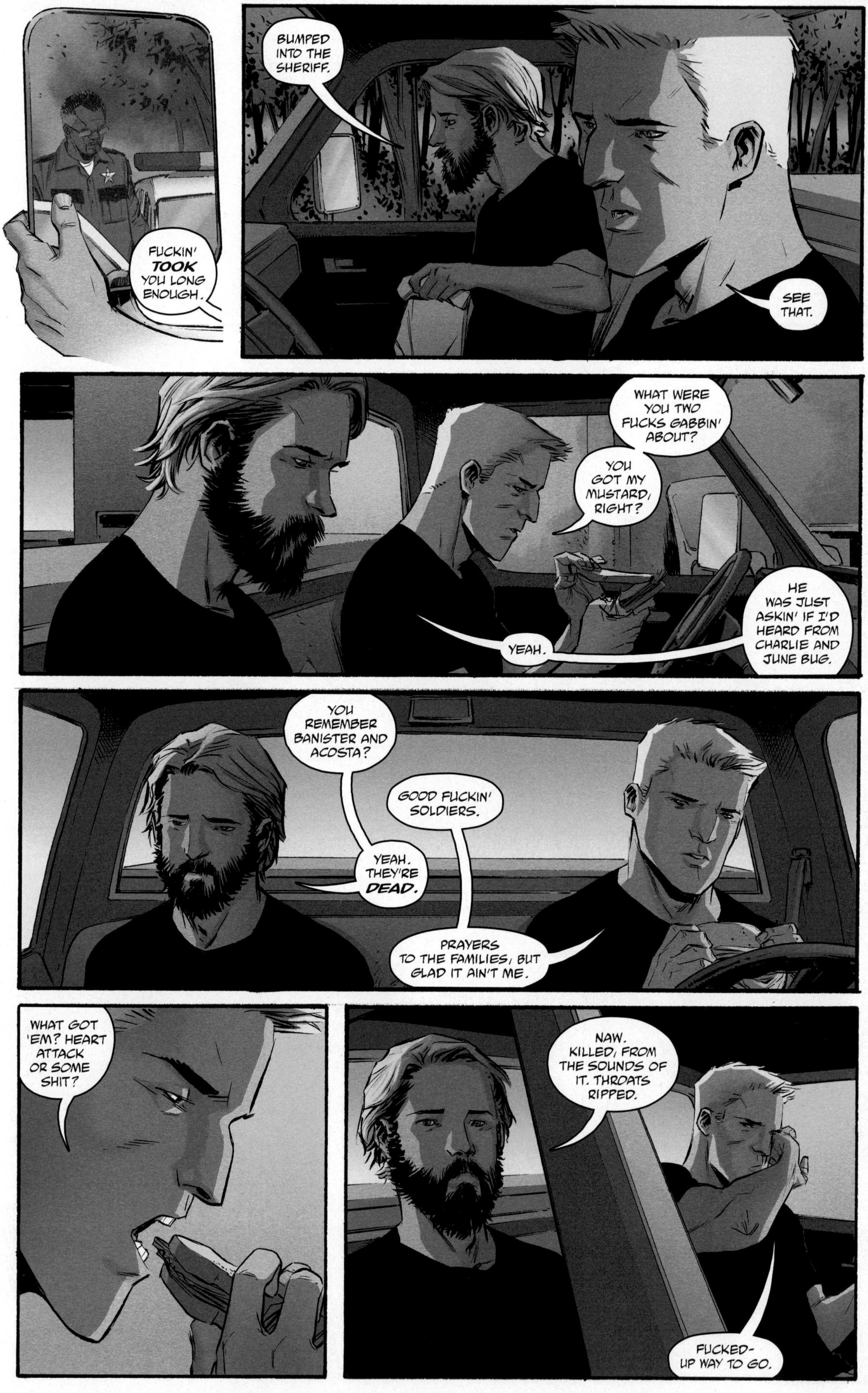
FUCKIN' **TOOK** YOU LONG ENOUGH.
BUMPED INTO THE SHERIFF.
SEE THAT.
WHAT WERE YOU TWO FUCKS GABBIN' ABOUT?
YOU GOT MY MUSTARD, RIGHT?
YEAH.
HE WAS JUST ASKIN' IF I'D HEARD FROM CHARLIE AND JUNE BUG.
YOU REMEMBER BANISTER AND ACOSTA?
GOOD FUCKIN' SOLDIERS.
YEAH. THEY'RE **DEAD.**
PRAYERS TO THE FAMILIES, BUT GLAD IT AIN'T ME.
WHAT GOT 'EM? HEART ATTACK OR SOME SHIT?
NAW. KILLED, FROM THE SOUNDS OF IT. THROATS RIPPED.
FUCKED-UP WAY TO GO.

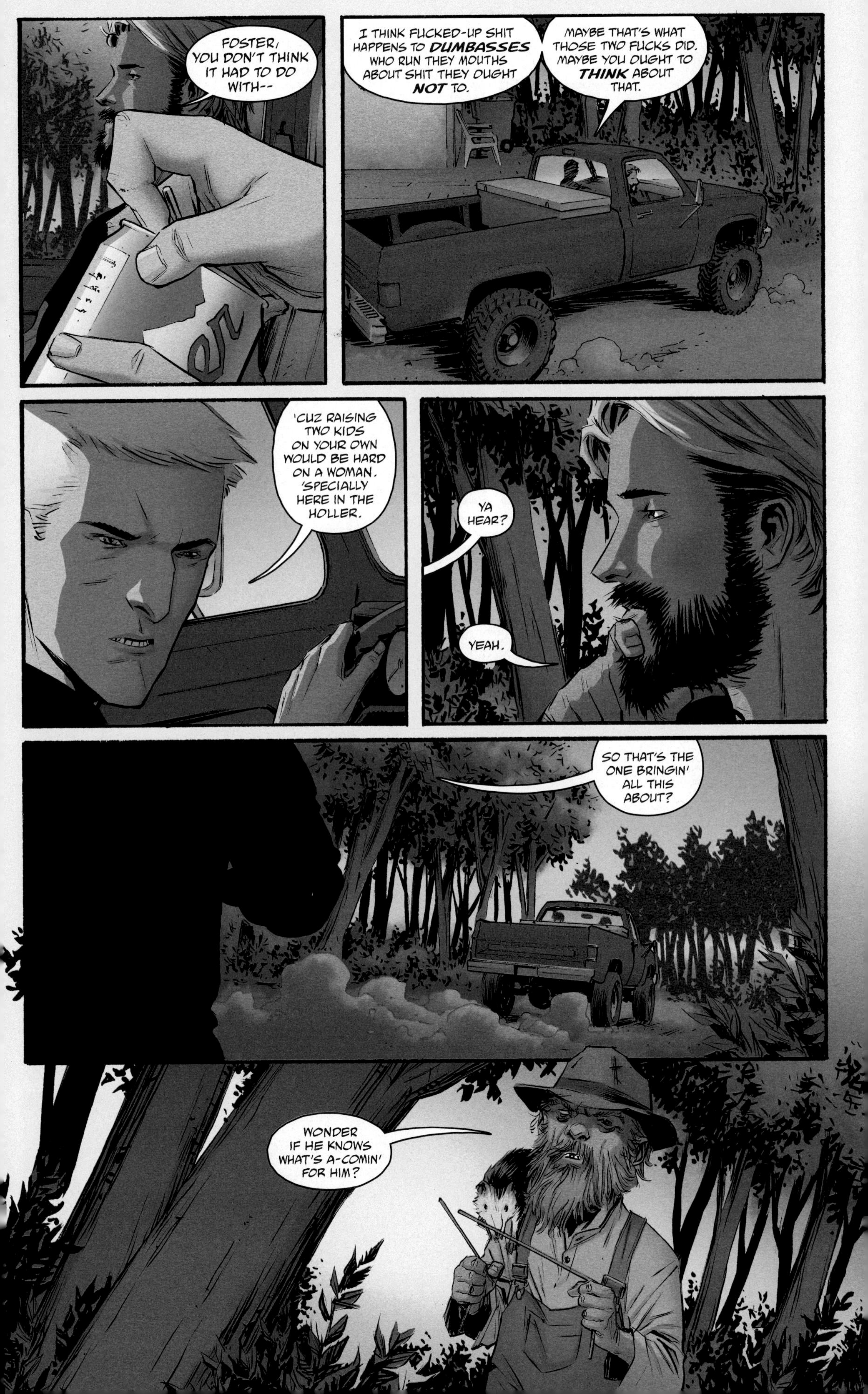
FOSTER, YOU DON'T THINK IT HAD TO DO WITH--
I THINK FUCKED-UP SHIT HAPPENS TO DUMBASSES WHO RUN THEY MOUTHS ABOUT SHIT THEY OUGHT NOT TO.
MAYBE THAT'S WHAT THOSE TWO FUCKS DID. MAYBE YOU OUGHT TO THINK ABOUT THAT.
'CUZ RAISING TWO KIDS ON YOUR OWN WOULD BE HARD ON A WOMAN. 'SPECIALLY HERE IN THE HOLLER.
YA HEAR?
YEAH.
SO THAT'S THE ONE BRINGIN' ALL THIS ABOUT?
WONDER IF HE KNOWS WHAT'S A-COMIN' FOR HIM?

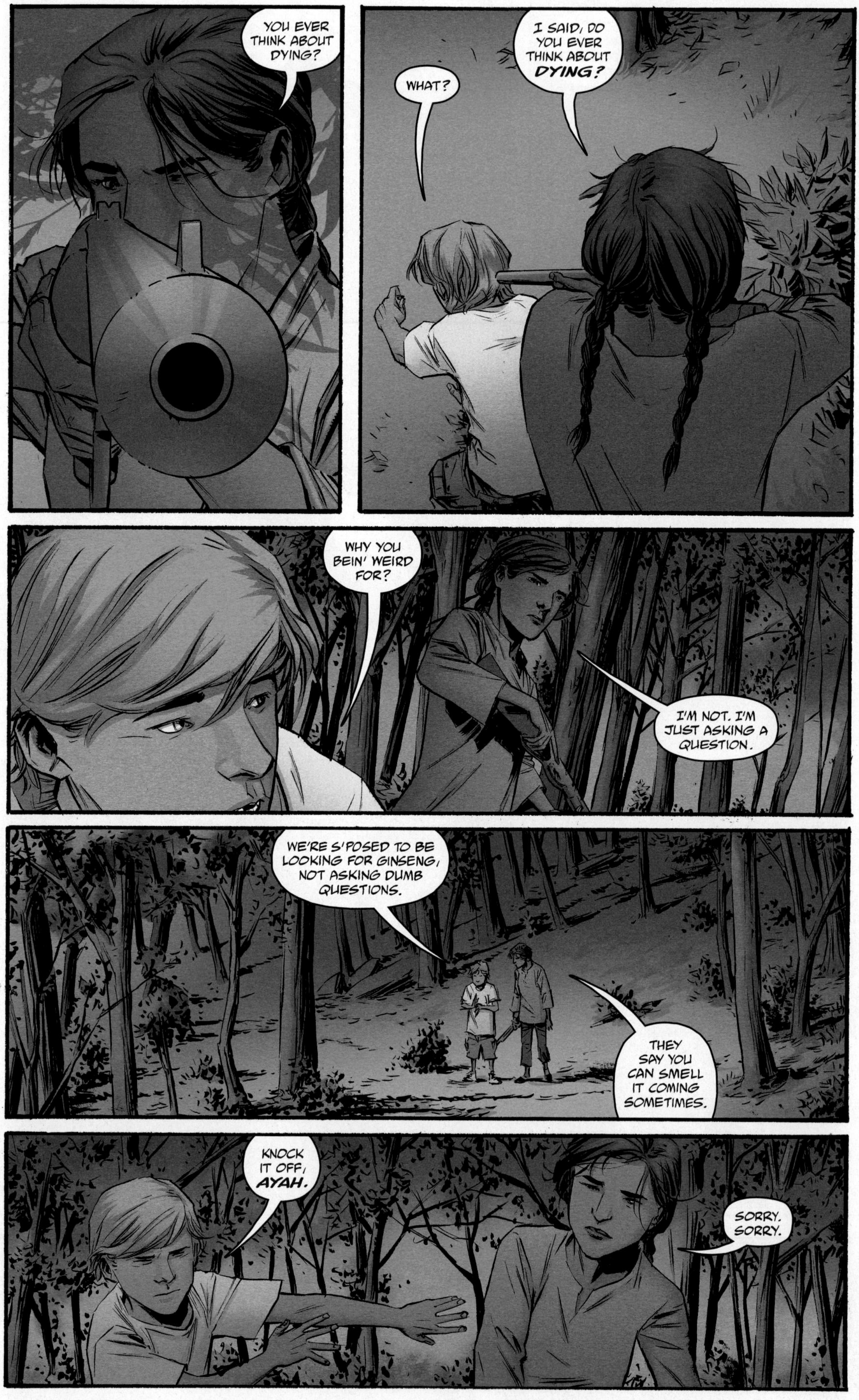
YOU EVER THINK ABOUT DYING?
WHAT?
I SAID, DO YOU EVER THINK ABOUT DYING?
WHY YOU BEIN' WEIRD FOR?
I'M NOT. I'M JUST ASKING A QUESTION.
WE'RE S'POSED TO BE LOOKING FOR GINSENG, NOT ASKING DUMB QUESTIONS.
THEY SAY YOU CAN SMELL IT COMING SOMETIMES.
KNOCK IT OFF, AYAH.
SORRY. SORRY.

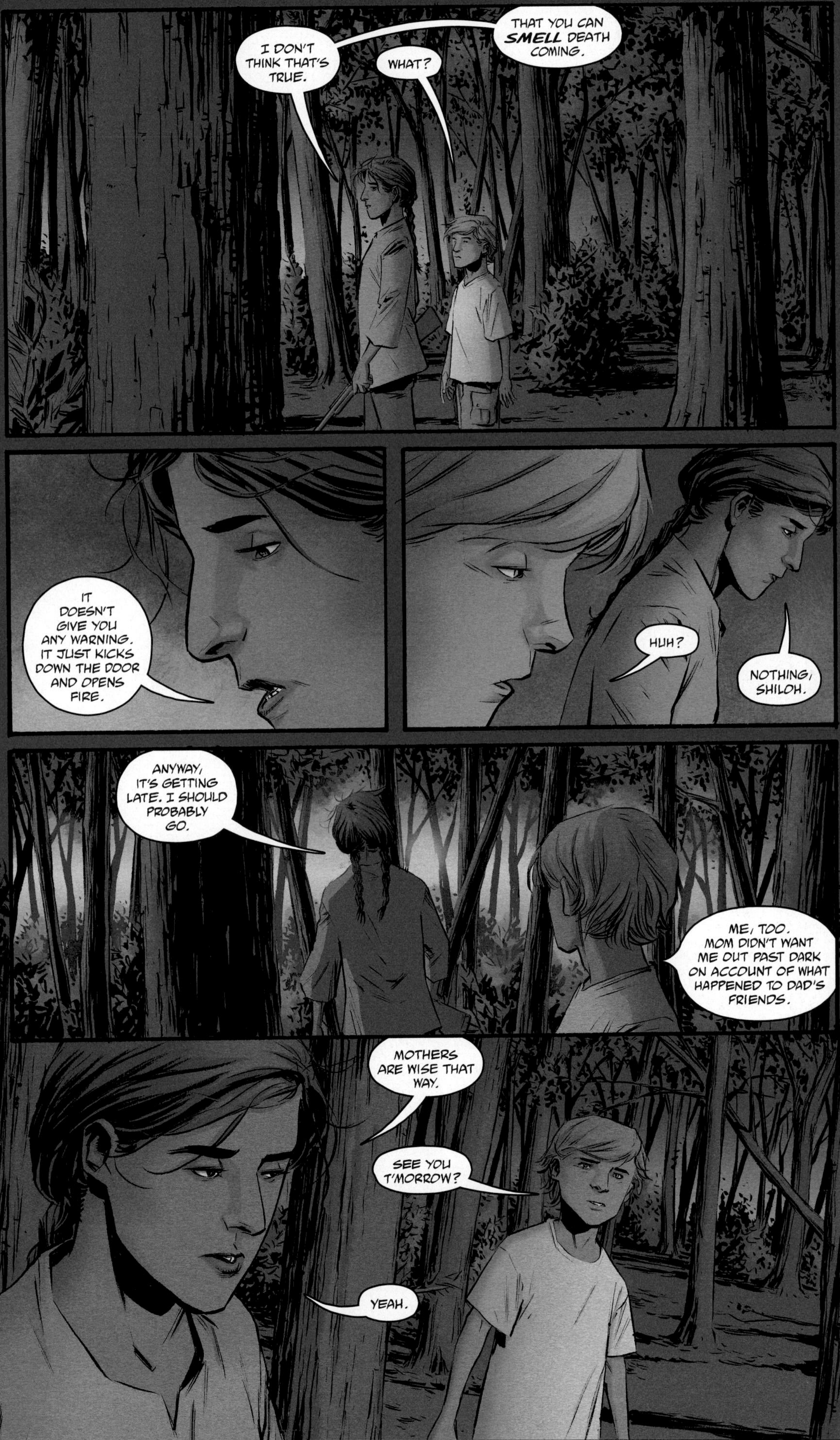
I DON'T THINK THAT'S TRUE.
WHAT?
THAT YOU CAN SMELL DEATH COMING.
IT DOESN'T GIVE YOU ANY WARNING. IT JUST KICKS DOWN THE DOOR AND OPENS FIRE.
HUH?
NOTHING, SHILOH.
ANYWAY, IT'S GETTING LATE. I SHOULD PROBABLY GO.
ME, TOO. MOM DIDN'T WANT ME OUT PAST DARK ON ACCOUNT OF WHAT HAPPENED TO DAD'S FRIENDS.
MOTHERS ARE WISE THAT WAY.
SEE YOU T'MORROW?
YEAH.

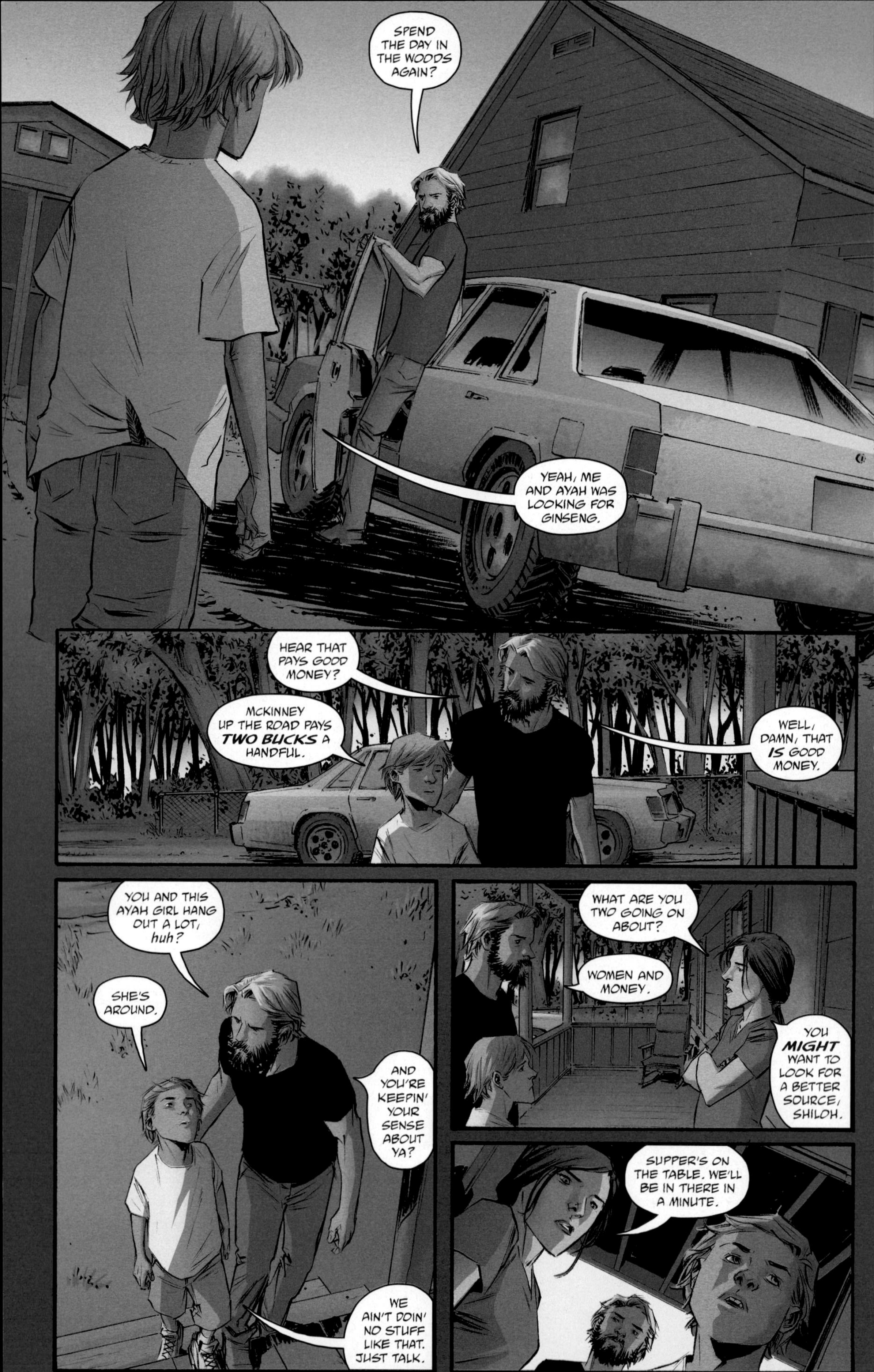
SPEND THE DAY IN THE WOODS AGAIN?
YEAH, ME AND AYAH WAS LOOKING FOR GINSENG.
HEAR THAT PAYS GOOD MONEY?
MCKINNEY UP THE ROAD PAYS **TWO BUCKS** A HANDFUL.
WELL, DAMN, THAT *IS* GOOD MONEY.
YOU AND THIS AYAH GIRL HANG OUT A LOT, *huh?*
SHE'S AROUND.
AND YOU'RE KEEPIN' YOUR SENSE ABOUT YA?
WE AIN'T DOIN' NO STUFF LIKE THAT. JUST TALK.
WHAT ARE YOU TWO GOING ON ABOUT?
WOMEN AND MONEY.
YOU **MIGHT** WANT TO LOOK FOR A BETTER SOURCE, SHILOH.
SUPPER'S ON THE TABLE. WE'LL BE IN THERE IN A MINUTE.

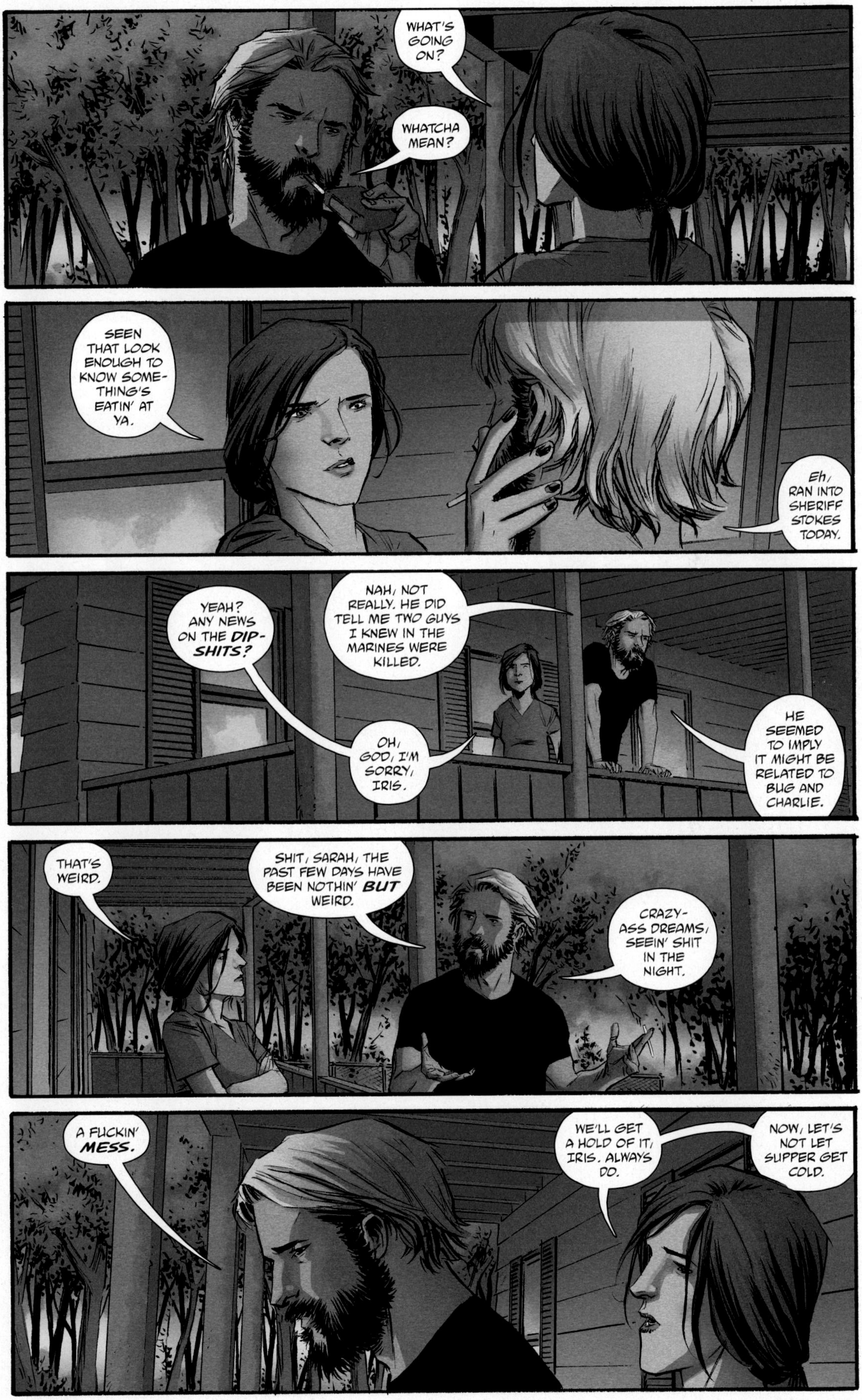

WHAT'S GOING ON?
WHATCHA MEAN?
SEEN THAT LOOK ENOUGH TO KNOW SOME-THING'S EATIN' AT YA.
Eh, RAN INTO SHERIFF STOKES TODAY.
YEAH? ANY NEWS ON THE **DIP-SHITS?**
NAH, NOT REALLY. HE DID TELL ME TWO GUYS I KNEW IN THE MARINES WERE KILLED.
OH, GOD, I'M SORRY, IRIS.
HE SEEMED TO IMPLY IT MIGHT BE RELATED TO BUG AND CHARLIE.
THAT'S WEIRD.
SHIT, SARAH, THE PAST FEW DAYS HAVE BEEN NOTHIN' **BUT** WEIRD.
CRAZY-ASS DREAMS, SEEIN' SHIT IN THE NIGHT.
A FUCKIN' **MESS.**
WE'LL GET A HOLD OF IT, IRIS. ALWAYS DO.
NOW, LET'S NOT LET SUPPER GET COLD.

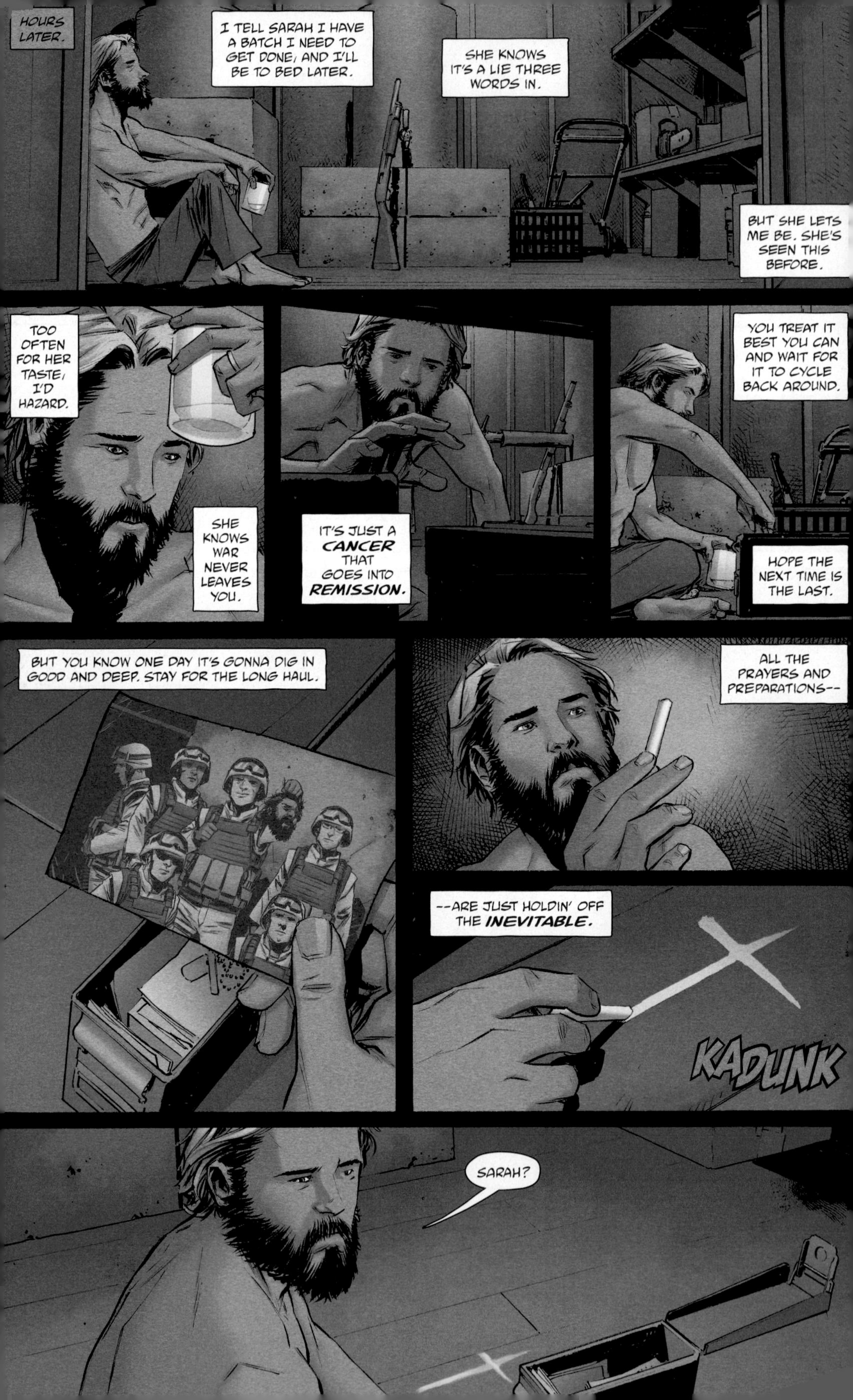

HOURS LATER.
I TELL SARAH I HAVE A BATCH I NEED TO GET DONE, AND I'LL BE TO BED LATER.
SHE KNOWS IT'S A LIE THREE WORDS IN.
BUT SHE LETS ME BE. SHE'S SEEN THIS BEFORE.
TOO OFTEN FOR HER TASTE, I'D HAZARD.
SHE KNOWS WAR NEVER LEAVES YOU.
IT'S JUST A CANCER THAT GOES INTO REMISSION.
YOU TREAT IT BEST YOU CAN AND WAIT FOR IT TO CYCLE BACK AROUND.
HOPE THE NEXT TIME IS THE LAST.
BUT YOU KNOW ONE DAY IT'S GONNA DIG IN GOOD AND DEEP. STAY FOR THE LONG HAUL.
ALL THE PRAYERS AND PREPARATIONS--
--ARE JUST HOLDIN' OFF THE INEVITABLE.
KADUNK
SARAH?

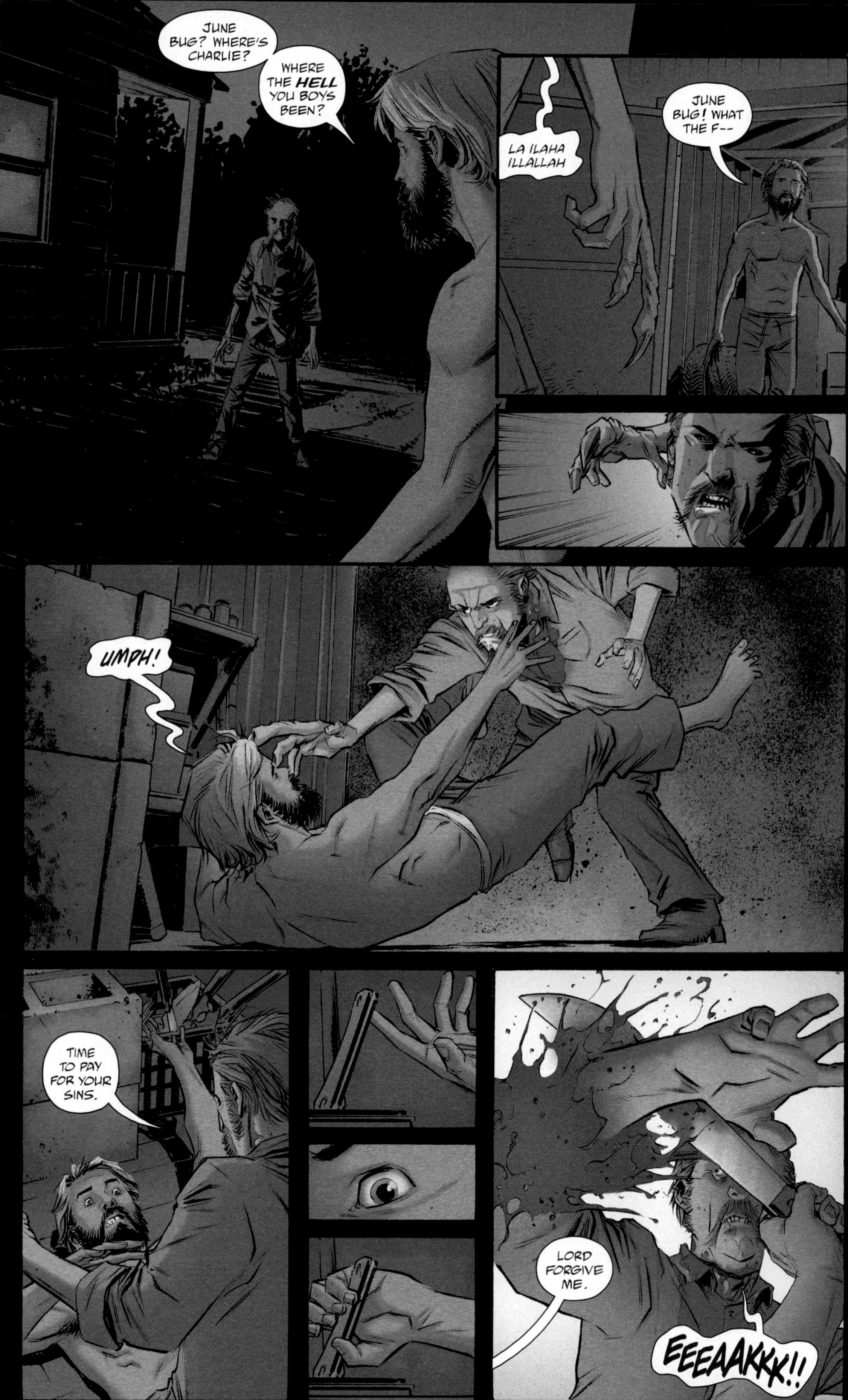
JUNE BUG? WHERE'S CHARLIE?
WHERE THE HELL YOU BOYS BEEN?
LA ILAHA ILLALLAH
JUNE BUG! WHAT THE F--
UMPH!
TIME TO PAY FOR YOUR SINS.
LORD FORGIVE ME.
EEEAAKKK!!

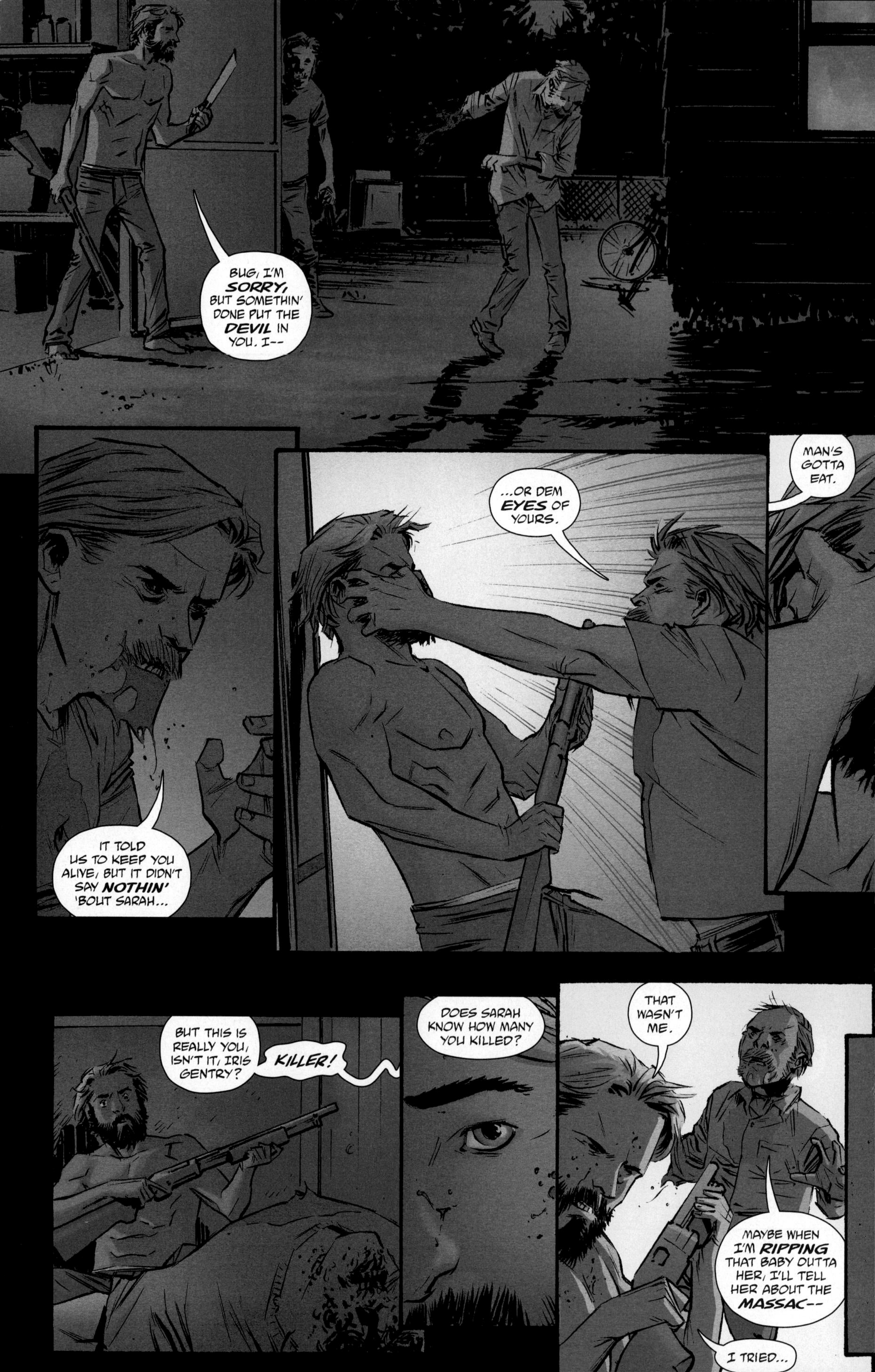
BUG, I'M SORRY, BUT SOMETHIN' DONE PUT THE DEVIL IN YOU. I--
IT TOLD US TO KEEP YOU ALIVE, BUT IT DIDN'T SAY NOTHIN' 'BOUT SARAH...
...OR DEM EYES OF YOURS.
MAN'S GOTTA EAT.
BUT THIS IS REALLY YOU, ISN'T IT, IRIS GENTRY?
KILLER!
DOES SARAH KNOW HOW MANY YOU KILLED?
THAT WASN'T ME.
MAYBE WHEN I'M RIPPING THAT BABY OUTTA HER, I'LL TELL HER ABOUT THE MASSAC--
I TRIED...

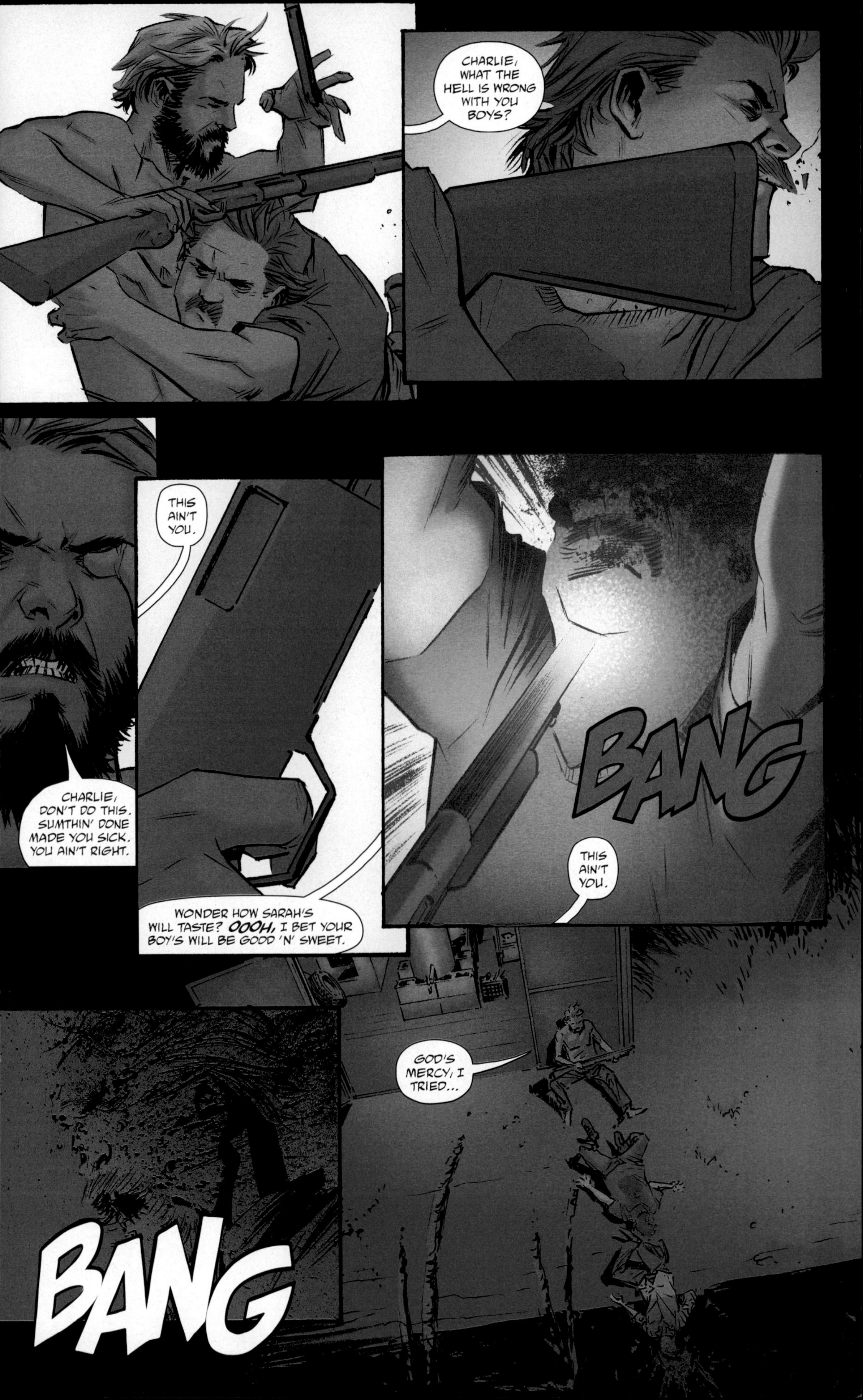
CHARLIE, WHAT THE HELL IS WRONG WITH YOU BOYS?
THIS AIN'T YOU.
CHARLIE, DON'T DO THIS. SUMTHIN' DONE MADE YOU SICK. YOU AIN'T RIGHT.
WONDER HOW SARAH'S WILL TASTE? OOOH, I BET YOUR BOY'S WILL BE GOOD 'N' SWEET.
BANG
THIS AIN'T YOU.
GOD'S MERCY, I TRIED...
BANG

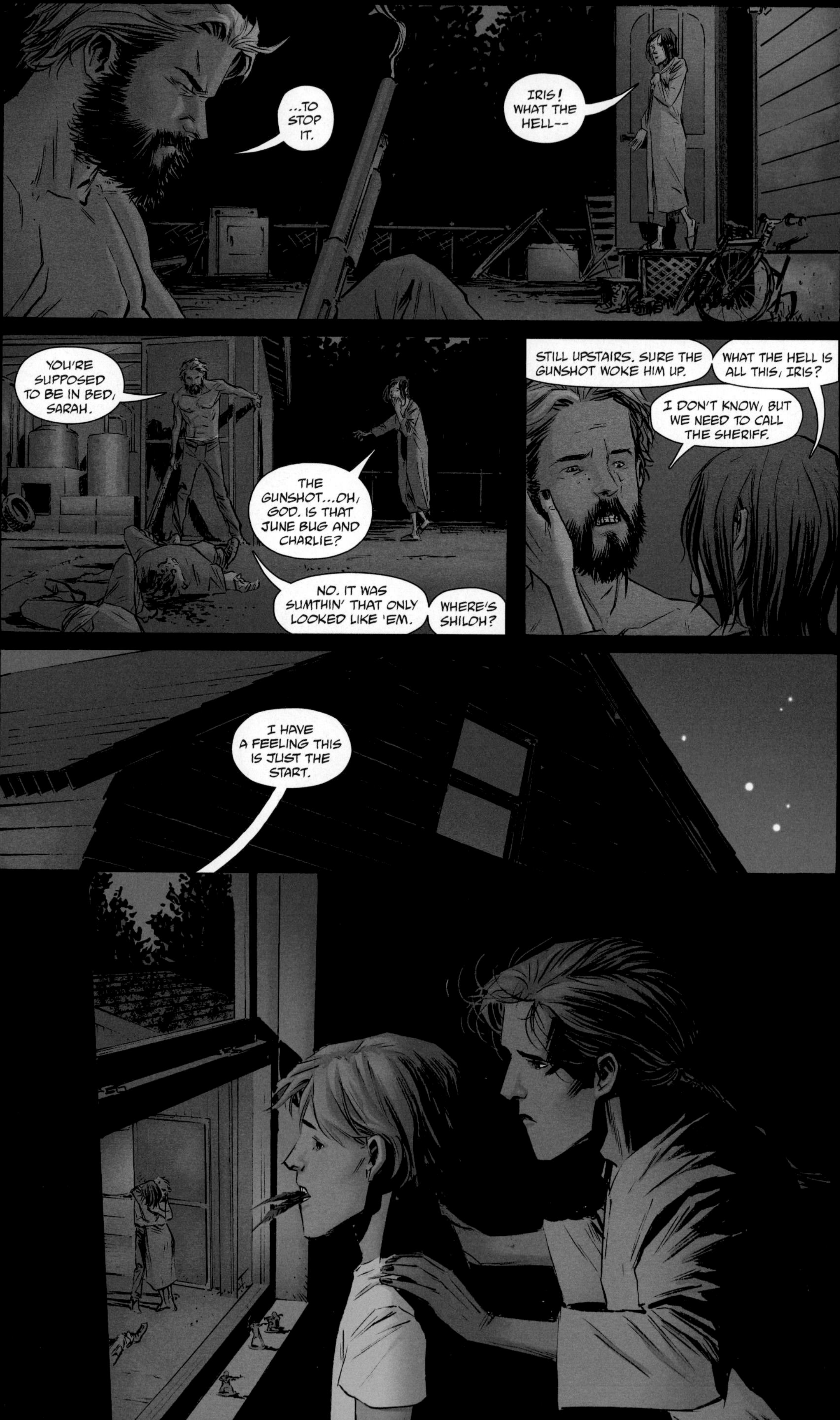
...TO STOP IT.
IRIS! WHAT THE HELL--
YOU'RE SUPPOSED TO BE IN BED, SARAH.
THE GUNSHOT...OH, GOD. IS THAT JUNE BUG AND CHARLIE?
NO. IT WAS SUMTHIN' THAT ONLY LOOKED LIKE 'EM.
WHERE'S SHILOH?
STILL UPSTAIRS. SURE THE GUNSHOT WOKE HIM UP.
WHAT THE HELL IS ALL THIS, IRIS?
I DON'T KNOW, BUT WE NEED TO CALL THE SHERIFF.
I HAVE A FEELING THIS IS JUST THE START.

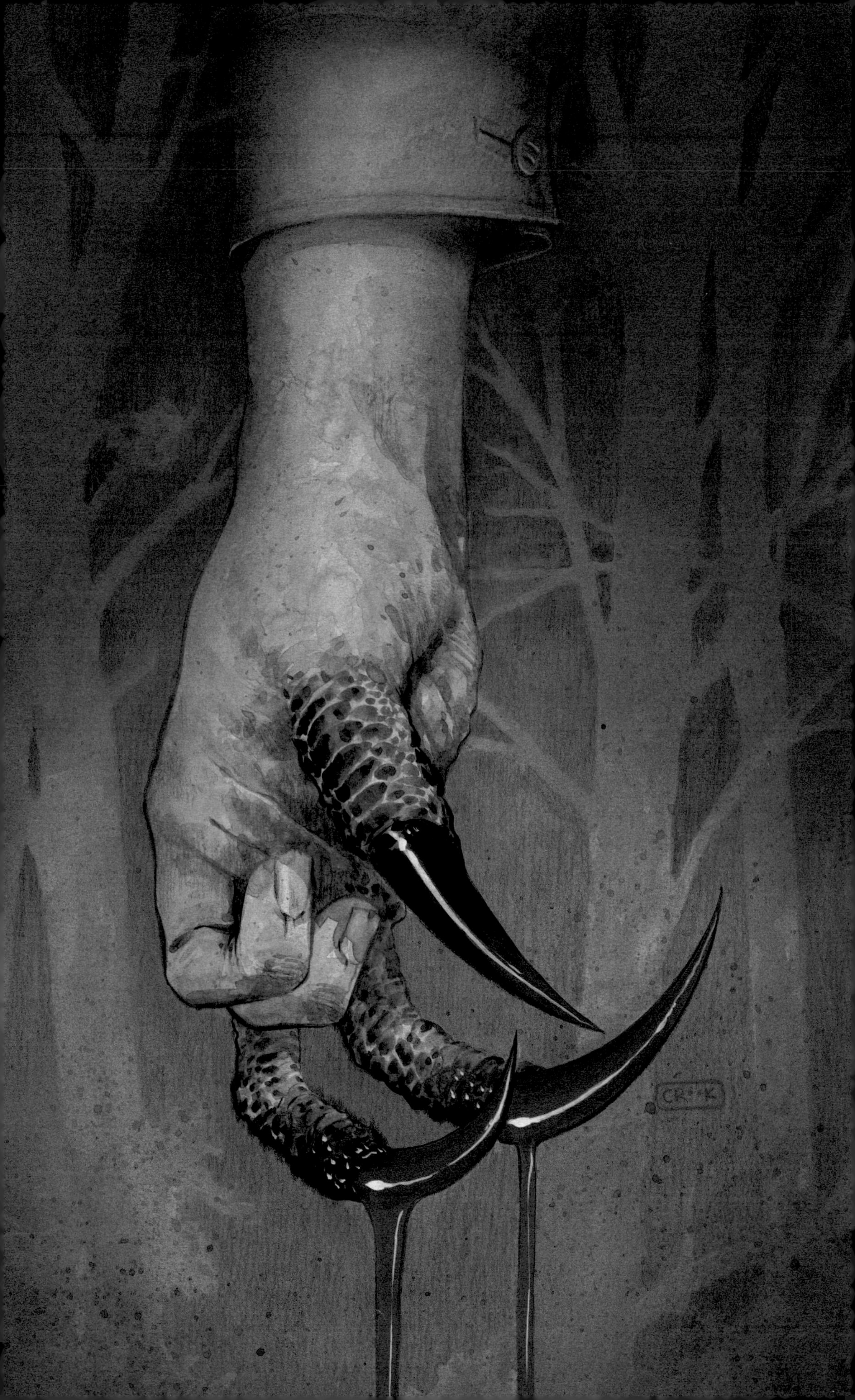

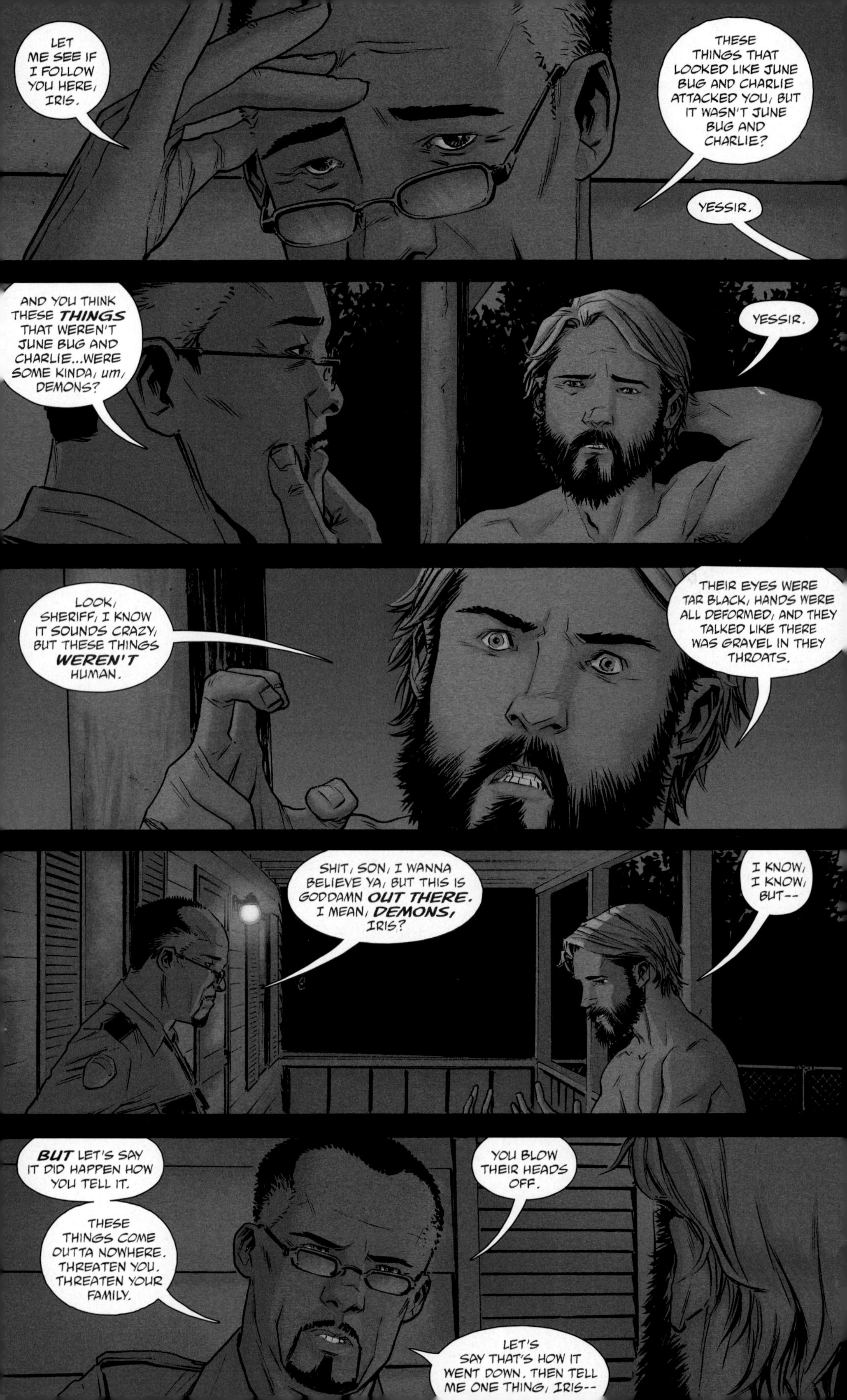
LET ME SEE IF I FOLLOW YOU HERE, IRIS.
THESE THINGS THAT LOOKED LIKE JUNE BUG AND CHARLIE ATTACKED YOU, BUT IT WASN'T JUNE BUG AND CHARLIE?
YESSIR.
AND YOU THINK THESE THINGS THAT WEREN'T JUNE BUG AND CHARLIE...WERE SOME KINDA, UM, DEMONS?
YESSIR.
LOOK, SHERIFF, I KNOW IT SOUNDS CRAZY, BUT THESE THINGS WEREN'T HUMAN.
THEIR EYES WERE TAR BLACK, HANDS WERE ALL DEFORMED, AND THEY TALKED LIKE THERE WAS GRAVEL IN THEY THROATS.
SHIT, SON, I WANNA BELIEVE YA, BUT THIS IS GODDAMN OUT THERE. I MEAN, DEMONS, IRIS?
I KNOW, I KNOW, BUT--
BUT LET'S SAY IT DID HAPPEN HOW YOU TELL IT.
THESE THINGS COME OUTTA NOWHERE. THREATEN YOU. THREATEN YOUR FAMILY.
YOU BLOW THEIR HEADS OFF.
LET'S SAY THAT'S HOW IT WENT DOWN. THEN TELL ME ONE THING, IRIS--

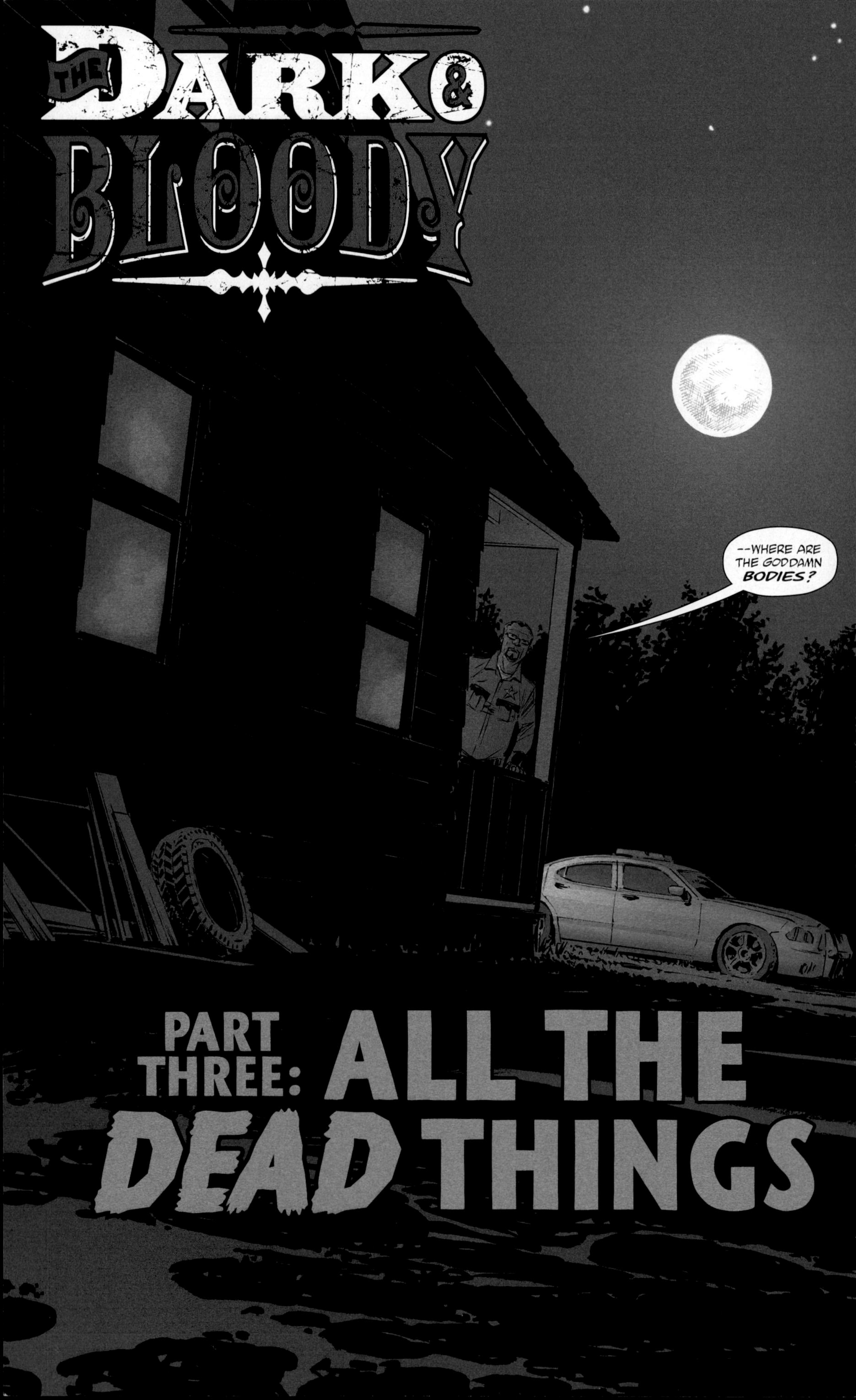
THE DARK & BLOODY
--WHERE ARE THE GODDAMN BODIES?
PART THREE: ALL THE DEAD THINGS

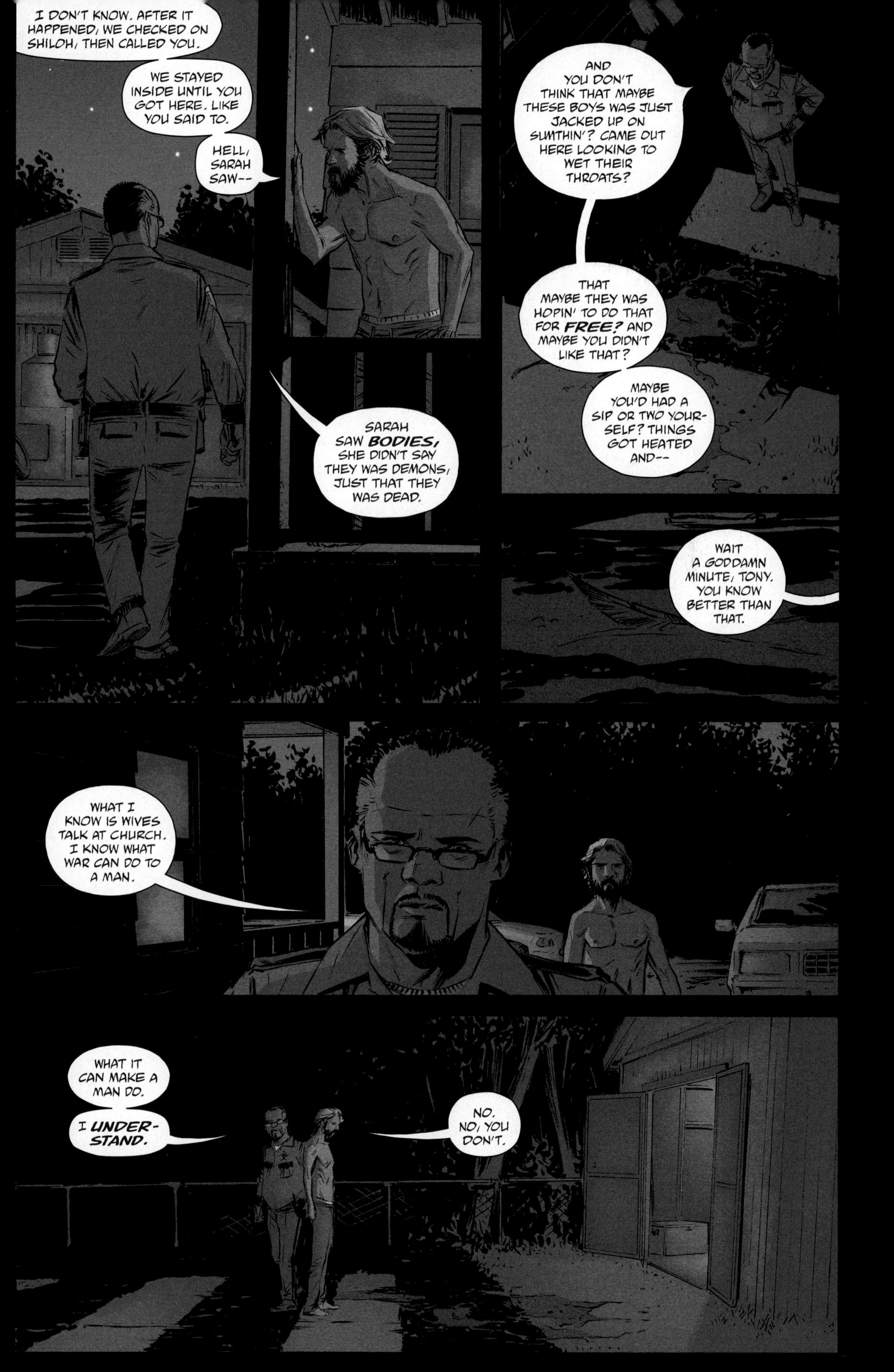
I DON'T KNOW. AFTER IT HAPPENED, WE CHECKED ON SHILOH, THEN CALLED YOU.
WE STAYED INSIDE UNTIL YOU GOT HERE. LIKE YOU SAID TO.
HELL, SARAH SAW--
SARAH SAW BODIES, SHE DIDN'T SAY THEY WAS DEMONS, JUST THAT THEY WAS DEAD.
AND YOU DON'T THINK THAT MAYBE THESE BOYS WAS JUST JACKED UP ON SUMTHIN'? CAME OUT HERE LOOKING TO WET THEIR THROATS?
THAT MAYBE THEY WAS HOPIN' TO DO THAT FOR FREE? AND MAYBE YOU DIDN'T LIKE THAT?
MAYBE YOU'D HAD A SIP OR TWO YOUR-SELF? THINGS GOT HEATED AND--
WAIT A GODDAMN MINUTE, TONY. YOU KNOW BETTER THAN THAT.
WHAT I KNOW IS WIVES TALK AT CHURCH. I KNOW WHAT WAR CAN DO TO A MAN.
WHAT IT CAN MAKE A MAN DO.
I UNDER-STAND.
NO. NO, YOU DON'T.

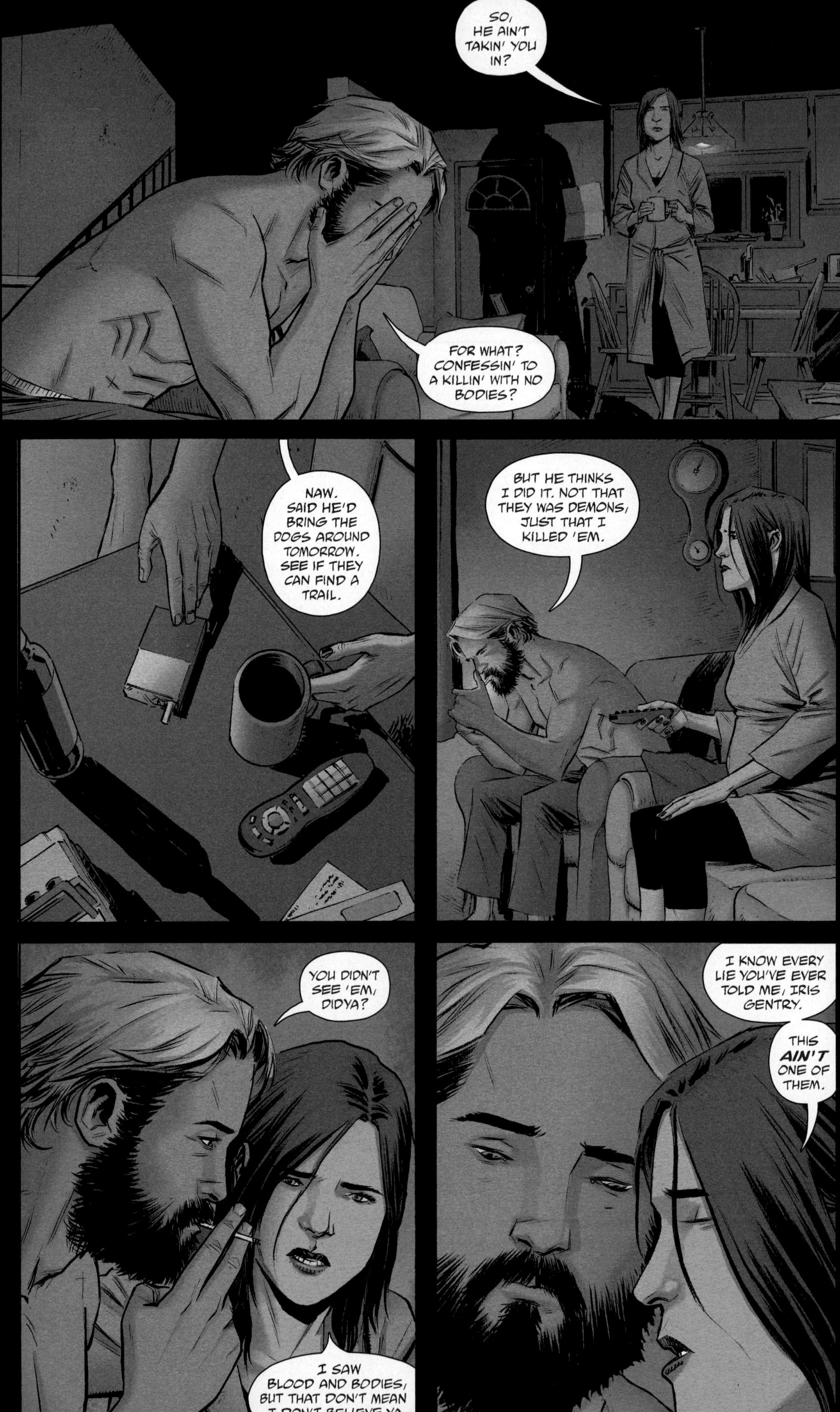
SO, HE AIN'T TAKIN' YOU IN?
FOR WHAT? CONFESSIN' TO A KILLIN' WITH NO BODIES?
NAW. SAID HE'D BRING THE DOGS AROUND TOMORROW. SEE IF THEY CAN FIND A TRAIL.
BUT HE THINKS I DID IT. NOT THAT THEY WAS DEMONS, JUST THAT I KILLED 'EM.
YOU DIDN'T SEE 'EM, DIDYA?
I SAW BLOOD AND BODIES, BUT THAT DON'T MEAN I DON'T BELIEVE YA.
I KNOW EVERY LIE YOU'VE EVER TOLD ME, IRIS GENTRY.
THIS AIN'T ONE OF THEM.

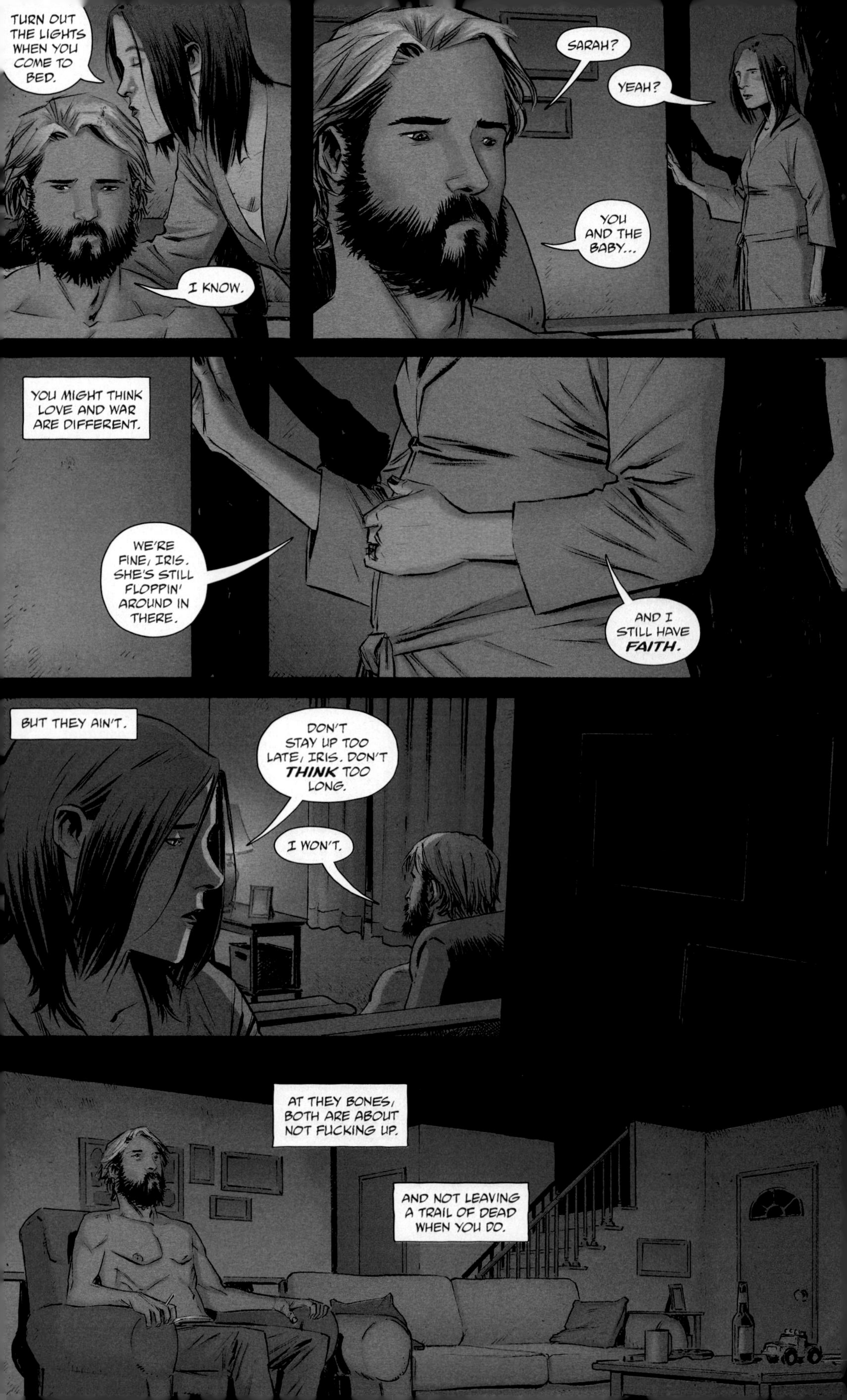
TURN OUT THE LIGHTS WHEN YOU COME TO BED.
I KNOW.
SARAH?
YEAH?
YOU AND THE BABY...
YOU MIGHT THINK LOVE AND WAR ARE DIFFERENT.
WE'RE FINE, IRIS. SHE'S STILL FLOPPIN' AROUND IN THERE.
AND I STILL HAVE FAITH.
BUT THEY AIN'T.
DON'T STAY UP TOO LATE, IRIS. DON'T THINK TOO LONG.
I WON'T.
AT THEY BONES, BOTH ARE ABOUT NOT FUCKING UP.
AND NOT LEAVING A TRAIL OF DEAD WHEN YOU DO.

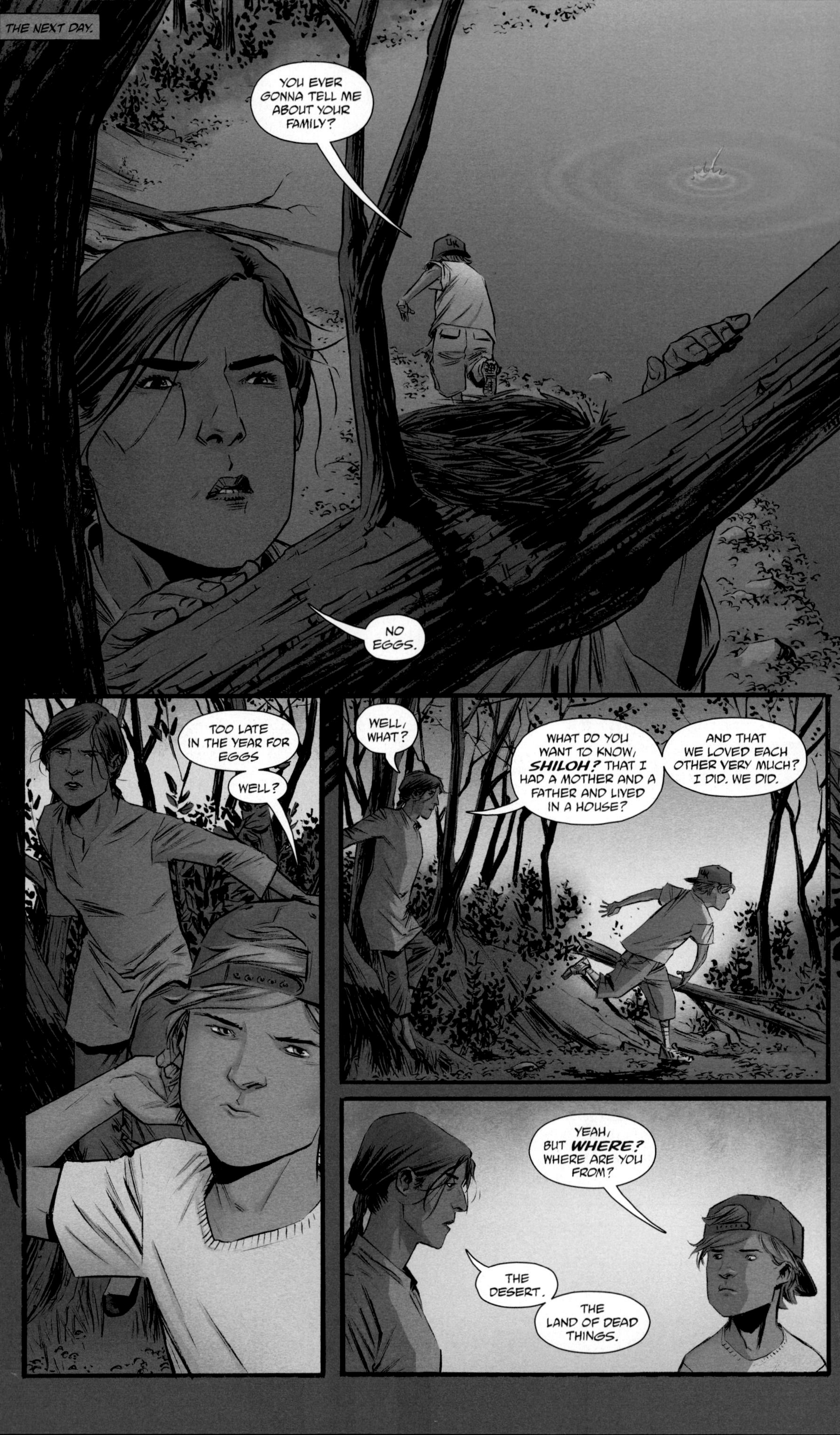
THE NEXT DAY.
YOU EVER GONNA TELL ME ABOUT YOUR FAMILY?
NO EGGS.
TOO LATE IN THE YEAR FOR EGGS
WELL?
WELL, WHAT?
WHAT DO YOU WANT TO KNOW, SHILOH? THAT I HAD A MOTHER AND A FATHER AND LIVED IN A HOUSE?
AND THAT WE LOVED EACH OTHER VERY MUCH? I DID. WE DID.
YEAH, BUT WHERE? WHERE ARE YOU FROM?
THE DESERT.
THE LAND OF DEAD THINGS.

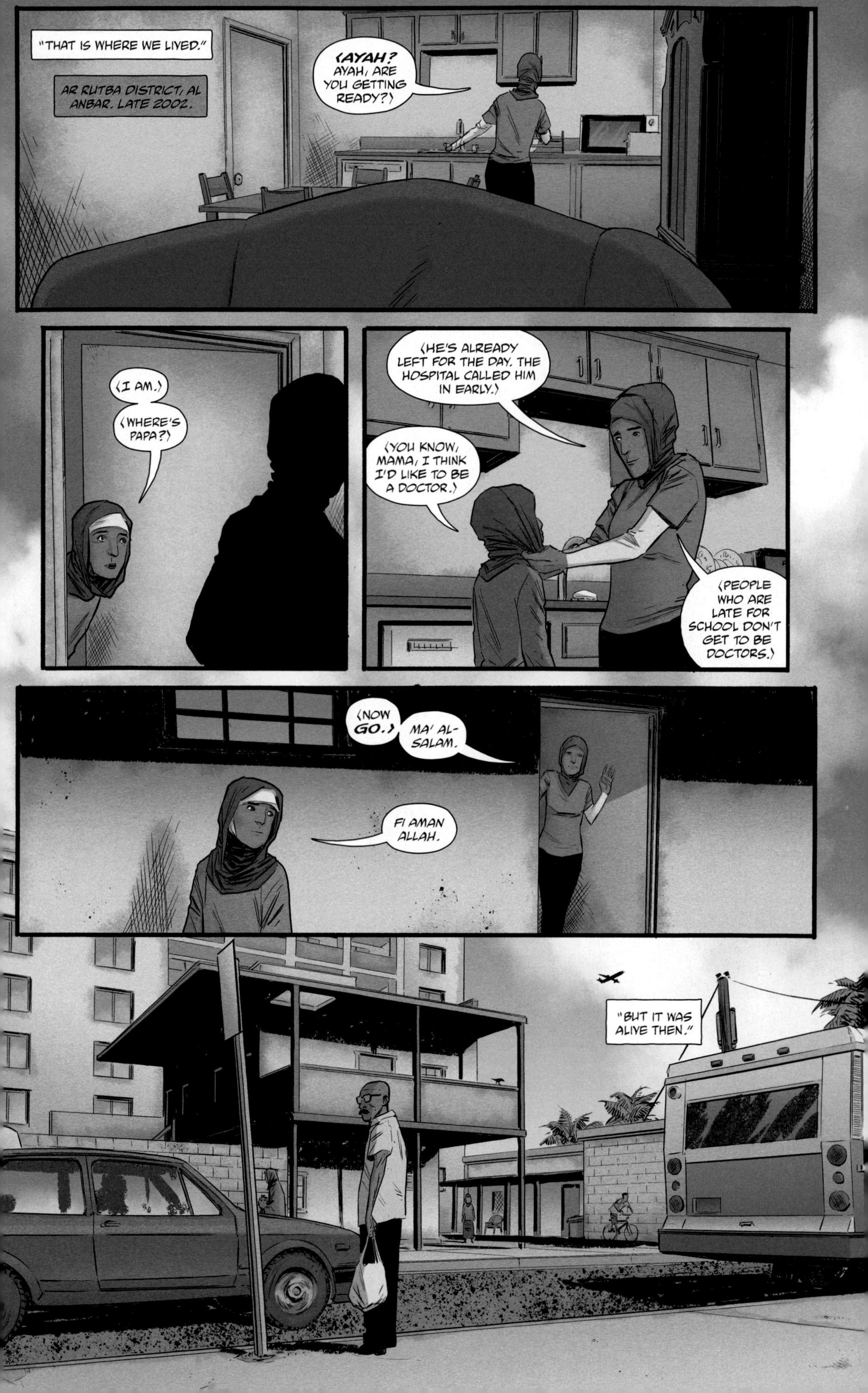
"THAT IS WHERE WE LIVED."
AR RUTBA DISTRICT, AL ANBAR. LATE 2002.
‹AYAH? AYAH, ARE YOU GETTING READY?›
‹I AM.›
‹WHERE'S PAPA?›
‹HE'S ALREADY LEFT FOR THE DAY. THE HOSPITAL CALLED HIM IN EARLY.›
‹YOU KNOW, MAMA, I THINK I'D LIKE TO BE A DOCTOR.›
‹PEOPLE WHO ARE LATE FOR SCHOOL DON'T GET TO BE DOCTORS.›
‹NOW GO.›
MA' AL-SALAM.
FI AMAN ALLAH.
"BUT IT WAS ALIVE THEN."

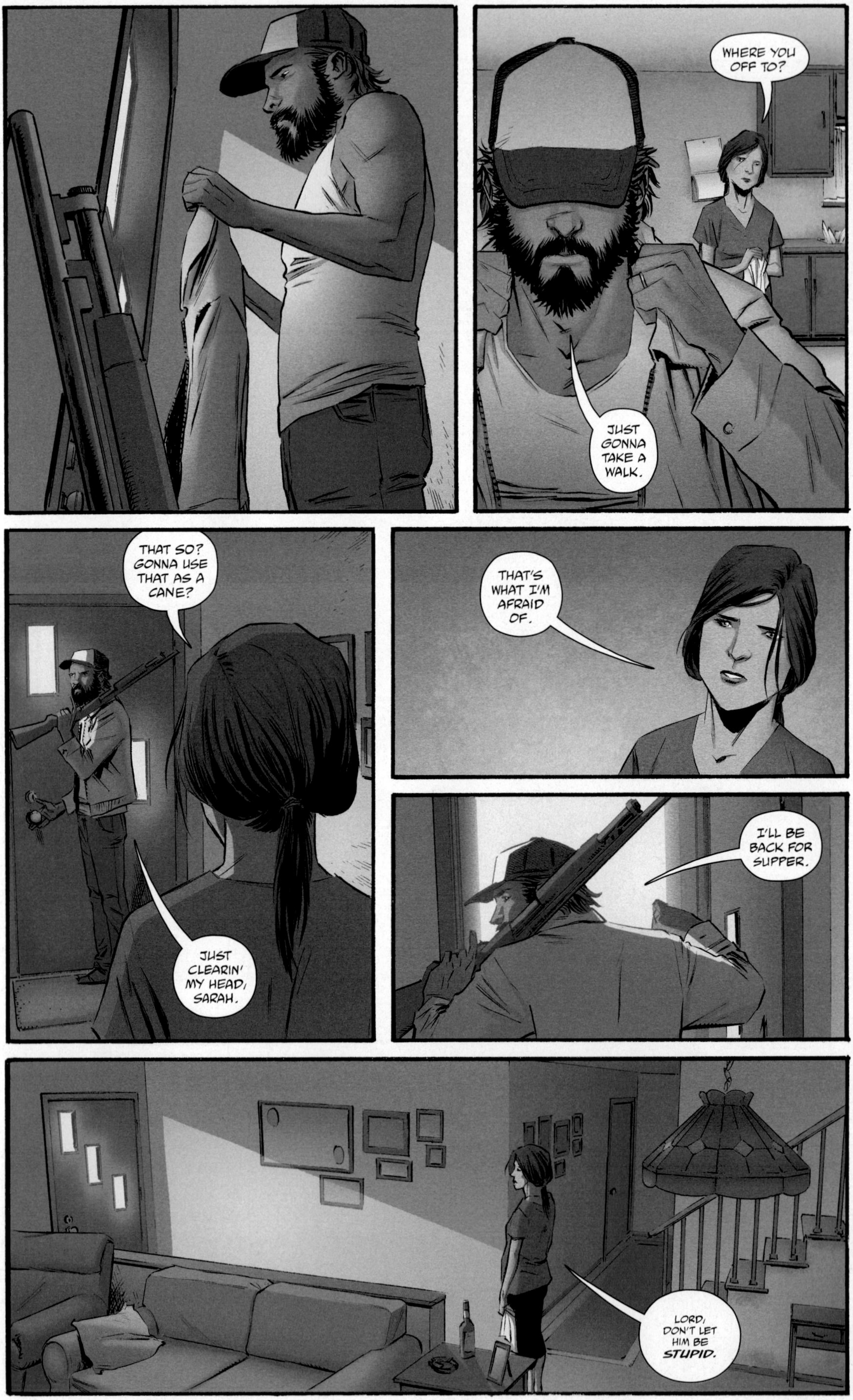
WHERE YOU OFF TO?
JUST GONNA TAKE A WALK.
THAT SO? GONNA USE THAT AS A CANE?
JUST CLEARIN' MY HEAD, SARAH.
THAT'S WHAT I'M AFRAID OF.
I'LL BE BACK FOR SUPPER.
LORD, DON'T LET HIM BE **STUPID**.

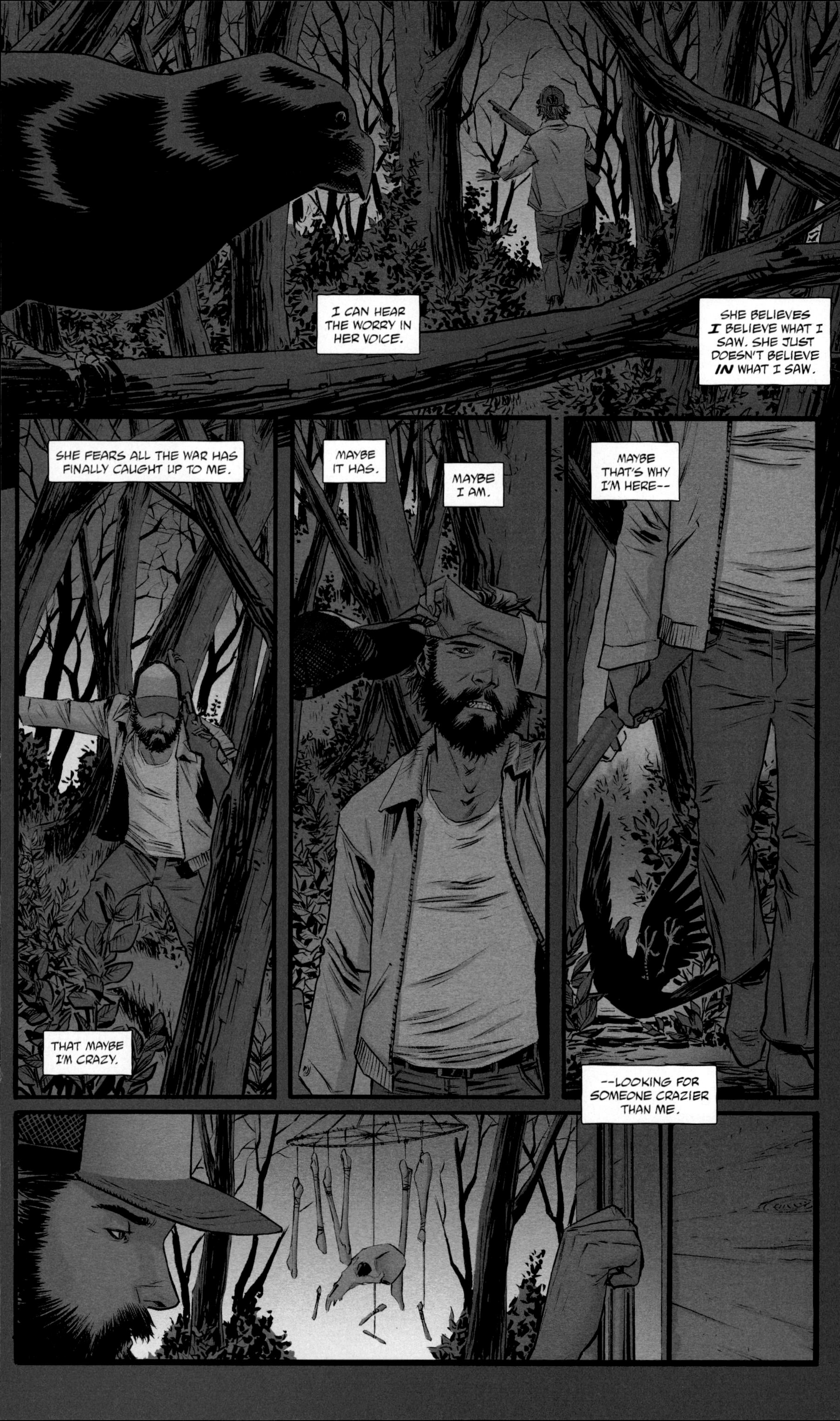
I CAN HEAR THE WORRY IN HER VOICE.
SHE BELIEVES *I* BELIEVE WHAT I SAW. SHE JUST DOESN'T BELIEVE *IN* WHAT I SAW.
SHE FEARS ALL THE WAR HAS FINALLY CAUGHT UP TO ME.
THAT MAYBE I'M CRAZY.
MAYBE IT HAS.
MAYBE I AM.
MAYBE THAT'S WHY I'M HERE--
--LOOKING FOR SOMEONE CRAZIER THAN ME.

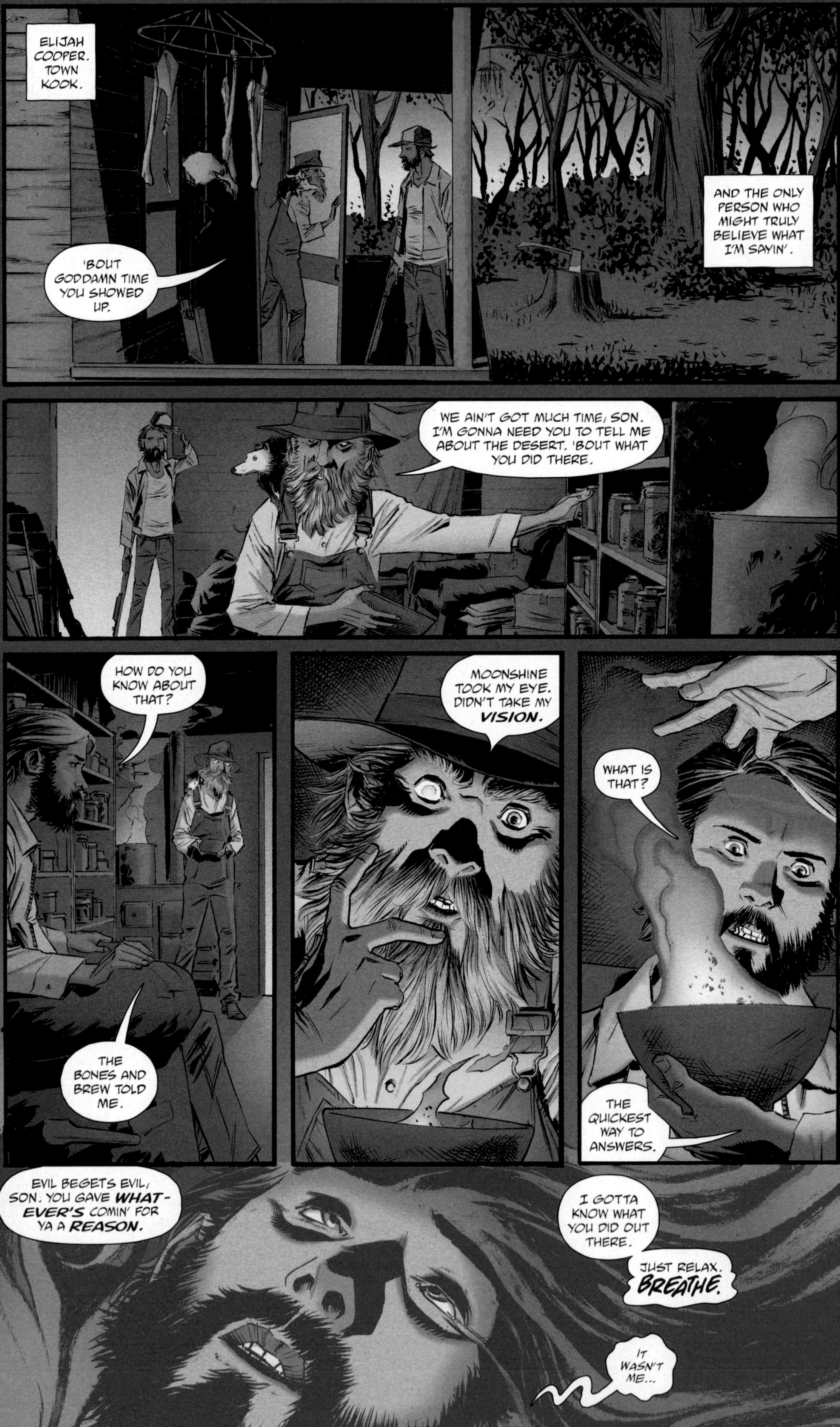
ELIJAH COOPER. TOWN KOOK.
'BOUT GODDAMN TIME YOU SHOWED UP.
AND THE ONLY PERSON WHO MIGHT TRULY BELIEVE WHAT I'M SAYIN'.
WE AIN'T GOT MUCH TIME, SON. I'M GONNA NEED YOU TO TELL ME ABOUT THE DESERT. 'BOUT WHAT YOU DID THERE.
HOW DO YOU KNOW ABOUT THAT?
THE BONES AND BREW TOLD ME.
MOONSHINE TOOK MY EYE. DIDN'T TAKE MY VISION.
WHAT IS THAT?
THE QUICKEST WAY TO ANSWERS.
EVIL BEGETS EVIL, SON. YOU GAVE WHAT-EVER'S COMIN' FOR YA A REASON.
I GOTTA KNOW WHAT YOU DID OUT THERE.
JUST RELAX. BREATHE.
IT WASN'T ME...

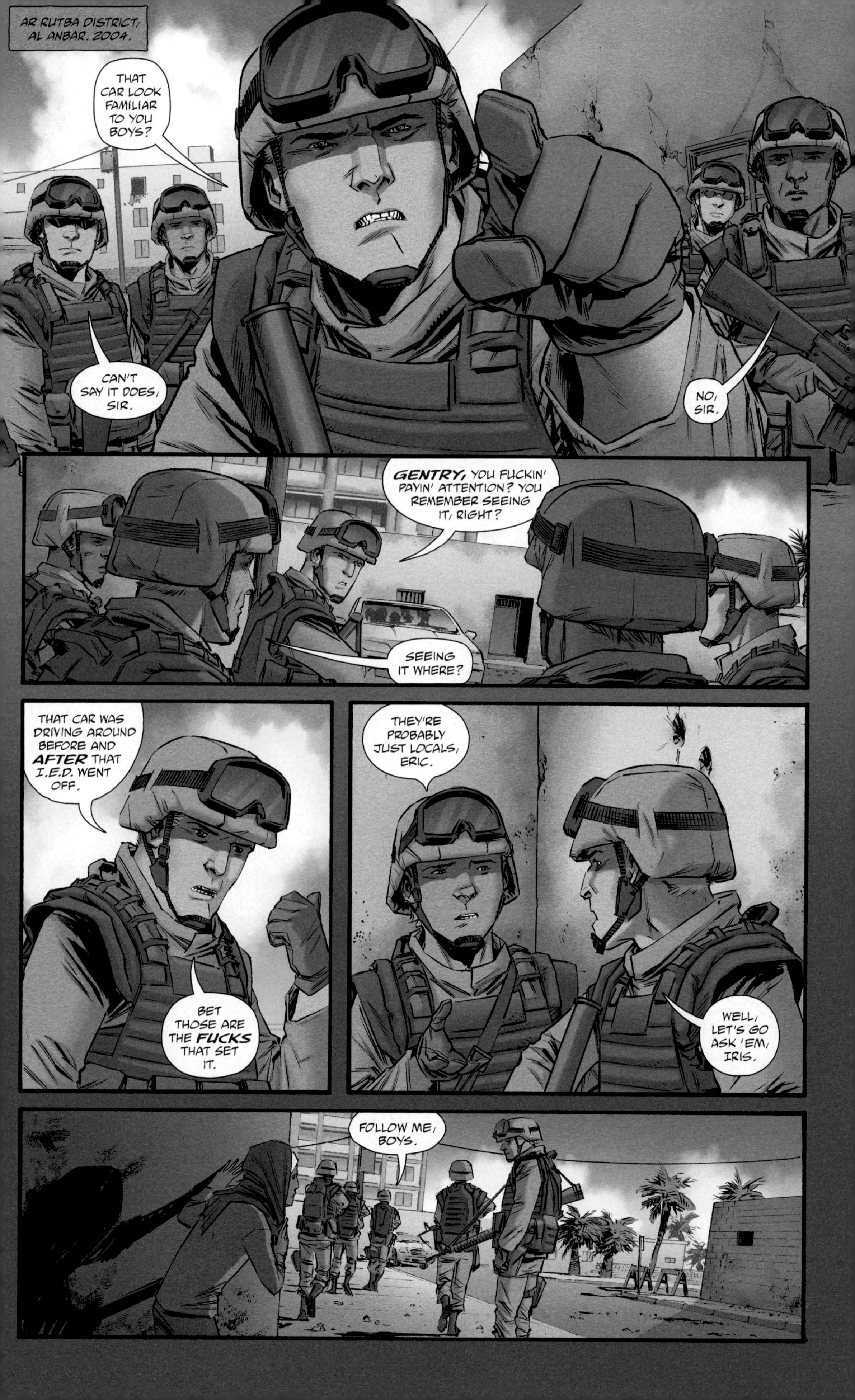
AR RUTBA DISTRICT, AL ANBAR. 2004.
THAT CAR LOOK FAMILIAR TO YOU BOYS?
CAN'T SAY IT DOES, SIR.
NO, SIR.
GENTRY, YOU FUCKIN' PAYIN' ATTENTION? YOU REMEMBER SEEING IT, RIGHT?
SEEING IT WHERE?
THAT CAR WAS DRIVING AROUND BEFORE AND AFTER THAT I.E.D. WENT OFF.
BET THOSE ARE THE FUCKS THAT SET IT.
THEY'RE PROBABLY JUST LOCALS, ERIC.
WELL, LET'S GO ASK 'EM, IRIS.
FOLLOW ME, BOYS.

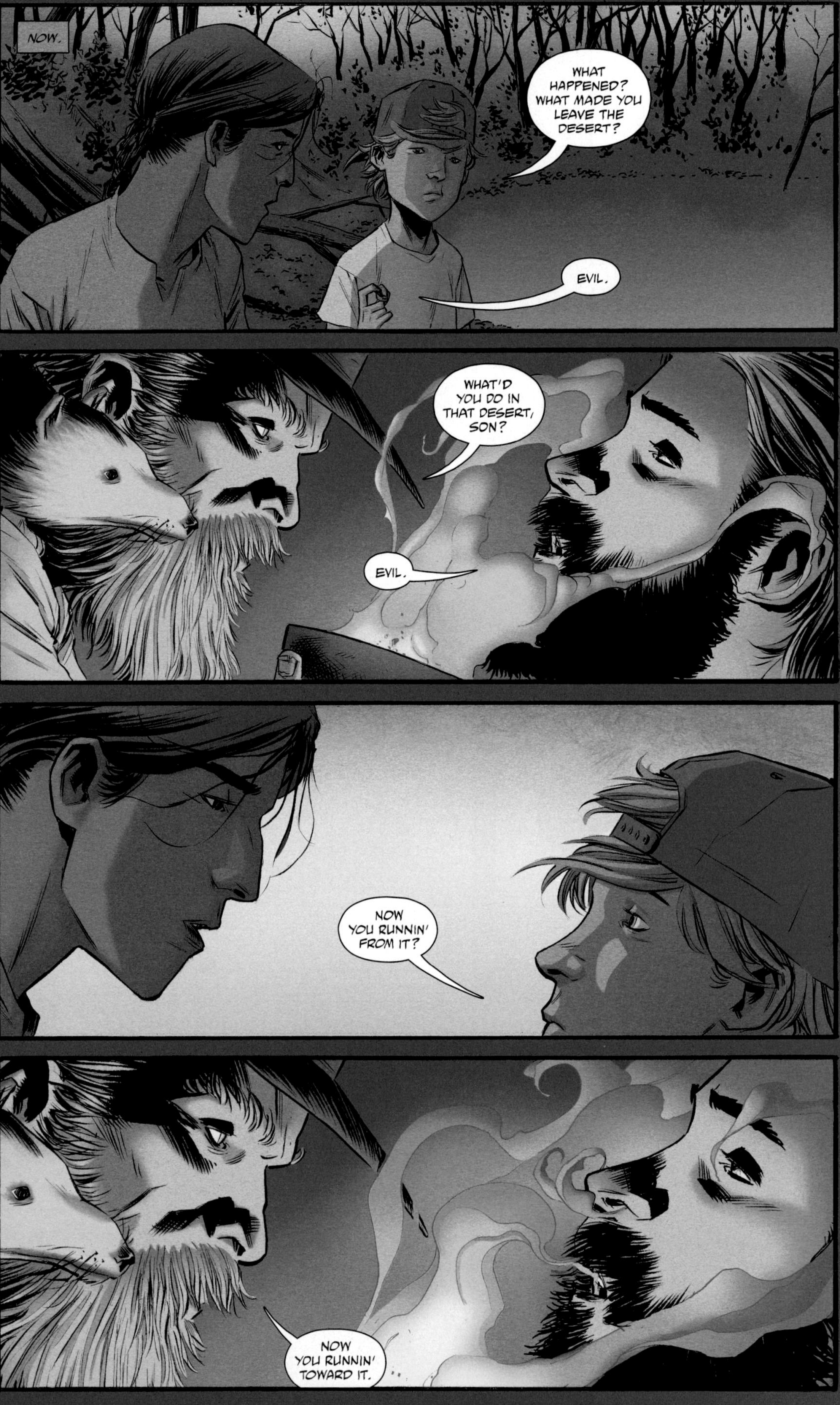
NOW.
WHAT HAPPENED? WHAT MADE YOU LEAVE THE DESERT?
EVIL.
WHAT'D YOU DO IN THAT DESERT, SON?
EVIL.
NOW YOU RUNNIN' FROM IT?
NOW YOU RUNNIN' TOWARD IT.

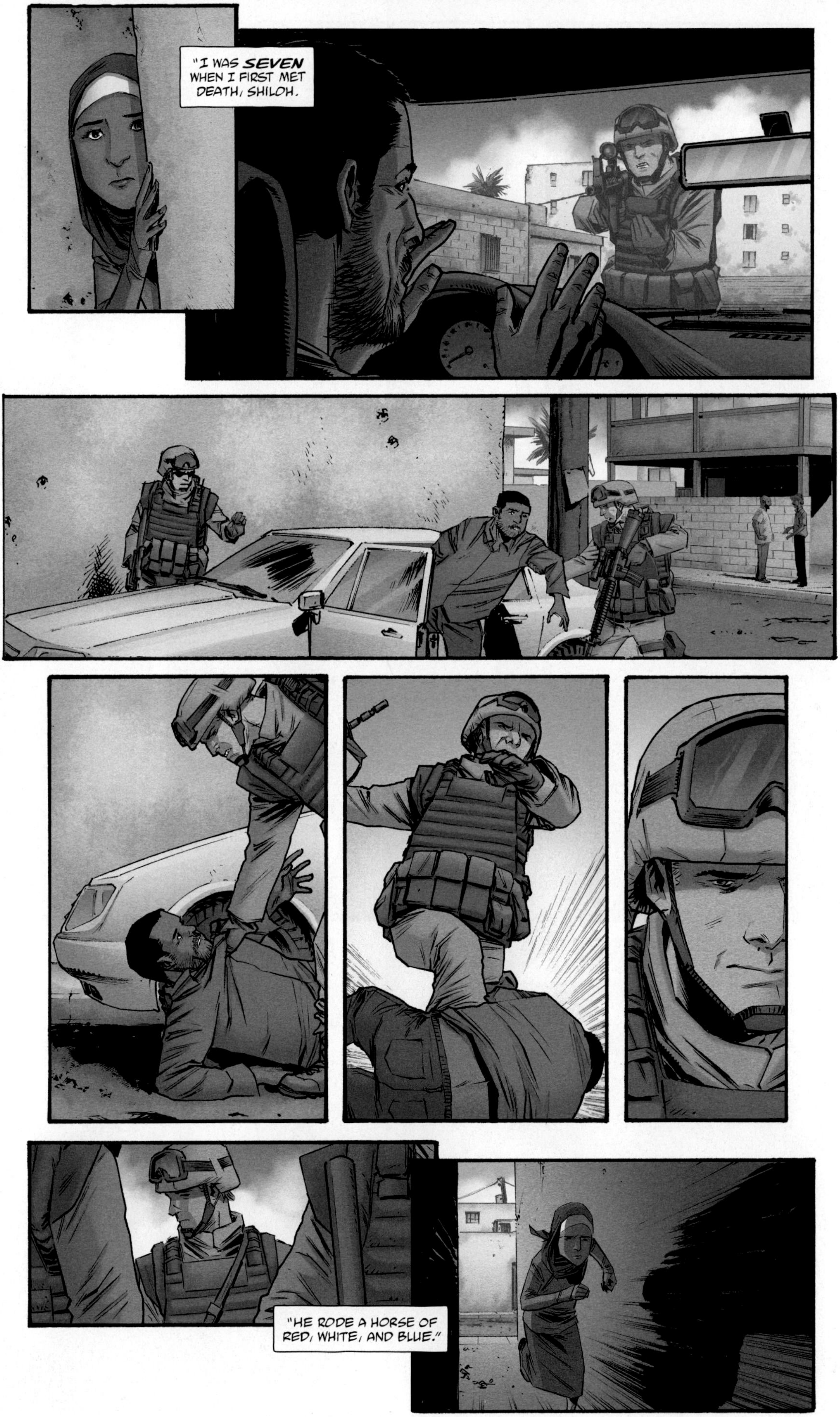
"I WAS SEVEN WHEN I FIRST MET DEATH, SHILOH.
"HE RODE A HORSE OF RED, WHITE, AND BLUE."

WHAT'S THIS, HAJJI? SHRAPNEL FOR ANOTHER BOMB?

GET THE OTHERS OUT. THINK WE HAVE US A CAR FULL OF *INSURGENTS,* FELLAS.

FOSTER, *SIR,* THIS ISN'T RIGHT. WE DON'T KNOW THESE PEOPLE HAVE ANY CONNECTION TO BOMBING.

I KNOW I SAW THAT CAR, AND I *KNOW* WHAT A FUCKIN' INSURGENT SMELLS LIKE.

LIKE FUCKIN' CAMEL PISS AND SAND.

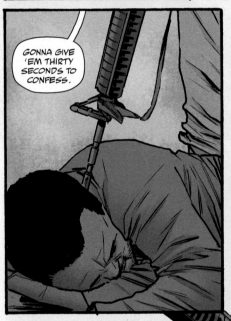

GONNA GIVE 'EM THIRTY SECONDS TO CONFESS.

HOW ABOUT IT?

ANY OF YOU *MUTHA-FUCKERS* WANNA *SPEAK?*

FINISH 'EM UP, FELLAS.

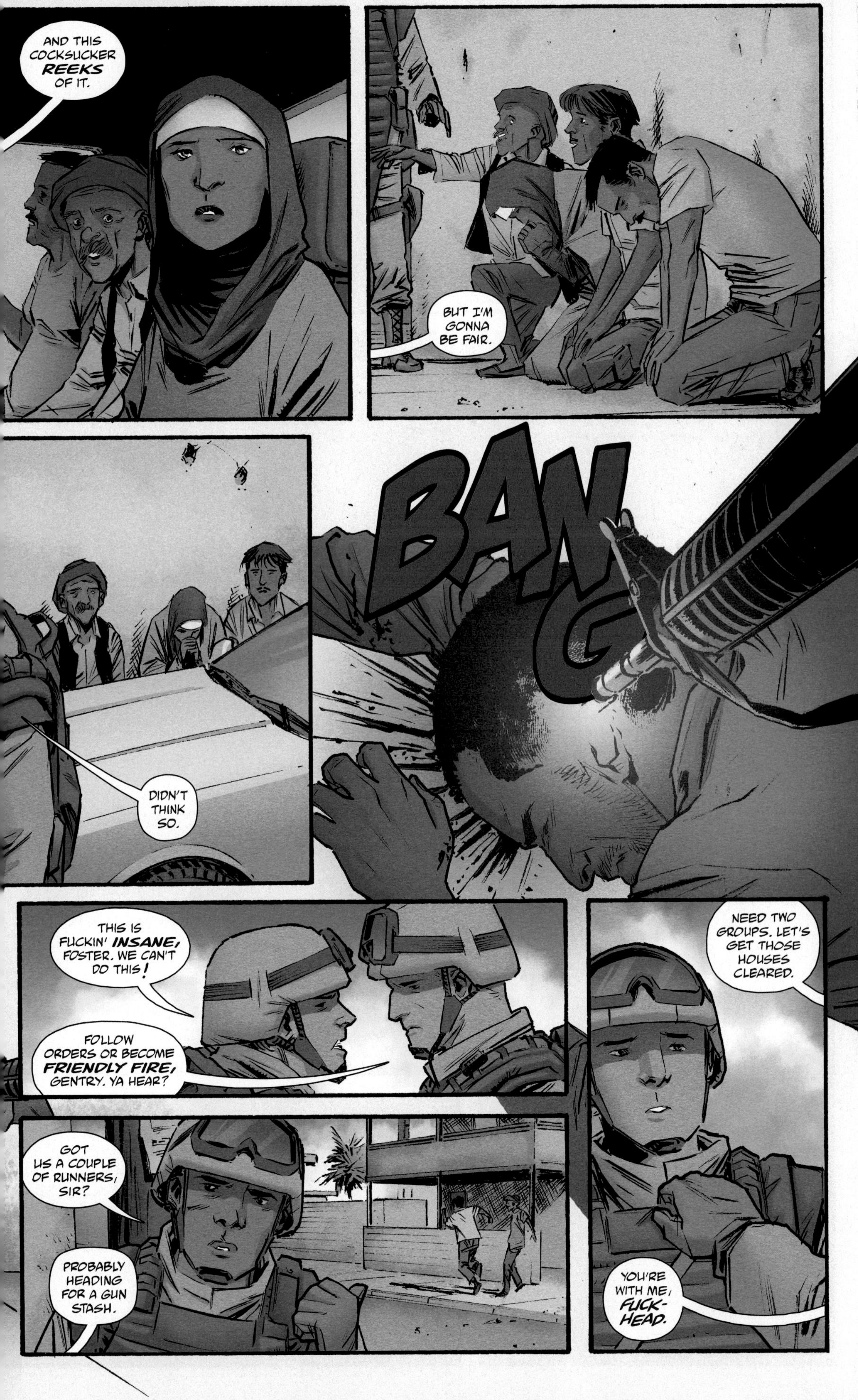
AND THIS COCKSUCKER REEKS OF IT.
BUT I'M GONNA BE FAIR.
DIDN'T THINK SO.
BANG
THIS IS FUCKIN' INSANE, FOSTER. WE CAN'T DO THIS!
FOLLOW ORDERS OR BECOME FRIENDLY FIRE, GENTRY. YA HEAR?
NEED TWO GROUPS. LET'S GET THOSE HOUSES CLEARED.
GOT US A COUPLE OF RUNNERS, SIR?
PROBABLY HEADING FOR A GUN STASH.
YOU'RE WITH ME, FUCK-HEAD.

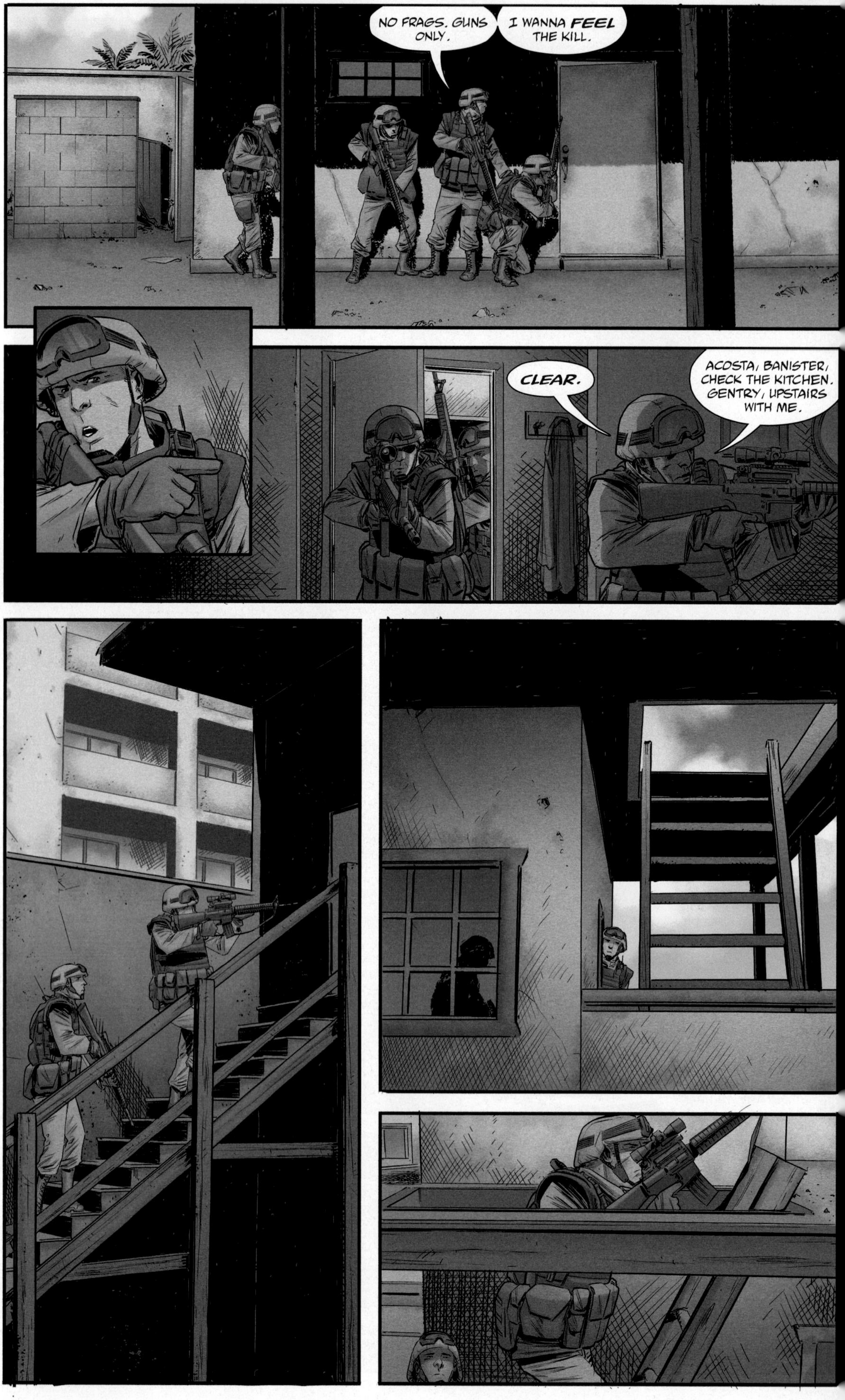
NO FRAGS. GUNS ONLY.
I WANNA FEEL THE KILL.
CLEAR.
ACOSTA, BANISTER, CHECK THE KITCHEN. GENTRY, UPSTAIRS WITH ME.

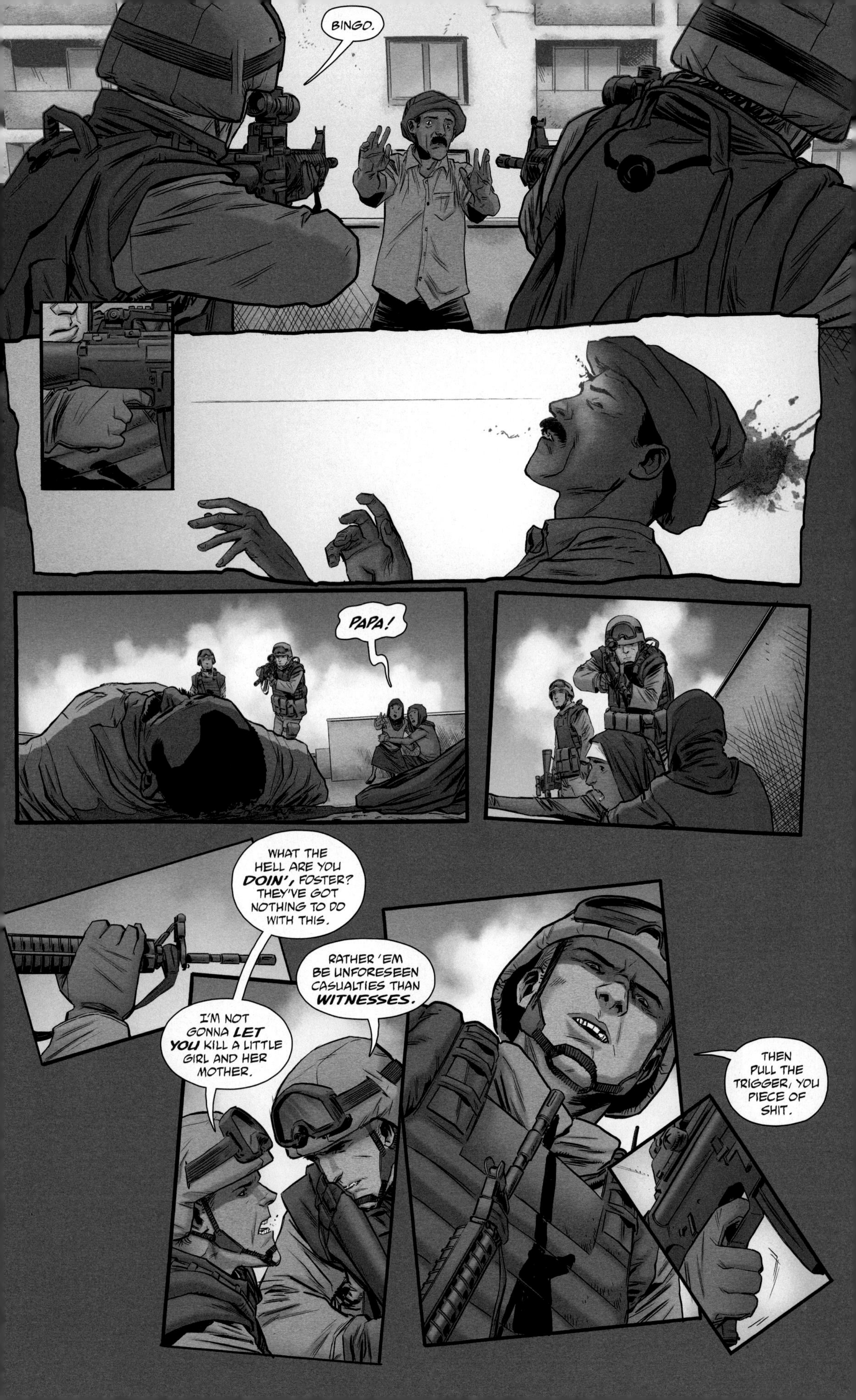
BINGO.
PAPA!
WHAT THE HELL ARE YOU DOIN', FOSTER? THEY'VE GOT NOTHING TO DO WITH THIS.
RATHER 'EM BE UNFORESEEN CASUALTIES THAN WITNESSES.
I'M NOT GONNA LET YOU KILL A LITTLE GIRL AND HER MOTHER.
THEN PULL THE TRIGGER, YOU PIECE OF SHIT.

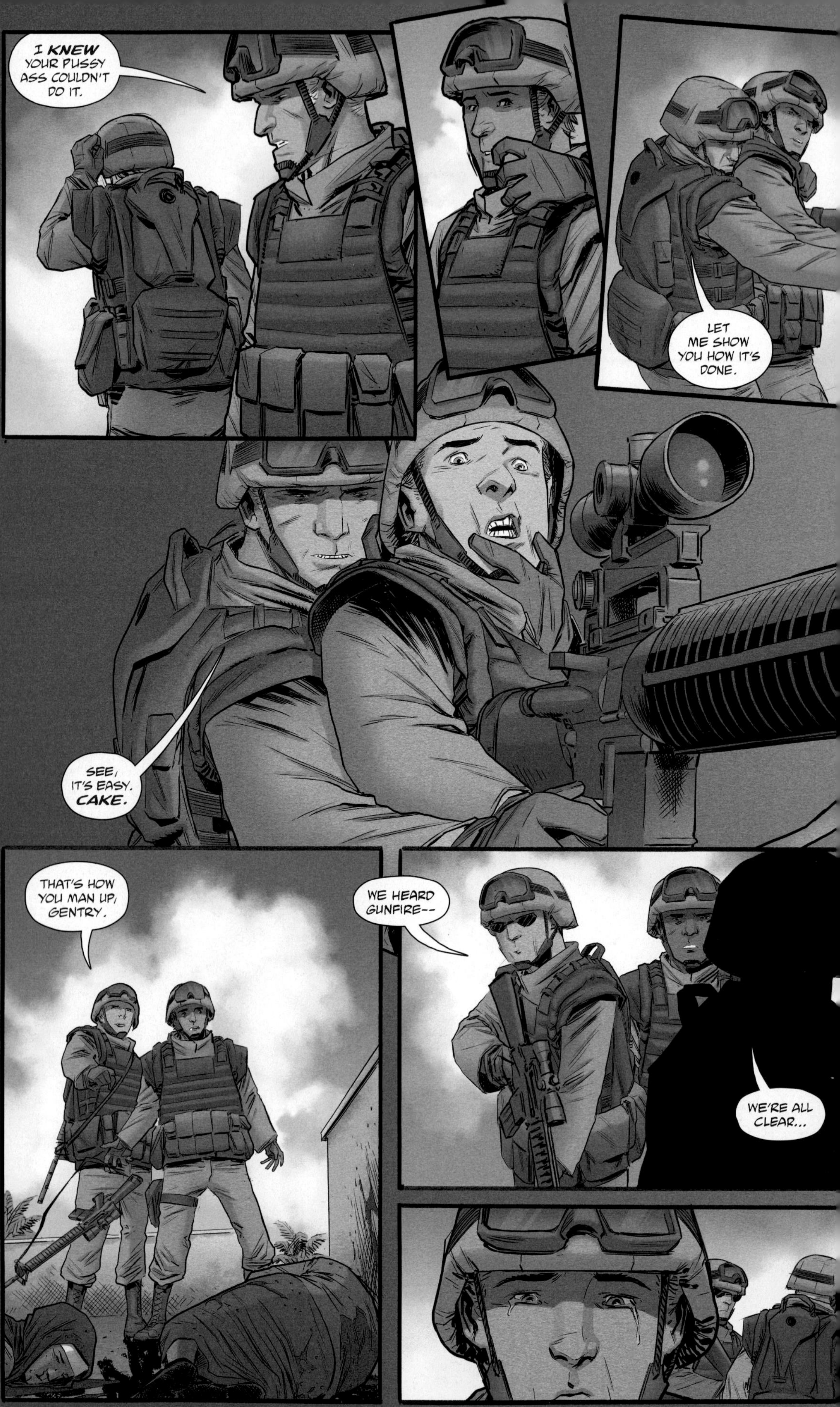
I KNEW YOUR PUSSY ASS COULDN'T DO IT.
LET ME SHOW YOU HOW IT'S DONE.
SEE, IT'S EASY. CAKE.
THAT'S HOW YOU MAN UP, GENTRY.
WE HEARD GUNFIRE--
WE'RE ALL CLEAR...

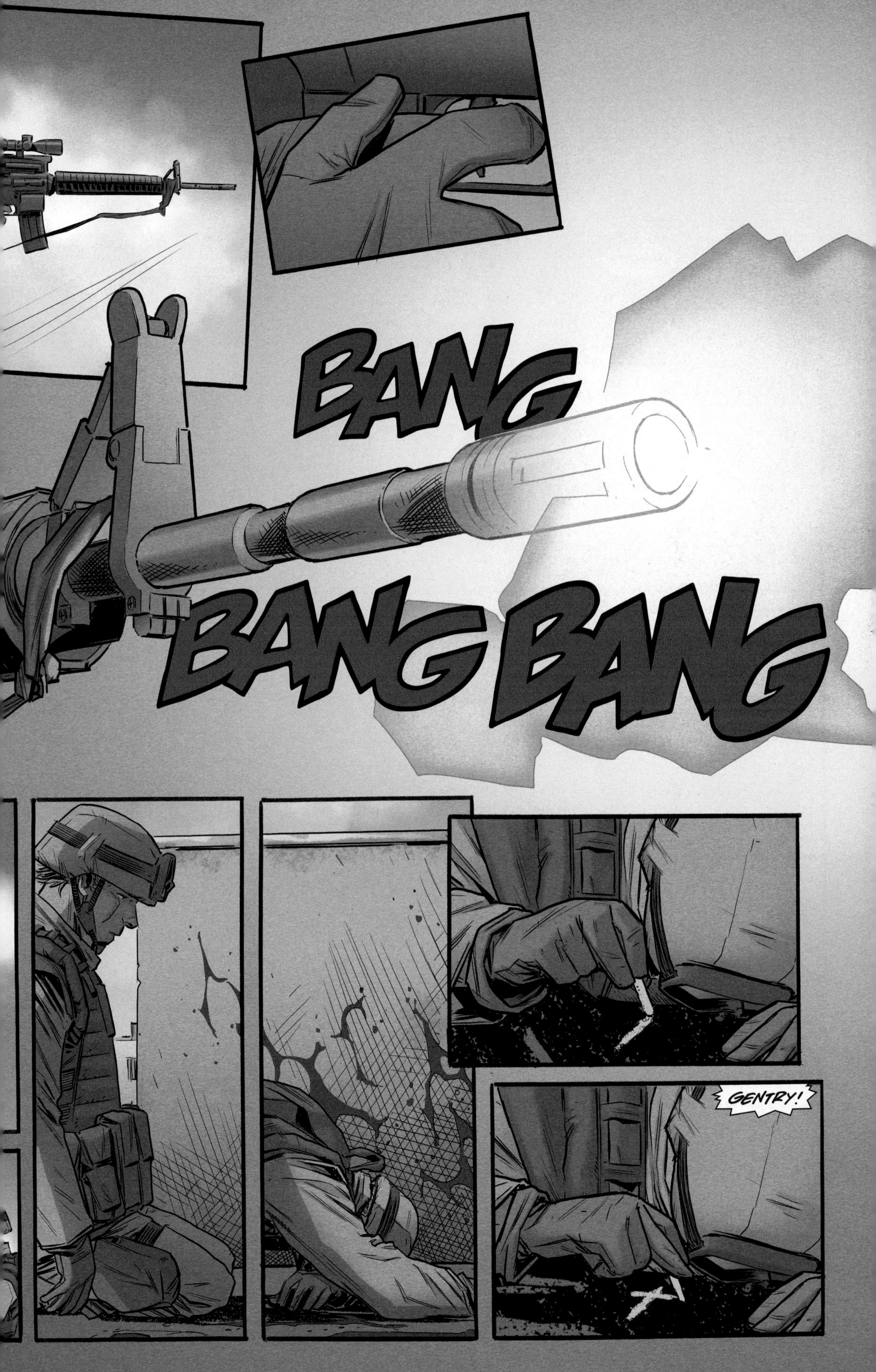
BANG
BANG BANG
GENTRY!

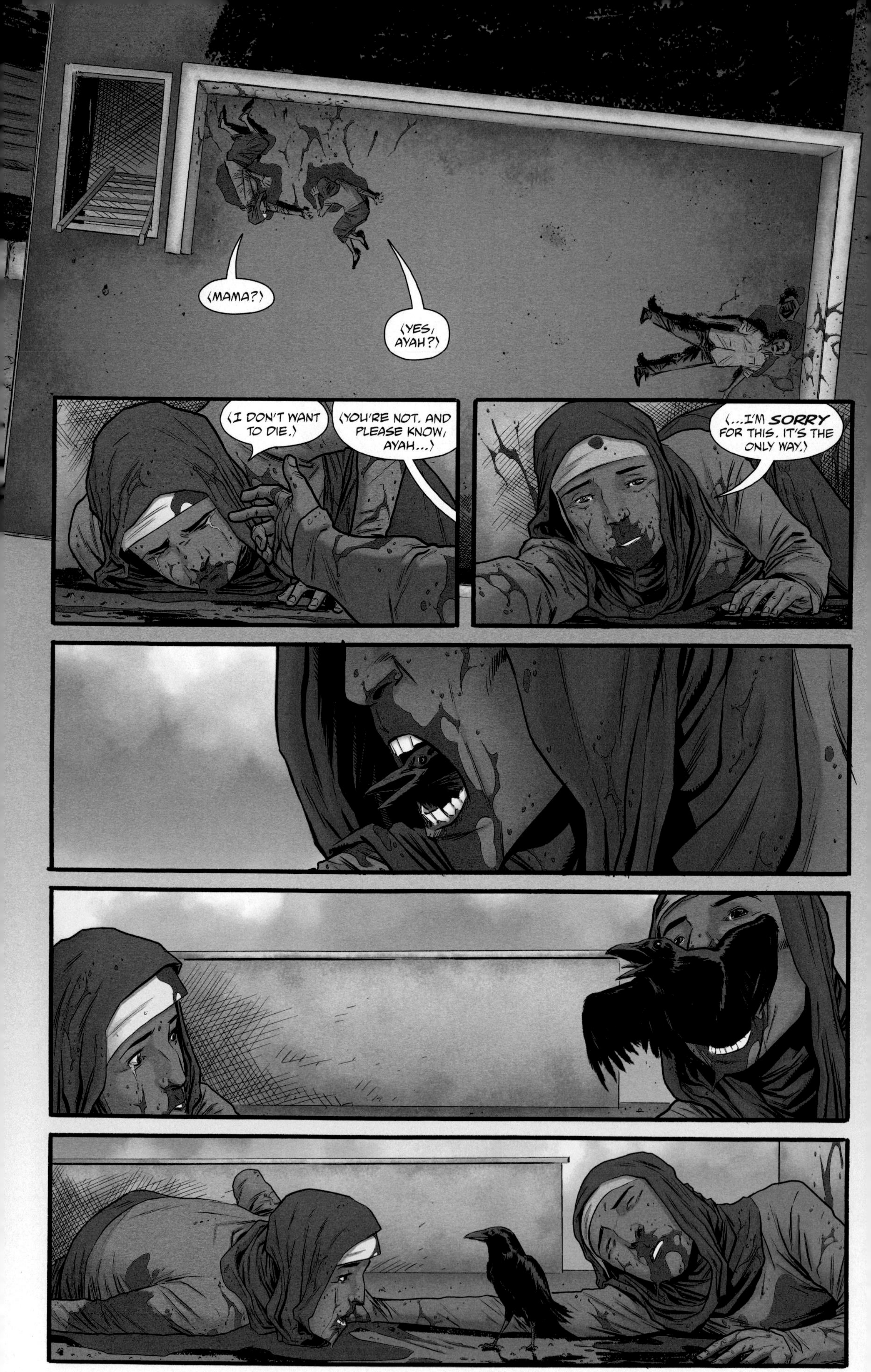
⟨MAMA?⟩
⟨YES, AYAH?⟩
⟨I DON'T WANT TO DIE.⟩
⟨YOU'RE NOT. AND PLEASE KNOW, AYAH...⟩
⟨...I'M **SORRY** FOR THIS. IT'S THE ONLY WAY.⟩

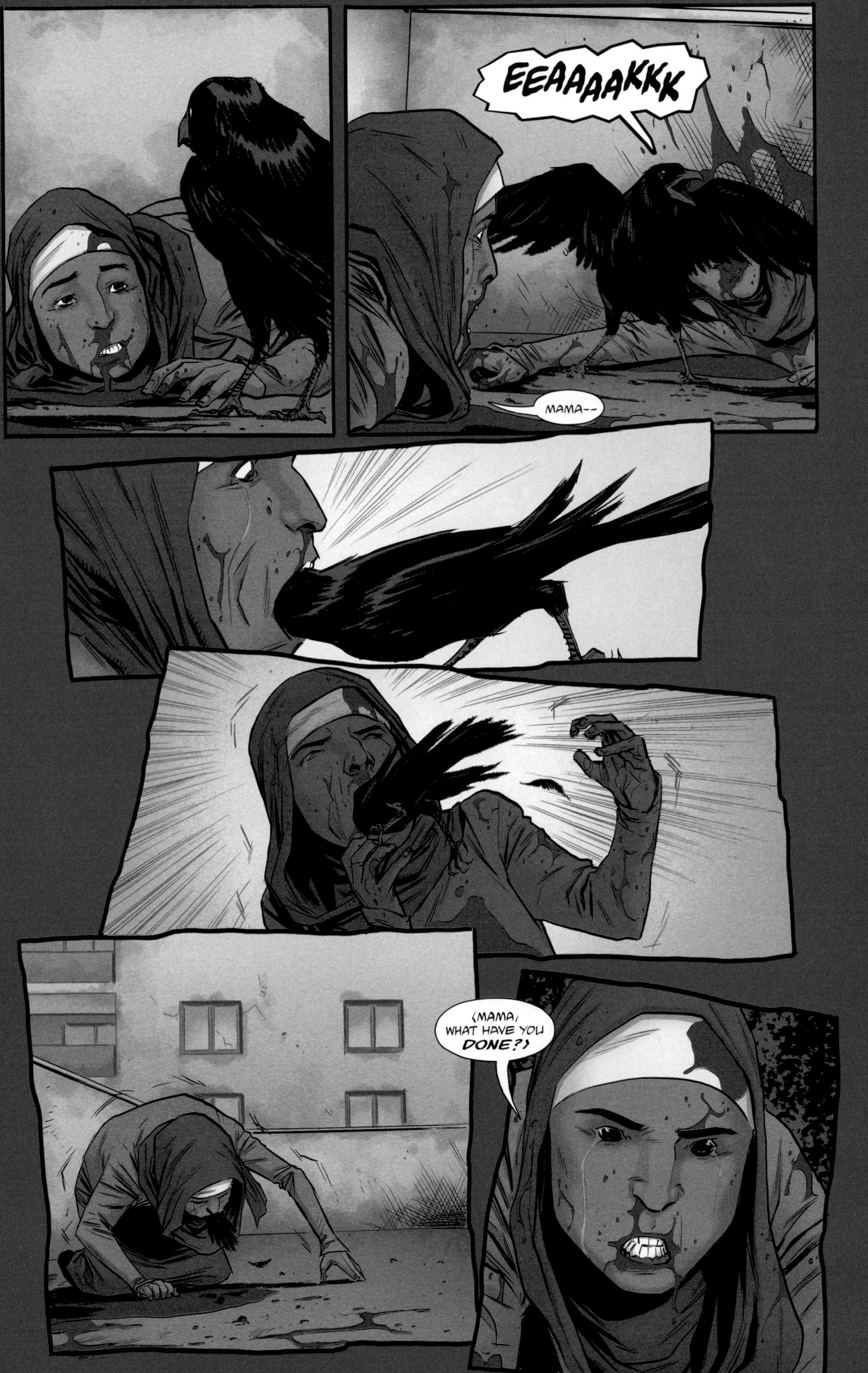
EEAAAAAKKK
MAMA--
(MAMA, WHAT HAVE YOU DONE?)

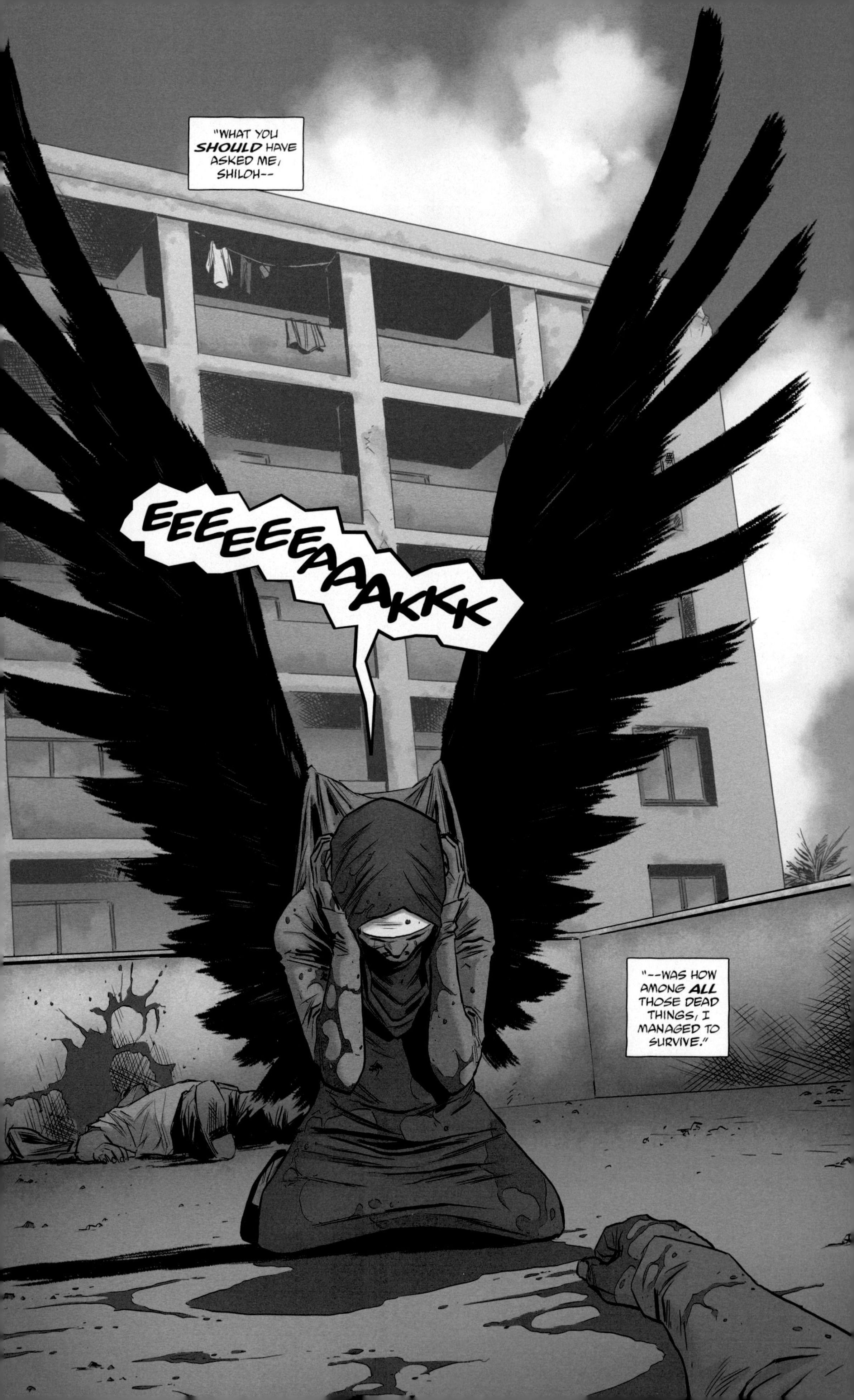
"WHAT YOU SHOULD HAVE ASKED ME, SHILOH--
EEEEEEEAAAAKKK
"--WAS HOW AMONG ALL THOSE DEAD THINGS, I MANAGED TO SURVIVE."

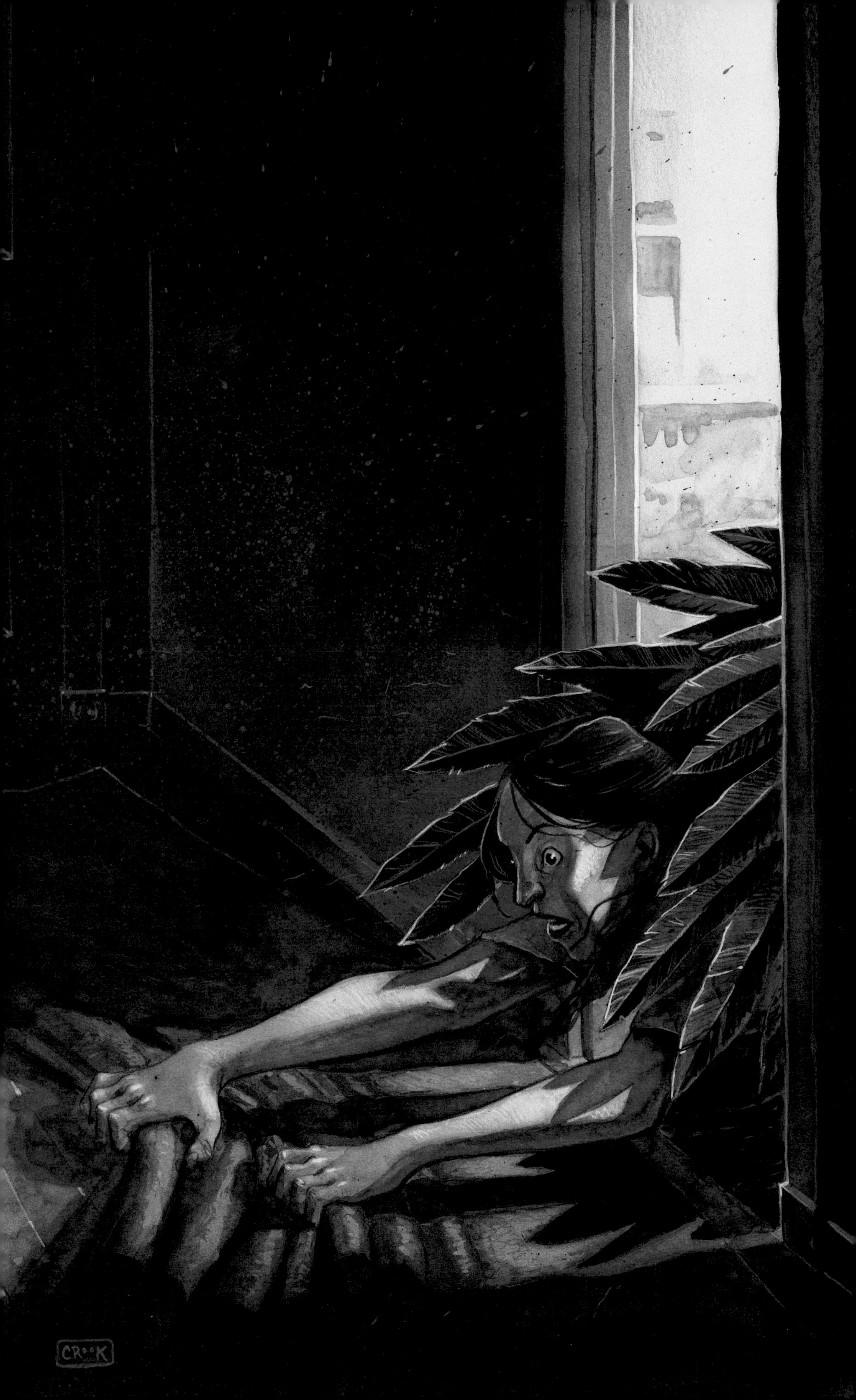
CROOK

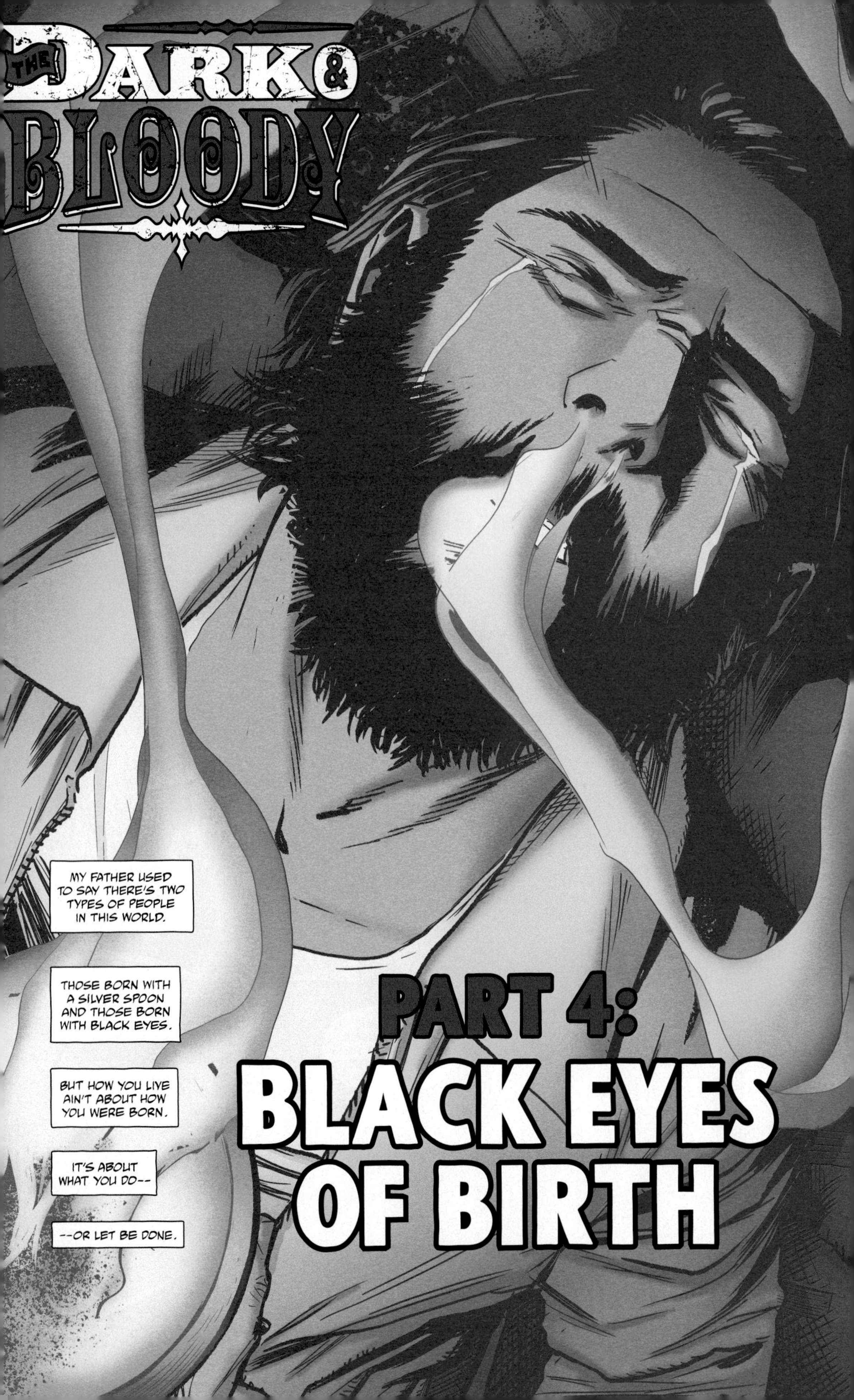
THE DARK & BLOODY
MY FATHER USED TO SAY THERE'S TWO TYPES OF PEOPLE IN THIS WORLD.
THOSE BORN WITH A SILVER SPOON AND THOSE BORN WITH BLACK EYES.
BUT HOW YOU LIVE AIN'T ABOUT HOW YOU WERE BORN.
IT'S ABOUT WHAT YOU DO--
--OR LET BE DONE.
PART 4:
BLACK EYES OF BIRTH

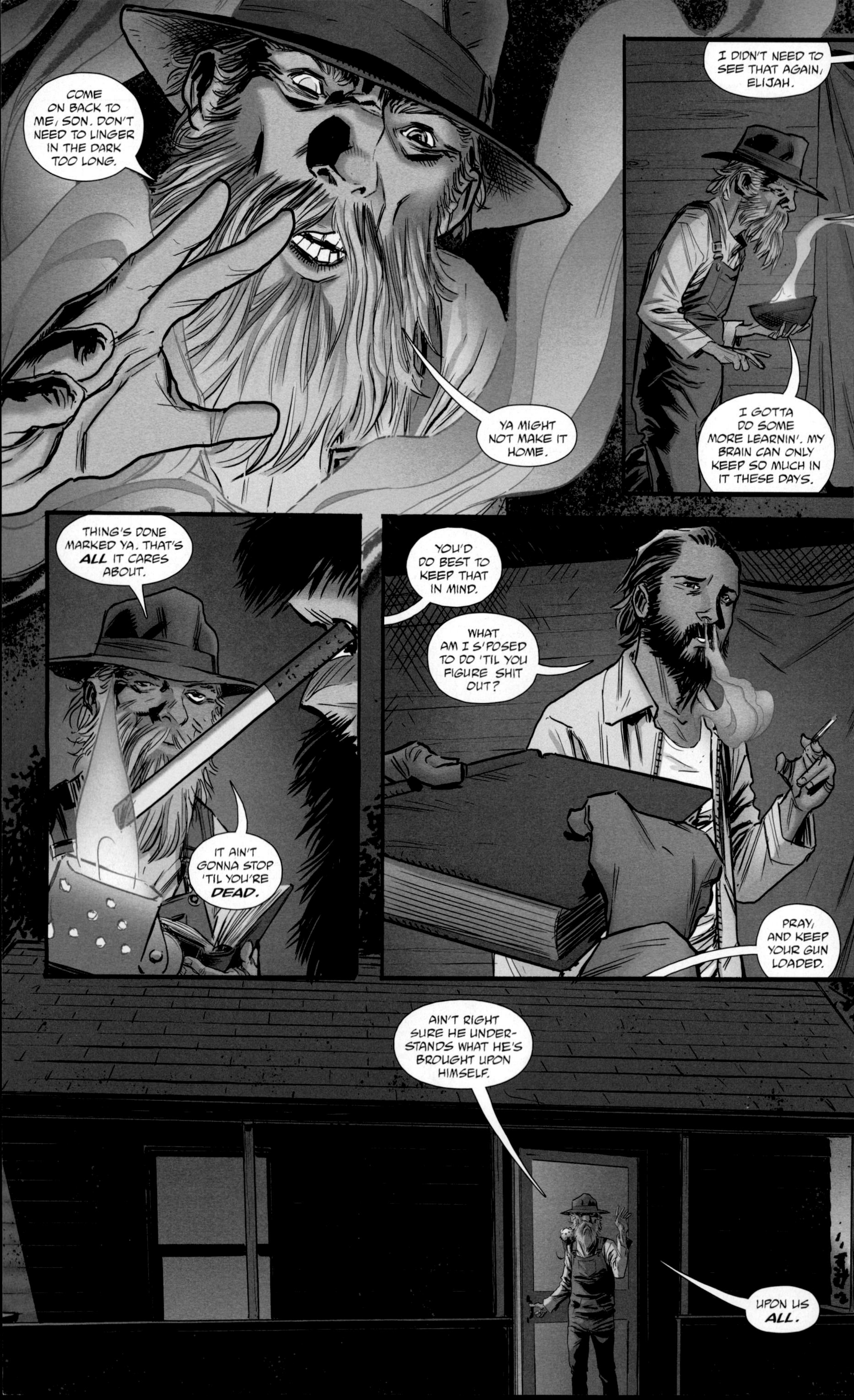
COME ON BACK TO ME, SON. DON'T NEED TO LINGER IN THE DARK TOO LONG.
YA MIGHT NOT MAKE IT HOME.
I DIDN'T NEED TO SEE THAT AGAIN, ELIJAH.
I GOTTA DO SOME MORE LEARNIN'. MY BRAIN CAN ONLY KEEP SO MUCH IN IT THESE DAYS.
THING'S DONE MARKED YA. THAT'S ALL IT CARES ABOUT.
IT AIN'T GONNA STOP 'TIL YOU'RE DEAD.
YOU'D DO BEST TO KEEP THAT IN MIND.
WHAT AM I S'POSED TO DO 'TIL YOU FIGURE SHIT OUT?
PRAY, AND KEEP YOUR GUN LOADED.
AIN'T RIGHT SURE HE UNDERSTANDS WHAT HE'S BROUGHT UPON HIMSELF.
UPON US ALL.

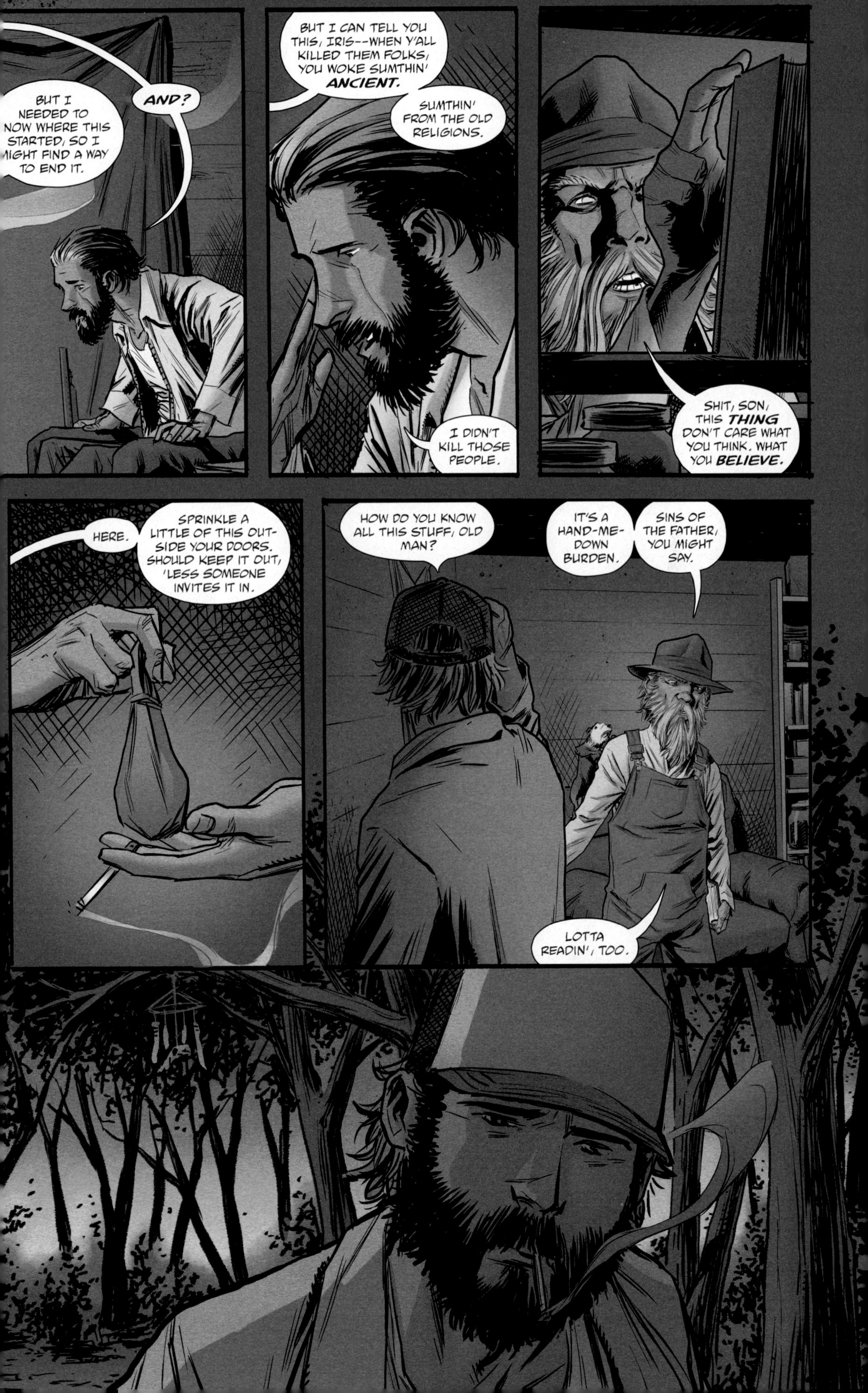
BUT I NEEDED TO NOW WHERE THIS STARTED, SO I MIGHT FIND A WAY TO END IT.
AND?
BUT I CAN TELL YOU THIS, IRIS--WHEN Y'ALL KILLED THEM FOLKS, YOU WOKE SUMTHIN' ANCIENT.
SUMTHIN' FROM THE OLD RELIGIONS.
I DIDN'T KILL THOSE PEOPLE.
SHIT, SON, THIS THING DON'T CARE WHAT YOU THINK. WHAT YOU BELIEVE.
HERE.
SPRINKLE A LITTLE OF THIS OUT-SIDE YOUR DOORS. SHOULD KEEP IT OUT, 'LESS SOMEONE INVITES IT IN.
HOW DO YOU KNOW ALL THIS STUFF, OLD MAN?
IT'S A HAND-ME-DOWN BURDEN.
SINS OF THE FATHER, YOU MIGHT SAY.
LOTTA READIN', TOO.

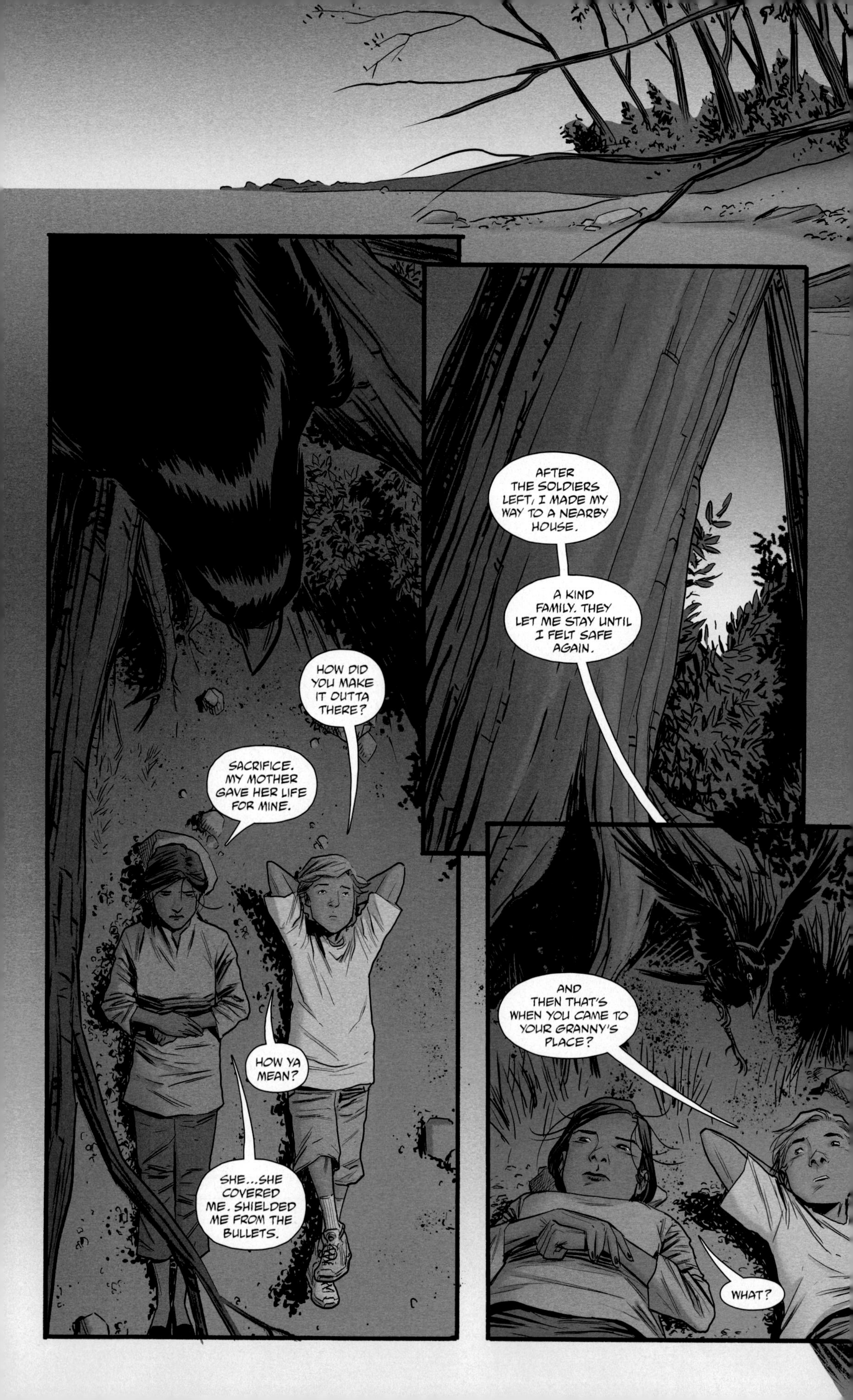
HOW DID YOU MAKE IT OUTTA THERE?
SACRIFICE. MY MOTHER GAVE HER LIFE FOR MINE.
HOW YA MEAN?
SHE...SHE COVERED ME. SHIELDED ME FROM THE BULLETS.
AFTER THE SOLDIERS LEFT, I MADE MY WAY TO A NEARBY HOUSE.
A KIND FAMILY. THEY LET ME STAY UNTIL I FELT SAFE AGAIN.
AND THEN THAT'S WHEN YOU CAME TO YOUR GRANNY'S PLACE?
WHAT?

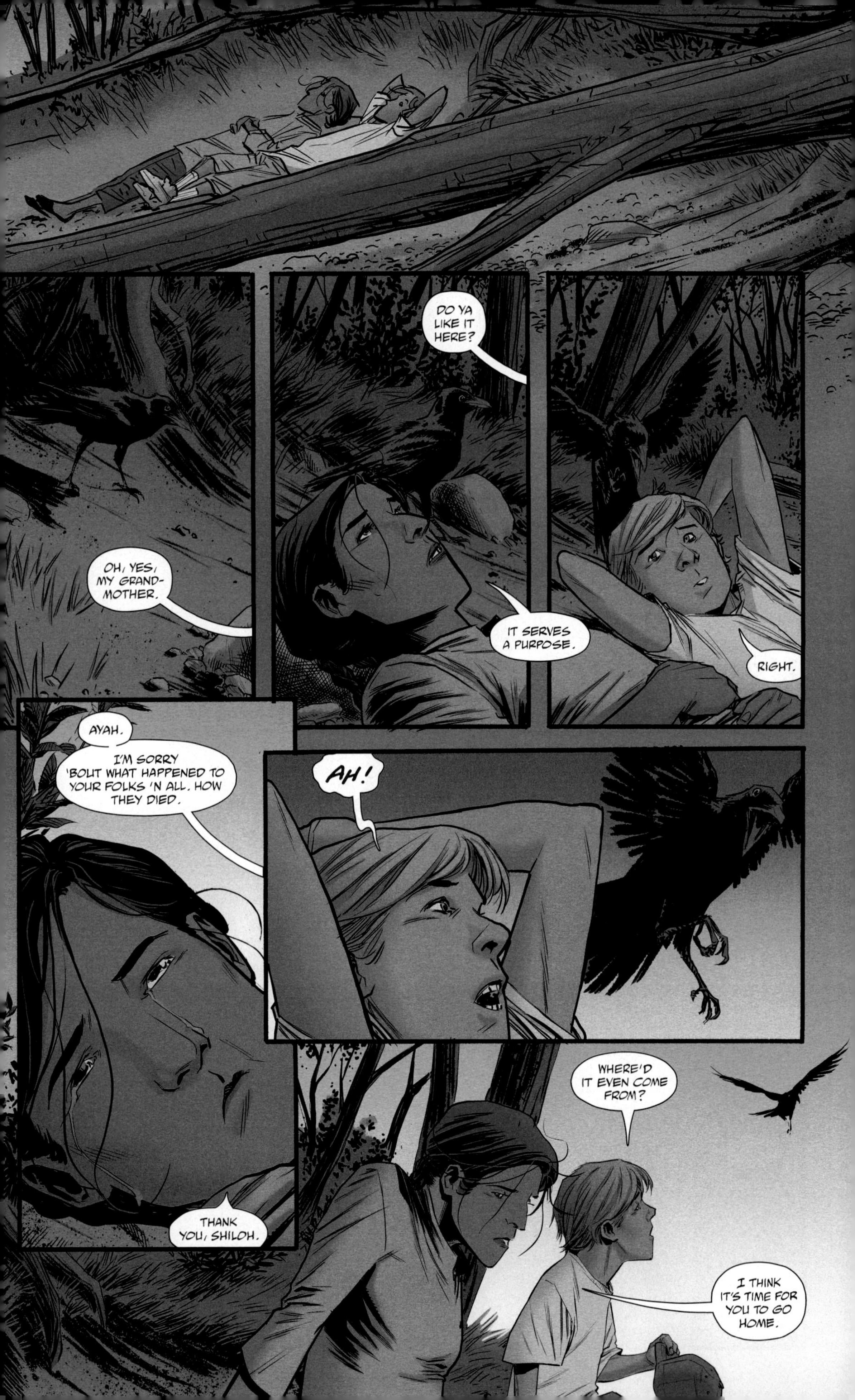
DO YA LIKE IT HERE?
OH, YES, MY GRAND-MOTHER.
IT SERVES A PURPOSE.
RIGHT.
AYAH.
I'M SORRY 'BOUT WHAT HAPPENED TO YOUR FOLKS 'N ALL. HOW THEY DIED.
THANK YOU, SHILOH.
AH!
WHERE'D IT EVEN COME FROM?
I THINK IT'S TIME FOR YOU TO GO HOME.

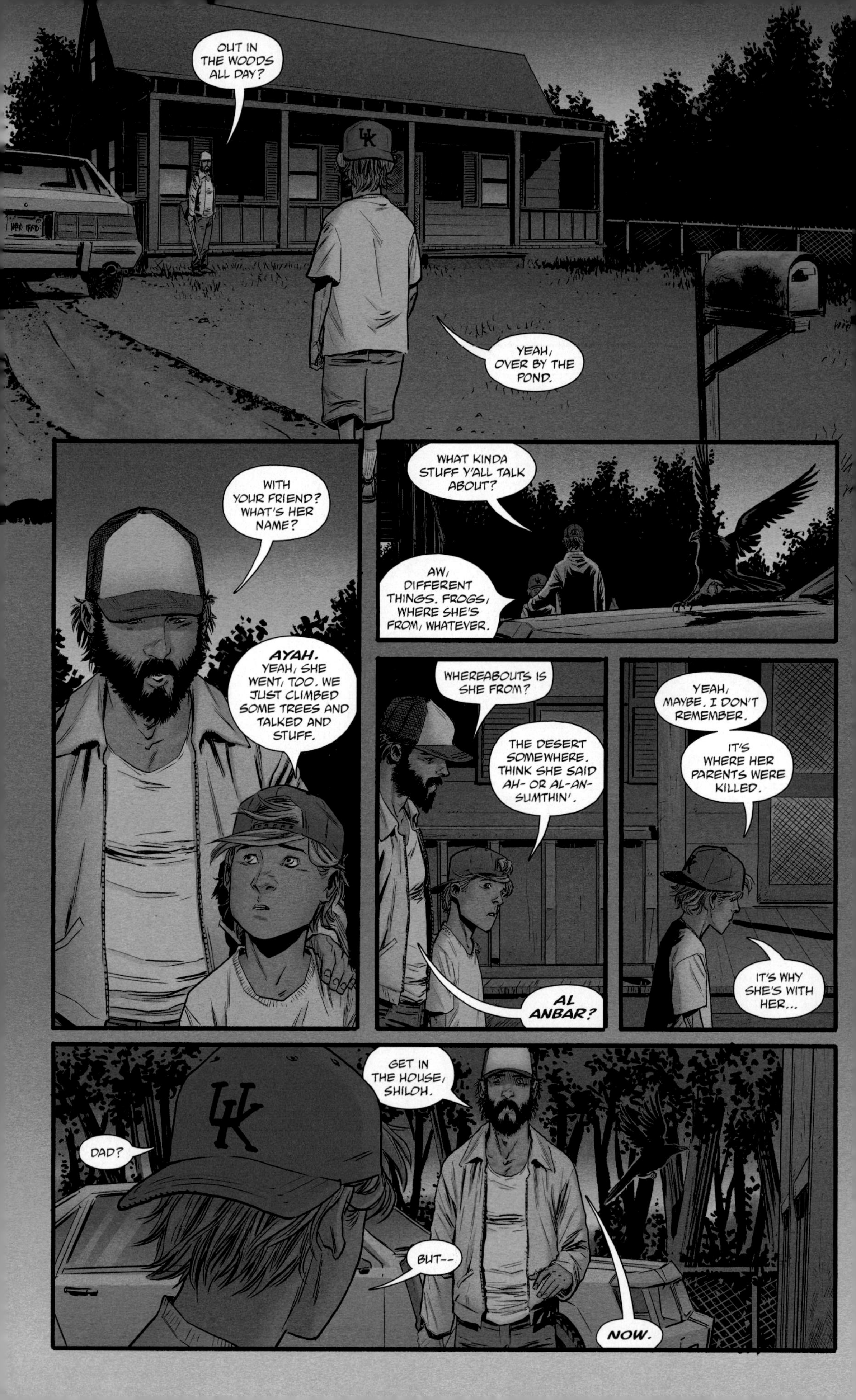
OUT IN THE WOODS ALL DAY?
YEAH, OVER BY THE POND.
WITH YOUR FRIEND? WHAT'S HER NAME?
AYAH. YEAH, SHE WENT, TOO. WE JUST CLIMBED SOME TREES AND TALKED AND STUFF.
WHAT KINDA STUFF Y'ALL TALK ABOUT?
AW, DIFFERENT THINGS. FROGS, WHERE SHE'S FROM, WHATEVER.
WHEREABOUTS IS SHE FROM?
THE DESERT SOMEWHERE. THINK SHE SAID AH- OR AL-AN-SUMTHIN'.
AL ANBAR?
YEAH, MAYBE. I DON'T REMEMBER.
IT'S WHERE HER PARENTS WERE KILLED.
IT'S WHY SHE'S WITH HER...
GET IN THE HOUSE, SHILOH.
DAD?
BUT--
NOW.

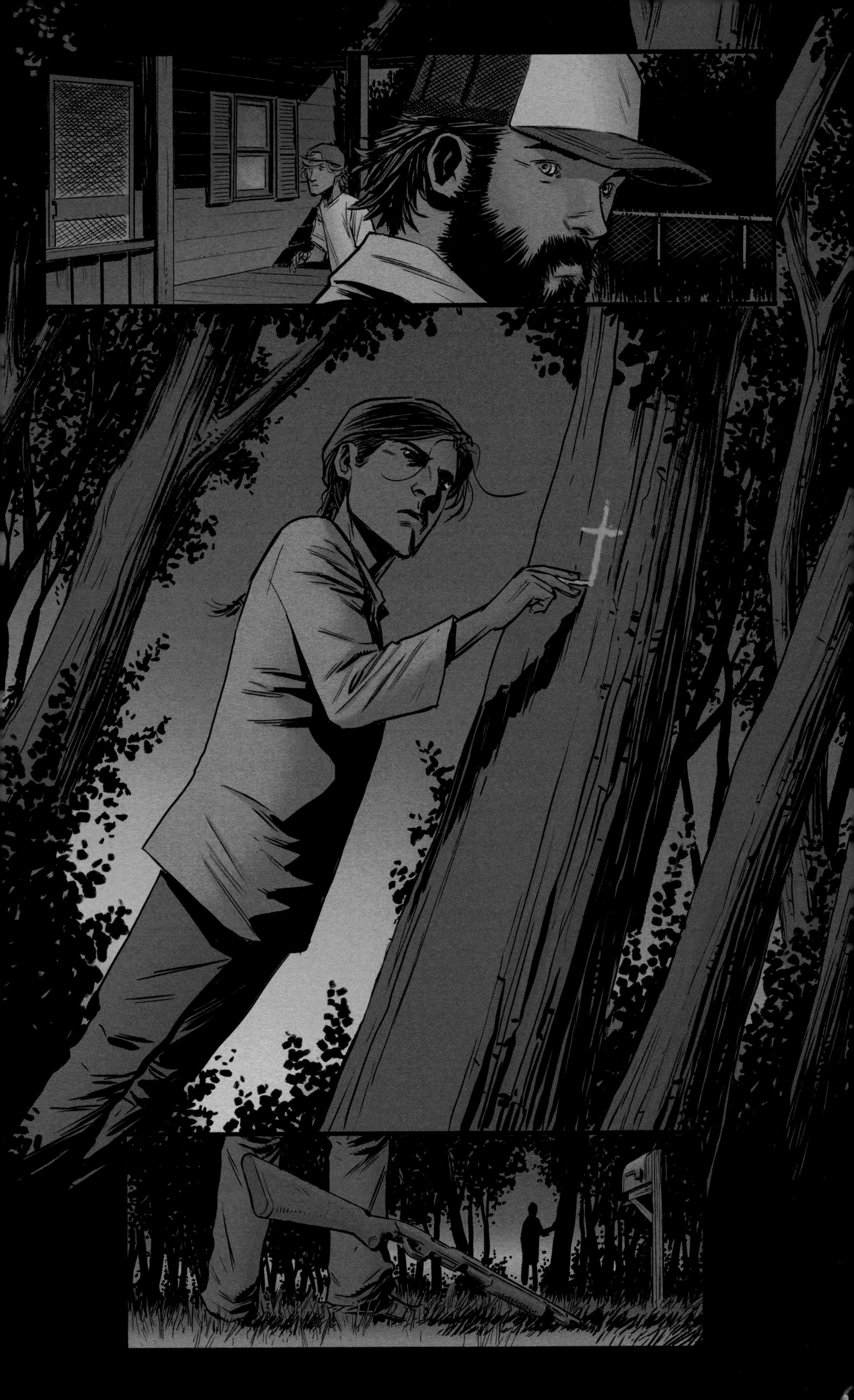

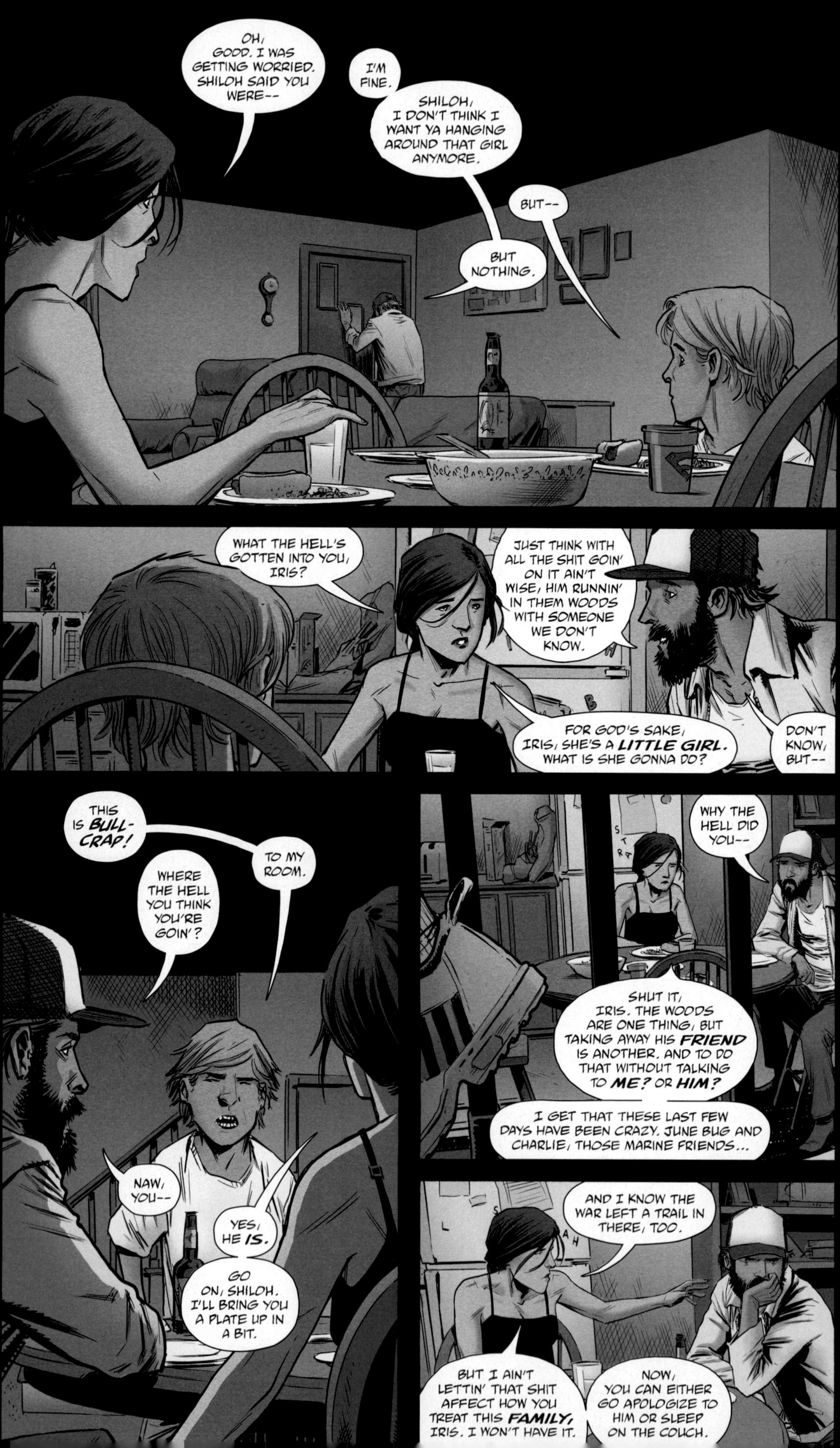
OH, GOOD. I WAS GETTING WORRIED. SHILOH SAID YOU WERE--
I'M FINE.
SHILOH, I DON'T THINK I WANT YA HANGING AROUND THAT GIRL ANYMORE.
BUT--
BUT NOTHING.
WHAT THE HELL'S GOTTEN INTO YOU, IRIS?
JUST THINK WITH ALL THE SHIT GOIN' ON IT AIN'T WISE, HIM RUNNIN' IN THEM WOODS WITH SOMEONE WE DON'T KNOW.
FOR GOD'S SAKE, IRIS, SHE'S A LITTLE GIRL. WHAT IS SHE GONNA DO?
DON'T KNOW, BUT--
THIS IS BULL-CRAP!
TO MY ROOM.
WHERE THE HELL YOU THINK YOU'RE GOIN'?
NAW, YOU--
YES, HE IS.
GO ON, SHILOH. I'LL BRING YOU A PLATE UP IN A BIT.
WHY THE HELL DID YOU--
SHUT IT, IRIS. THE WOODS ARE ONE THING, BUT TAKING AWAY HIS FRIEND IS ANOTHER. AND TO DO THAT WITHOUT TALKING TO ME? OR HIM?
I GET THAT THESE LAST FEW DAYS HAVE BEEN CRAZY. JUNE BUG AND CHARLIE, THOSE MARINE FRIENDS...
AND I KNOW THE WAR LEFT A TRAIL IN THERE, TOO.
BUT I AIN'T LETTIN' THAT SHIT AFFECT HOW YOU TREAT THIS FAMILY, IRIS. I WON'T HAVE IT.
NOW, YOU CAN EITHER GO APOLOGIZE TO HIM OR SLEEP ON THE COUCH.

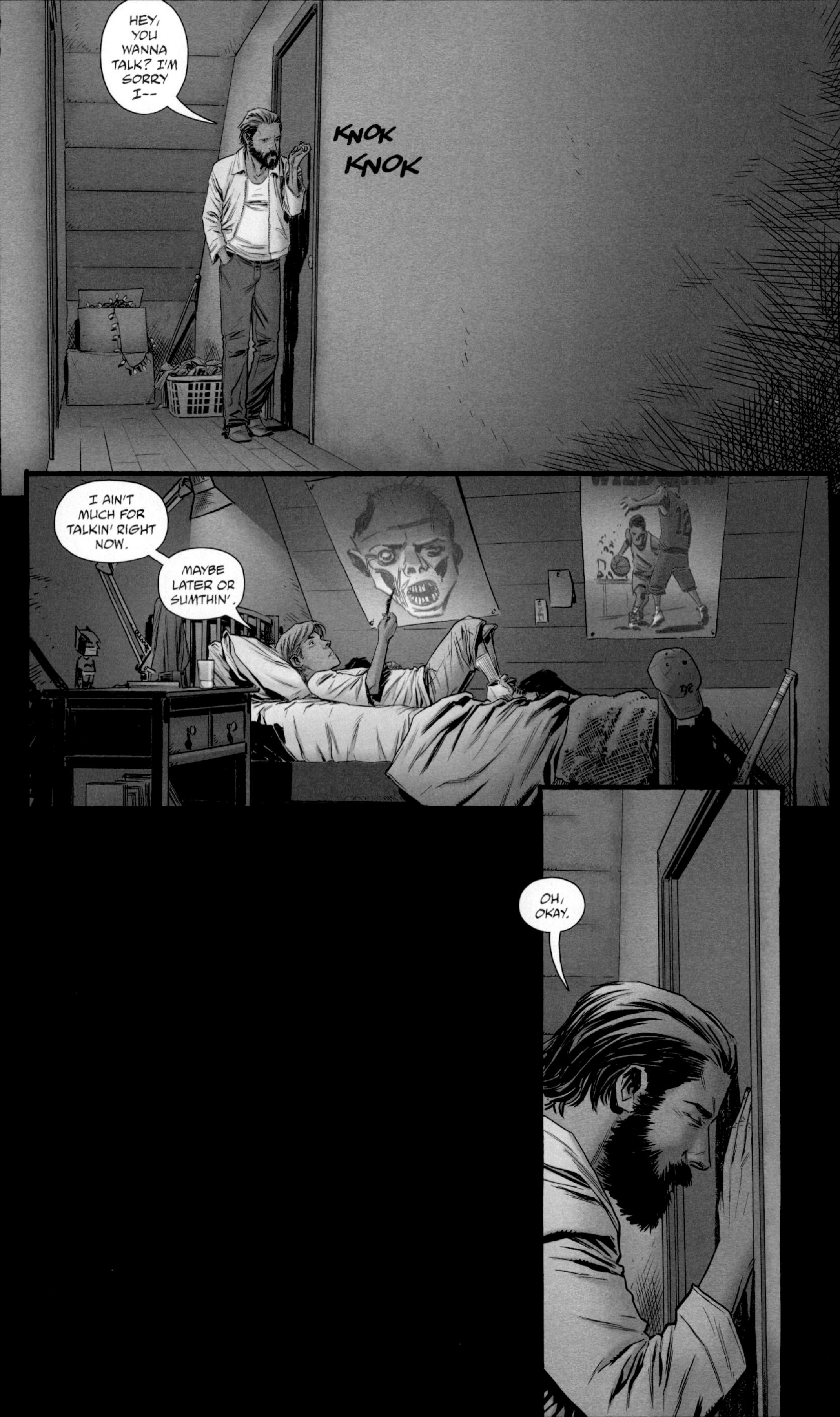
HEY, YOU WANNA TALK? I'M SORRY I--
KNOK KNOK
I AIN'T MUCH FOR TALKIN' RIGHT NOW.
MAYBE LATER OR SUMTHIN'.
OH, OKAY.

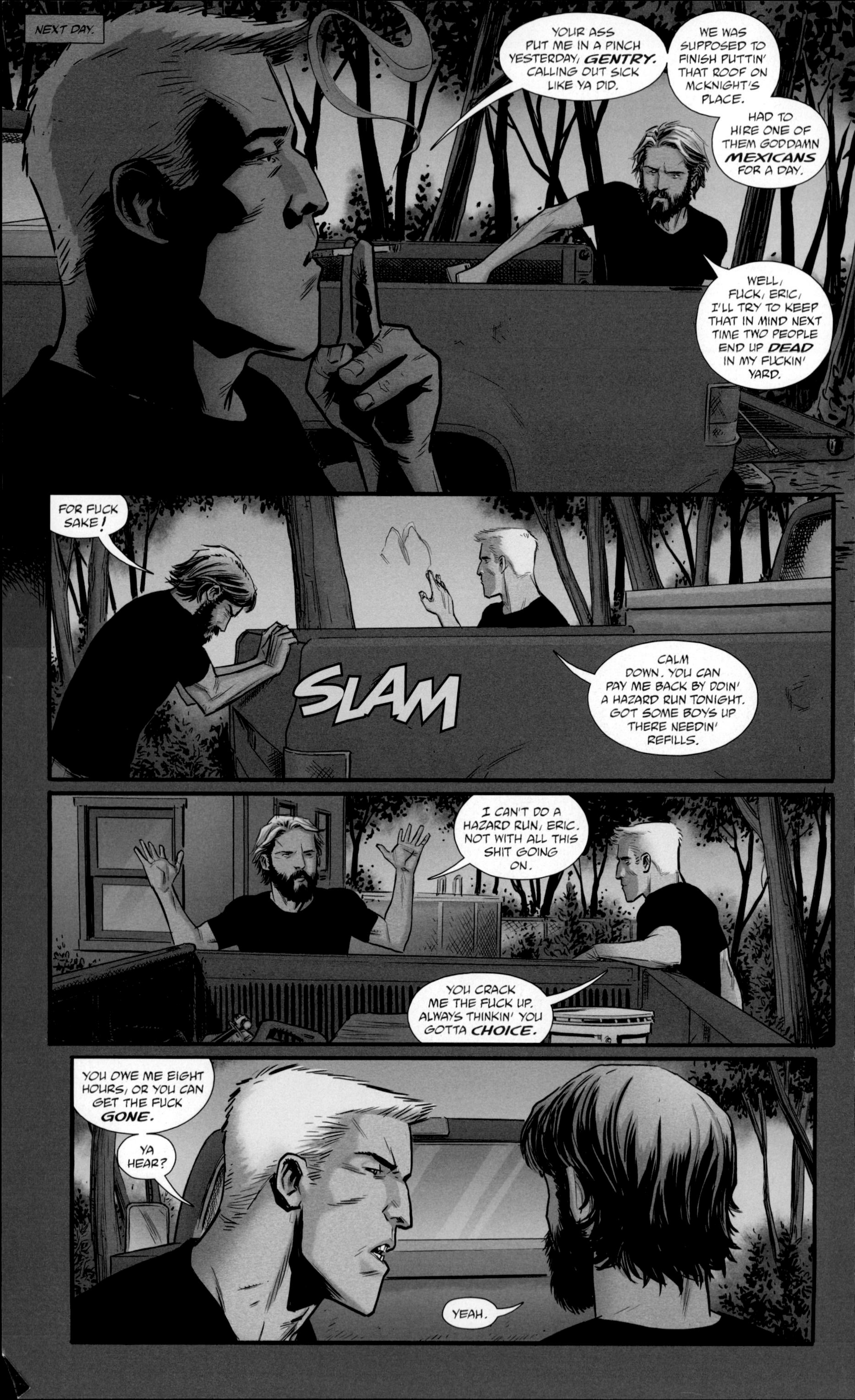
NEXT DAY.
YOUR ASS PUT ME IN A PINCH YESTERDAY, GENTRY. CALLING OUT SICK LIKE YA DID.
WE WAS SUPPOSED TO FINISH PUTTIN' THAT ROOF ON McKNIGHT'S PLACE.
HAD TO HIRE ONE OF THEM GODDAMN MEXICANS FOR A DAY.
WELL, FUCK, ERIC, I'LL TRY TO KEEP THAT IN MIND NEXT TIME TWO PEOPLE END UP DEAD IN MY FUCKIN' YARD.
FOR FUCK SAKE!
SLAM
CALM DOWN. YOU CAN PAY ME BACK BY DOIN' A HAZARD RUN TONIGHT. GOT SOME BOYS UP THERE NEEDIN' REFILLS.
I CAN'T DO A HAZARD RUN, ERIC. NOT WITH ALL THIS SHIT GOING ON.
YOU CRACK ME THE FUCK UP. ALWAYS THINKIN' YOU GOTTA CHOICE.
YOU OWE ME EIGHT HOURS, OR YOU CAN GET THE FUCK GONE.
YA HEAR?
YEAH.

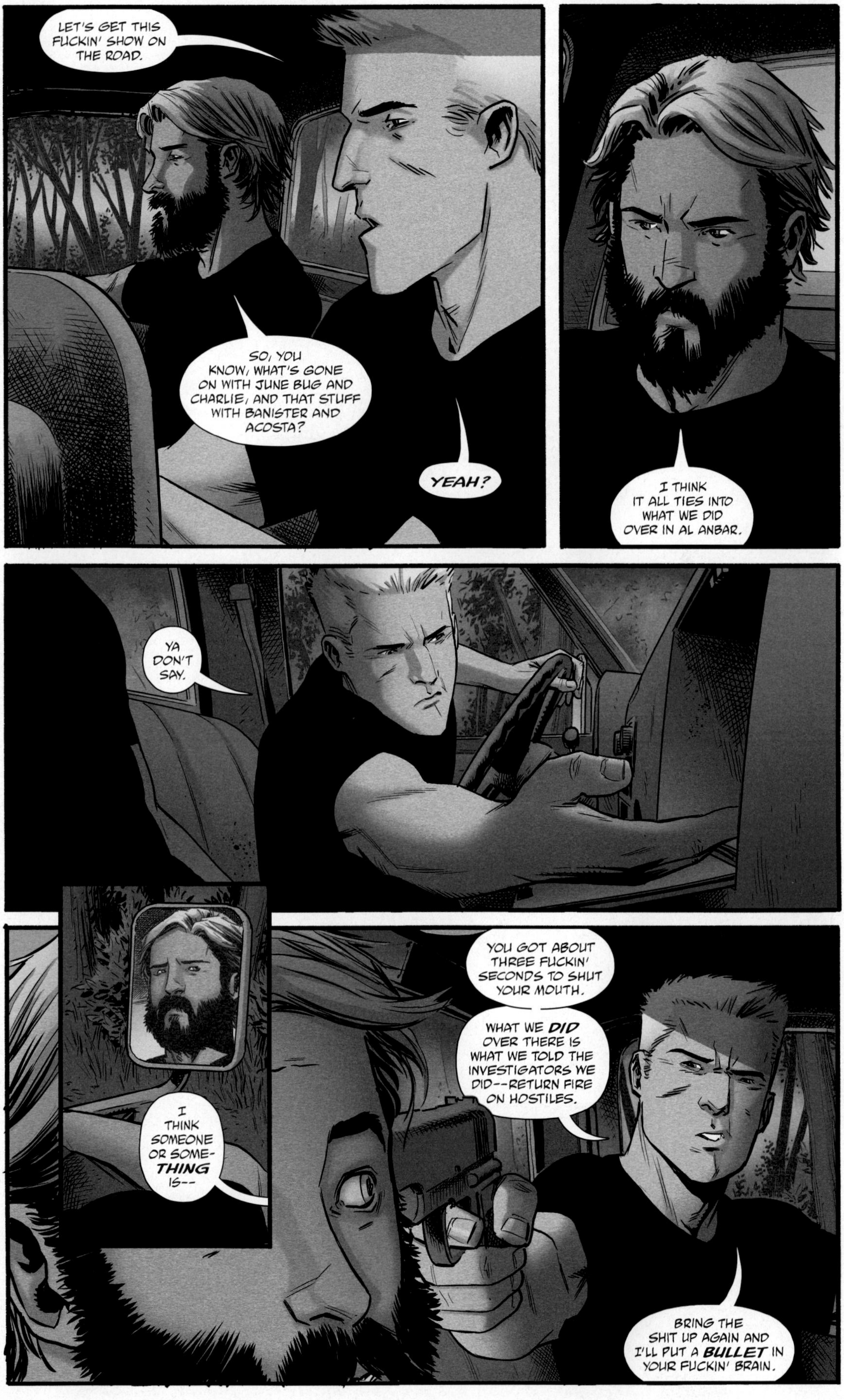
LET'S GET THIS FUCKIN' SHOW ON THE ROAD.
SO, YOU KNOW, WHAT'S GONE ON WITH JUNE BUG AND CHARLIE, AND THAT STUFF WITH BANISTER AND ACOSTA?
YEAH?
I THINK IT ALL TIES INTO WHAT WE DID OVER IN AL ANBAR.
YA DON'T SAY.
I THINK SOMEONE OR SOME-THING IS--
YOU GOT ABOUT THREE FUCKIN' SECONDS TO SHUT YOUR MOUTH.
WHAT WE DID OVER THERE IS WHAT WE TOLD THE INVESTIGATORS WE DID--RETURN FIRE ON HOSTILES.
BRING THE SHIT UP AGAIN AND I'LL PUT A BULLET IN YOUR FUCKIN' BRAIN.

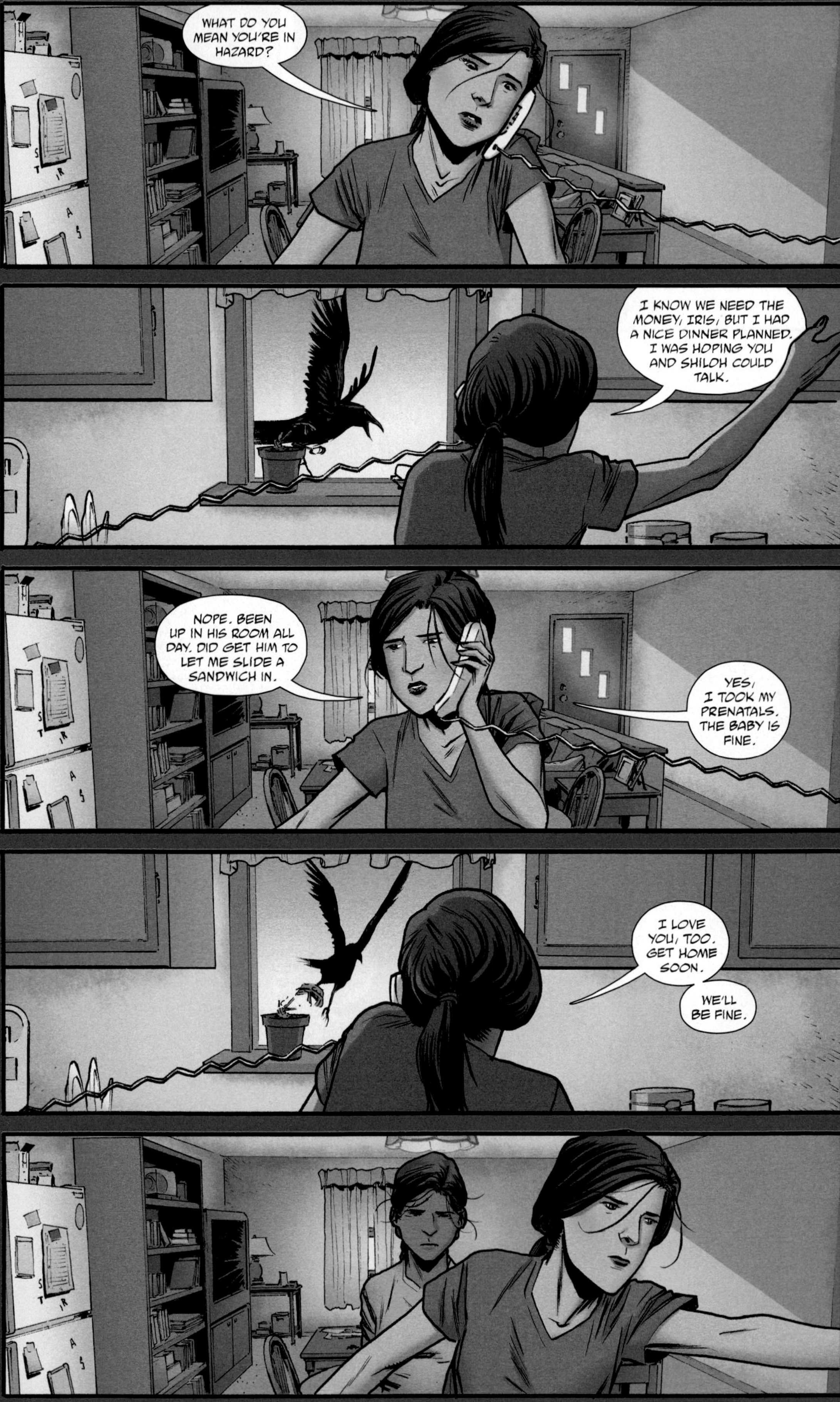
WHAT DO YOU MEAN YOU'RE IN HAZARD?
I KNOW WE NEED THE MONEY, IRIS, BUT I HAD A NICE DINNER PLANNED. I WAS HOPING YOU AND SHILOH COULD TALK.
NOPE. BEEN UP IN HIS ROOM ALL DAY. DID GET HIM TO LET ME SLIDE A SANDWICH IN.
YES, I TOOK MY PRENATALS. THE BABY IS FINE.
I LOVE YOU, TOO. GET HOME SOON.
WE'LL BE FINE.

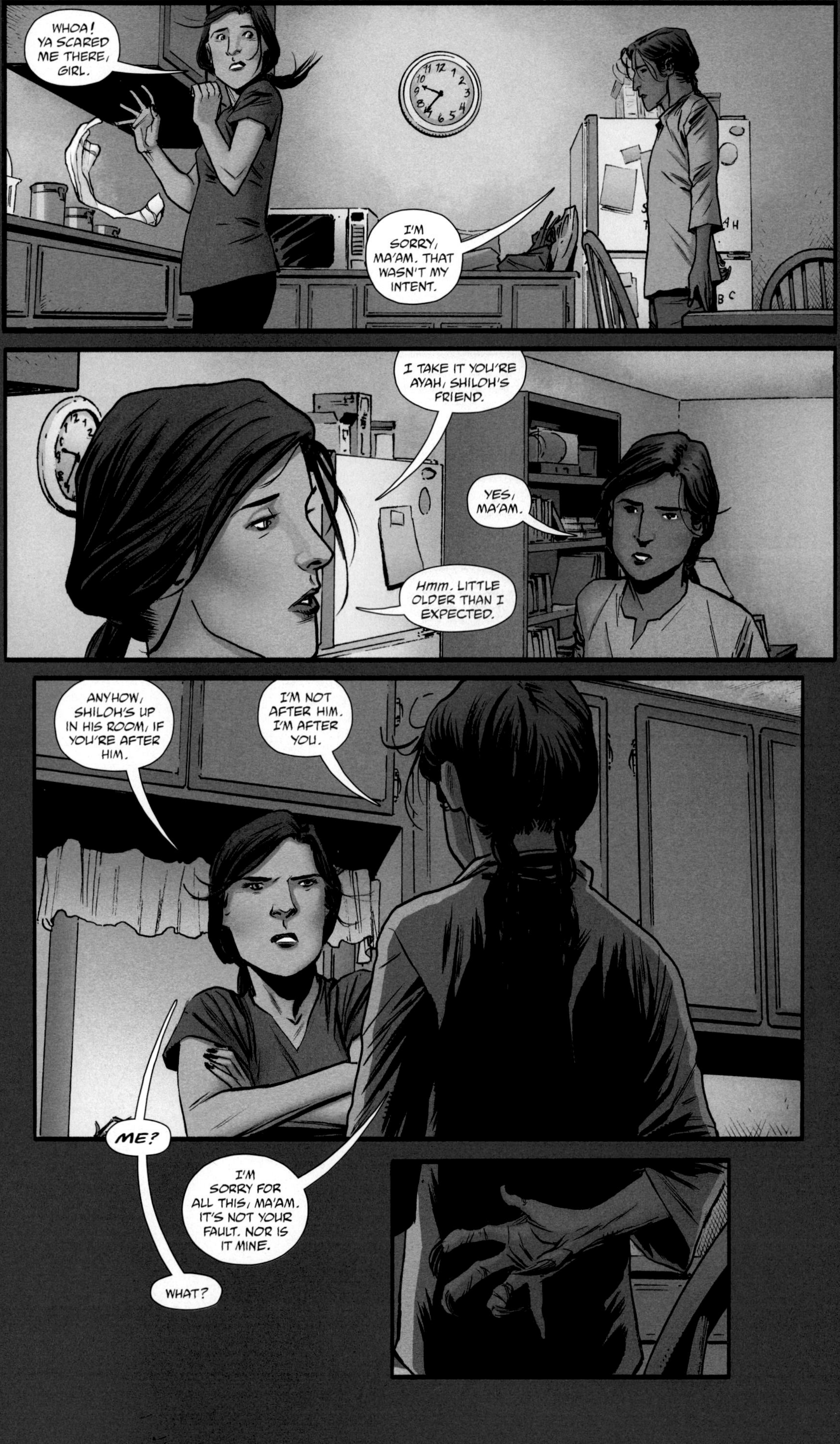
WHOA! YA SCARED ME THERE, GIRL.
I'M SORRY, MA'AM. THAT WASN'T MY INTENT.
I TAKE IT YOU'RE AYAH, SHILOH'S FRIEND.
YES, MA'AM.
Hmm. LITTLE OLDER THAN I EXPECTED.
ANYHOW, SHILOH'S UP IN HIS ROOM, IF YOU'RE AFTER HIM.
I'M NOT AFTER HIM. I'M AFTER YOU.
ME?
I'M SORRY FOR ALL THIS, MA'AM. IT'S NOT YOUR FAULT. NOR IS IT MINE.
WHAT?

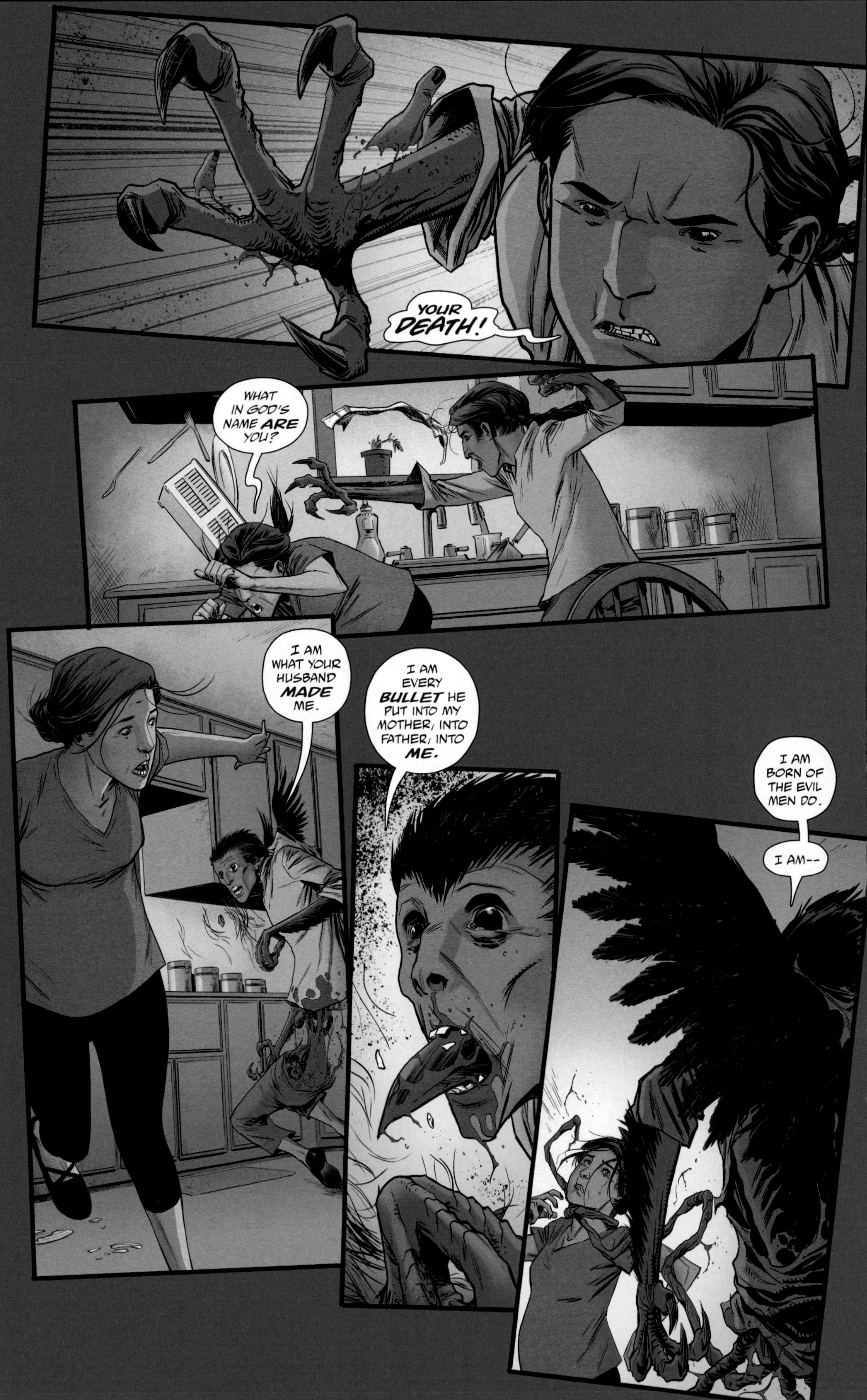
YOUR DEATH!
WHAT IN GOD'S NAME ARE YOU?
I AM WHAT YOUR HUSBAND MADE ME.
I AM EVERY BULLET HE PUT INTO MY MOTHER, INTO FATHER, INTO ME.
I AM BORN OF THE EVIL MEN DO.
I AM--

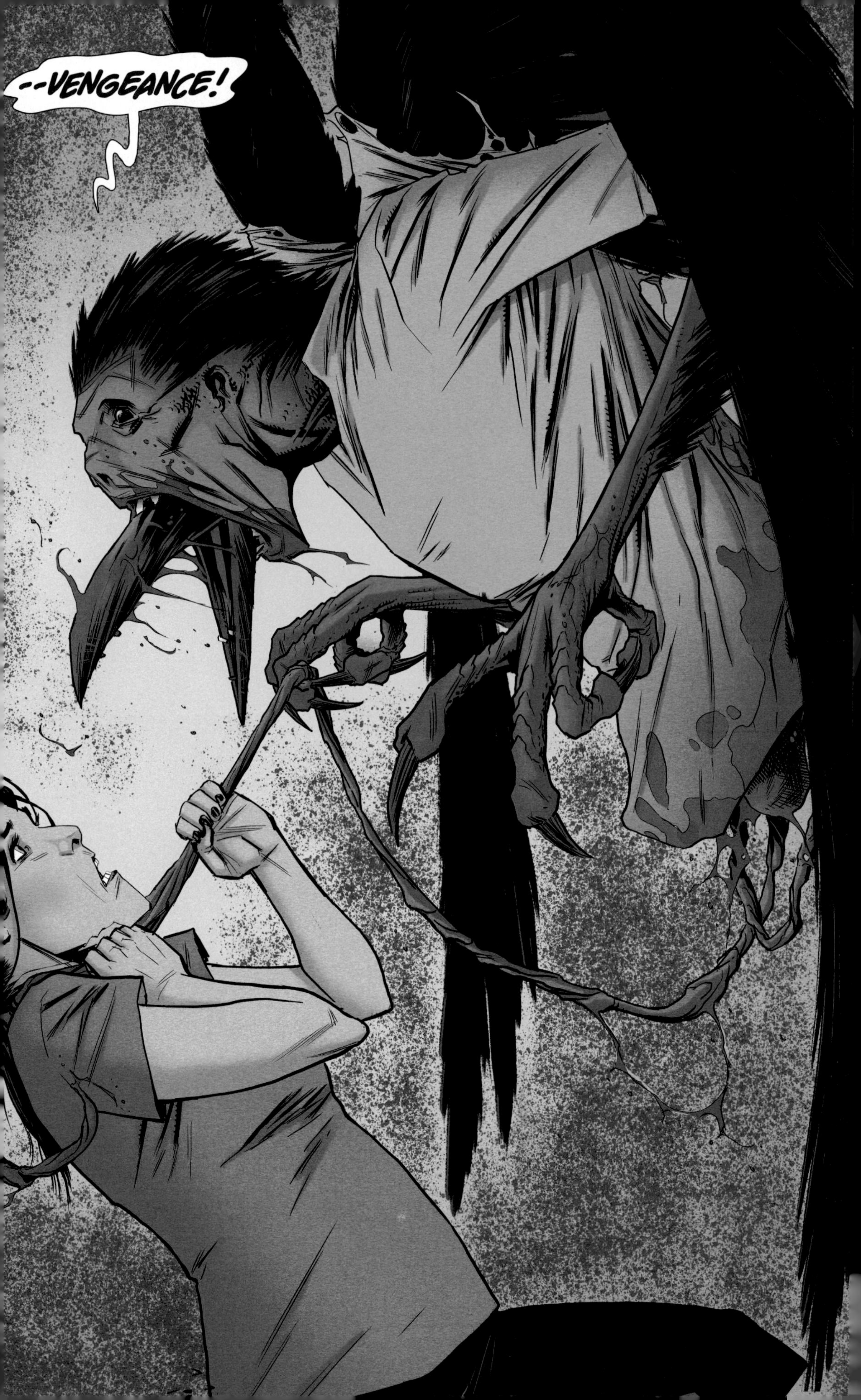
--VENGEANCE!

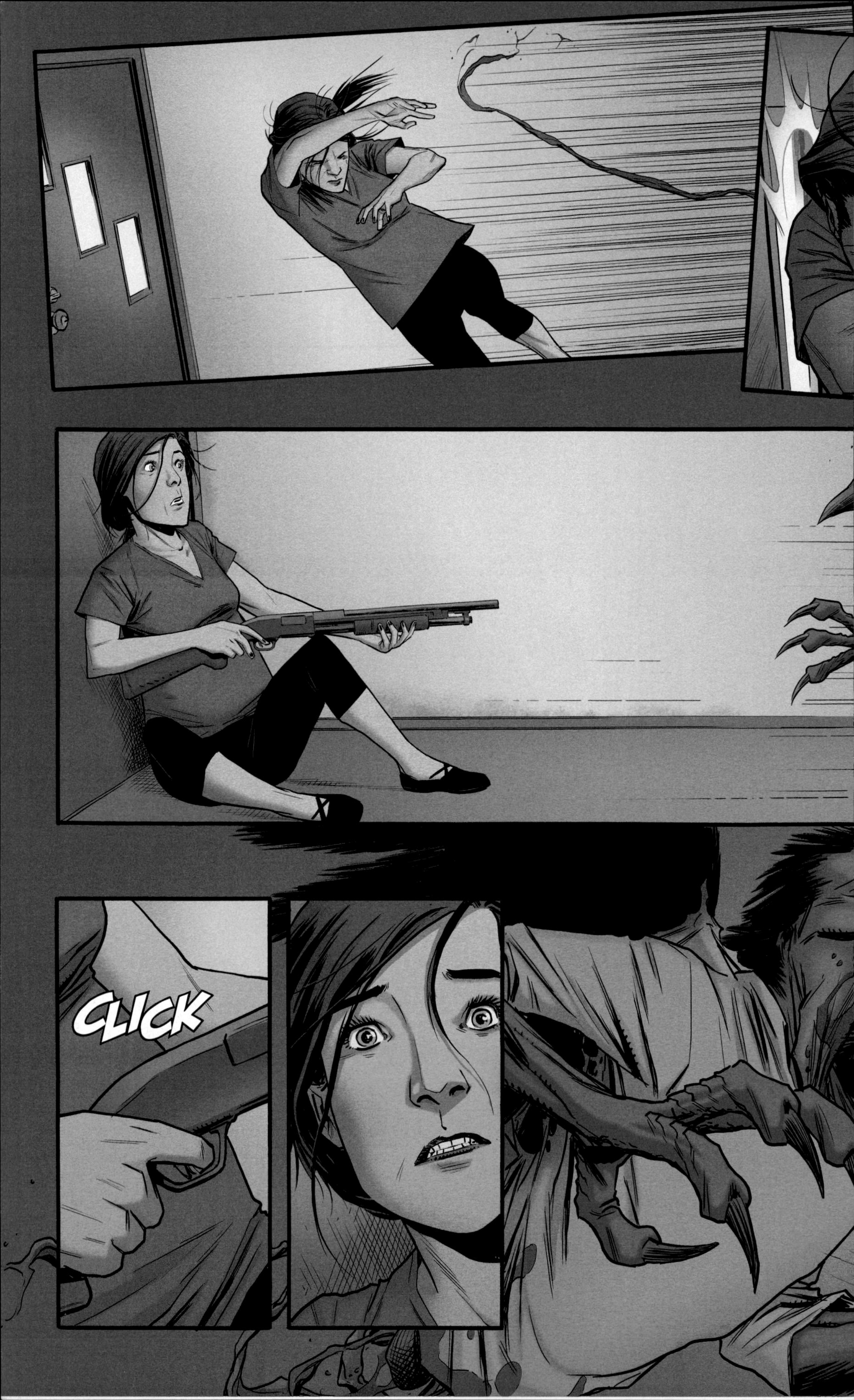
CLICK

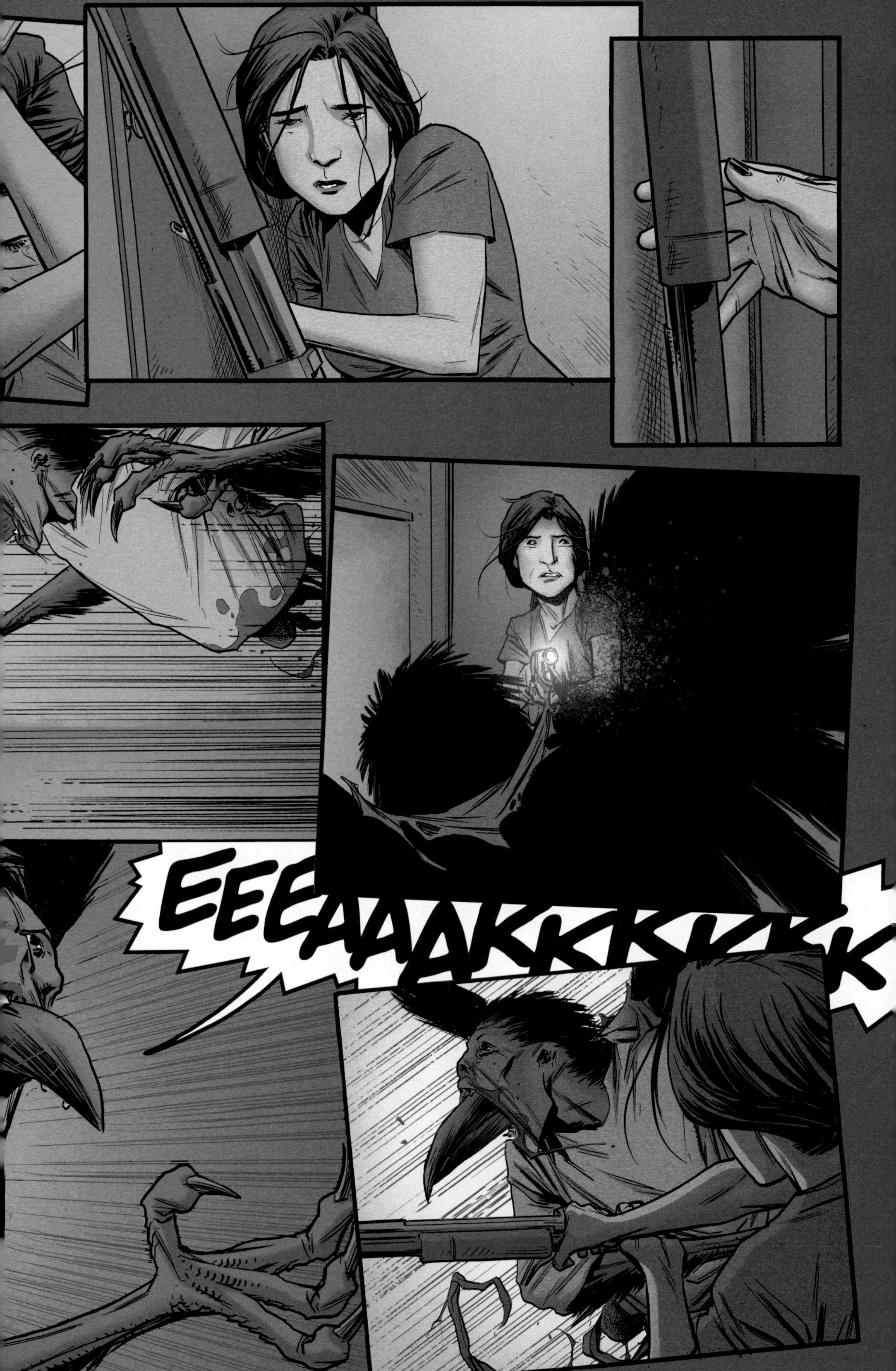
EEEAAAKKKKKKK

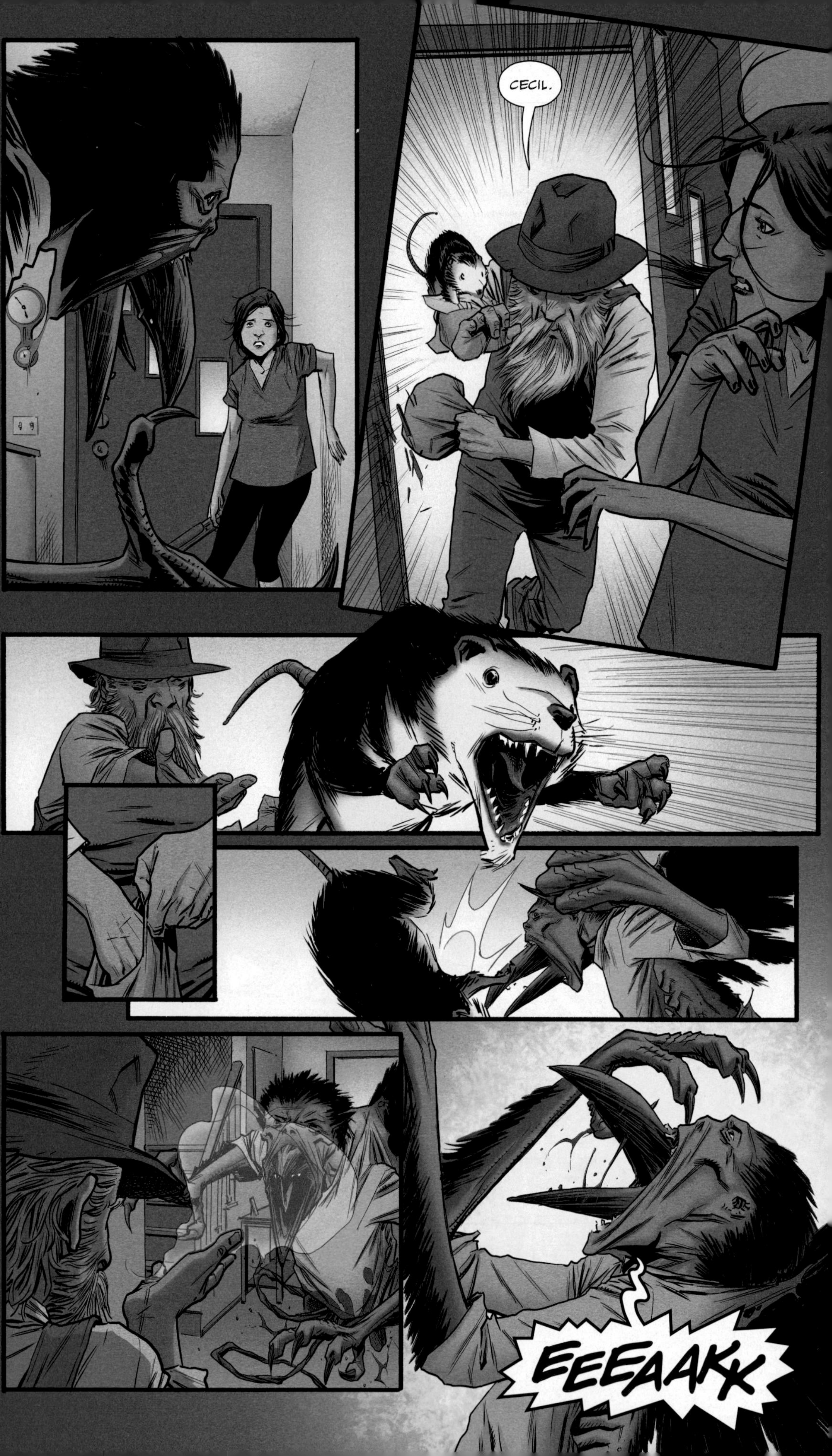
CECIL.
EEEAAKK

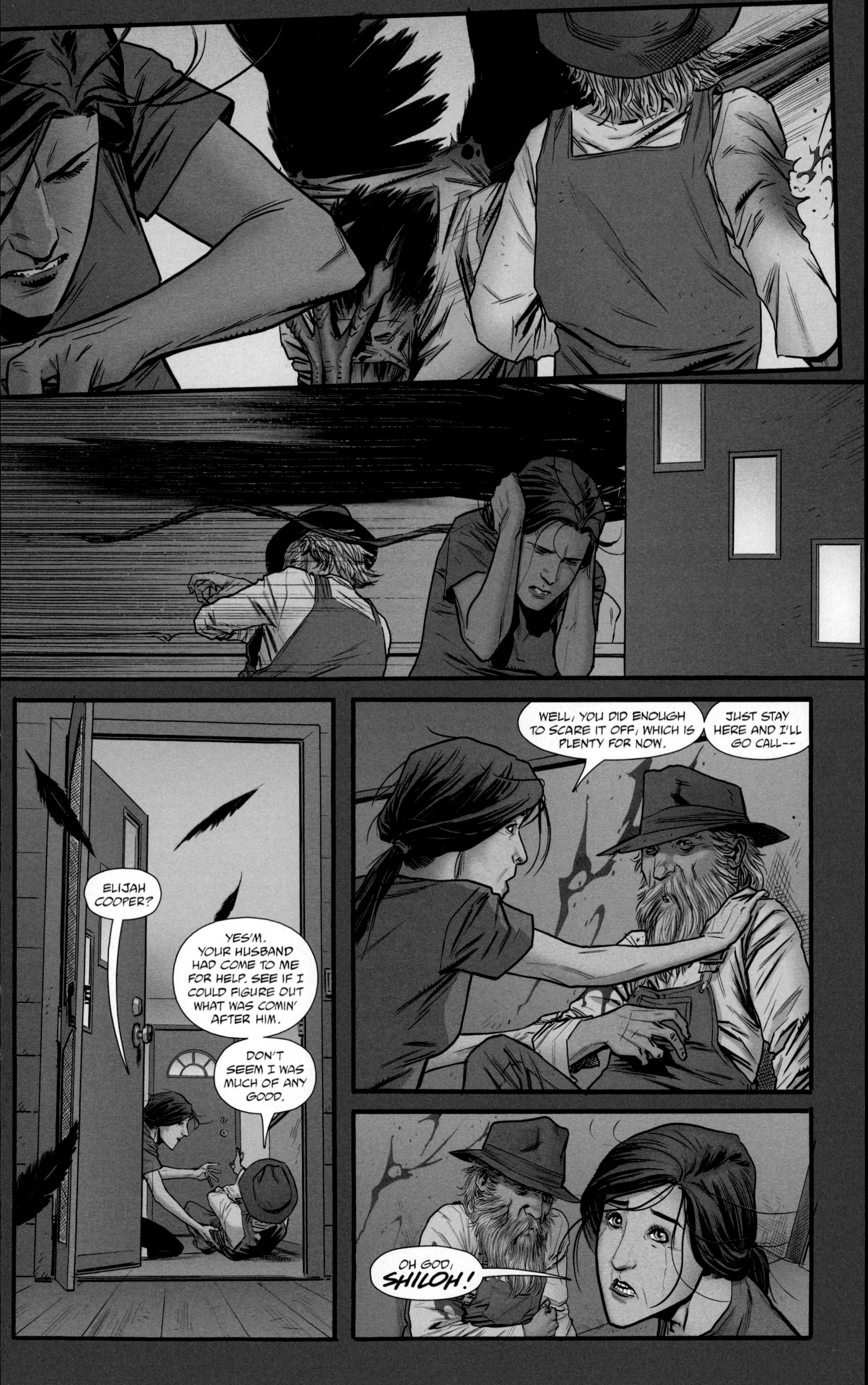
ELIJAH COOPER?
YES'M. YOUR HUSBAND HAD COME TO ME FOR HELP. SEE IF I COULD FIGURE OUT WHAT WAS COMIN' AFTER HIM.
DON'T SEEM I WAS MUCH OF ANY GOOD.
WELL, YOU DID ENOUGH TO SCARE IT OFF, WHICH IS PLENTY FOR NOW.
JUST STAY HERE AND I'LL GO CALL--
OH GOD, SHILOH!

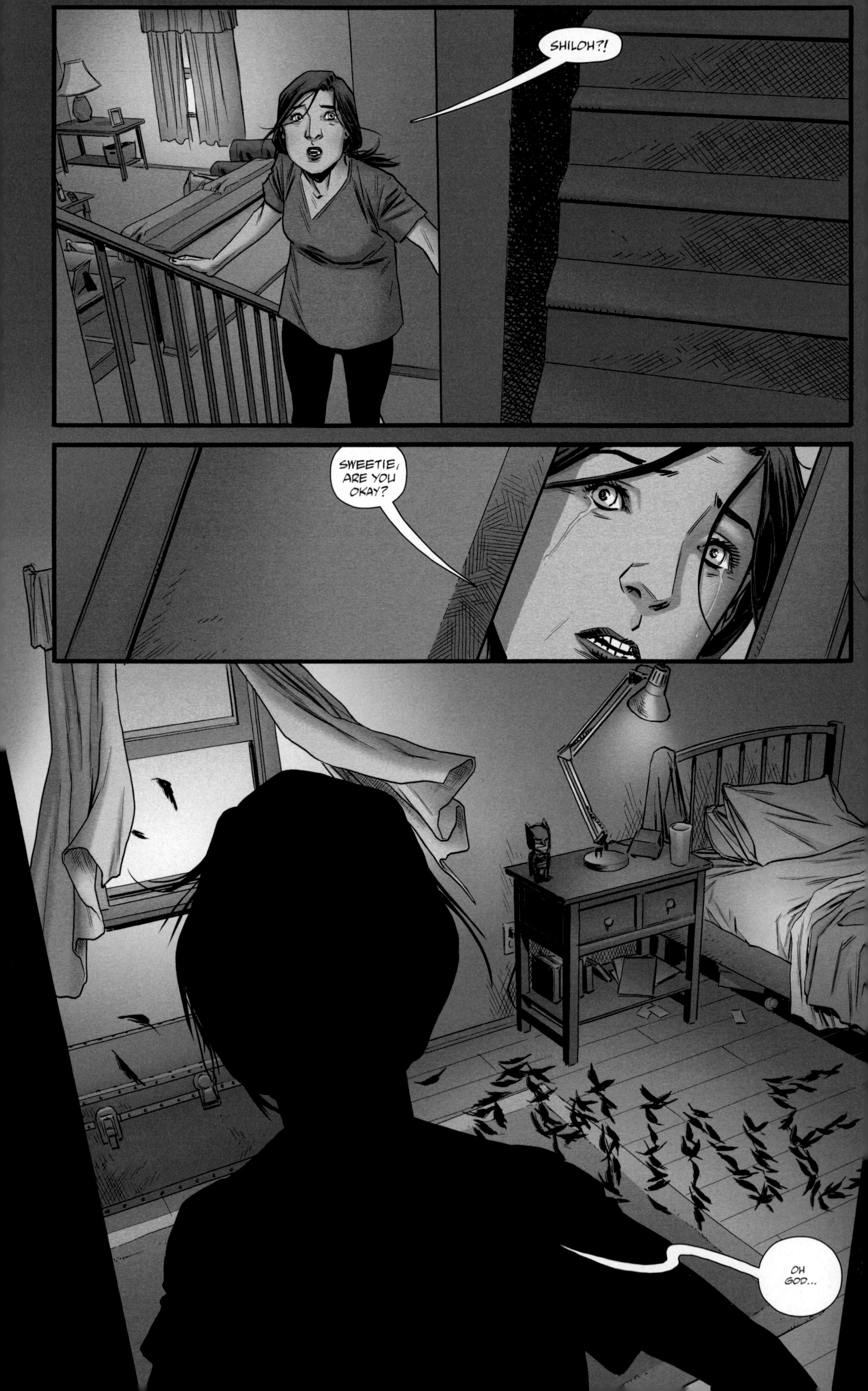
SHILOH?!
SWEETIE, ARE YOU OKAY?
OH GOD...

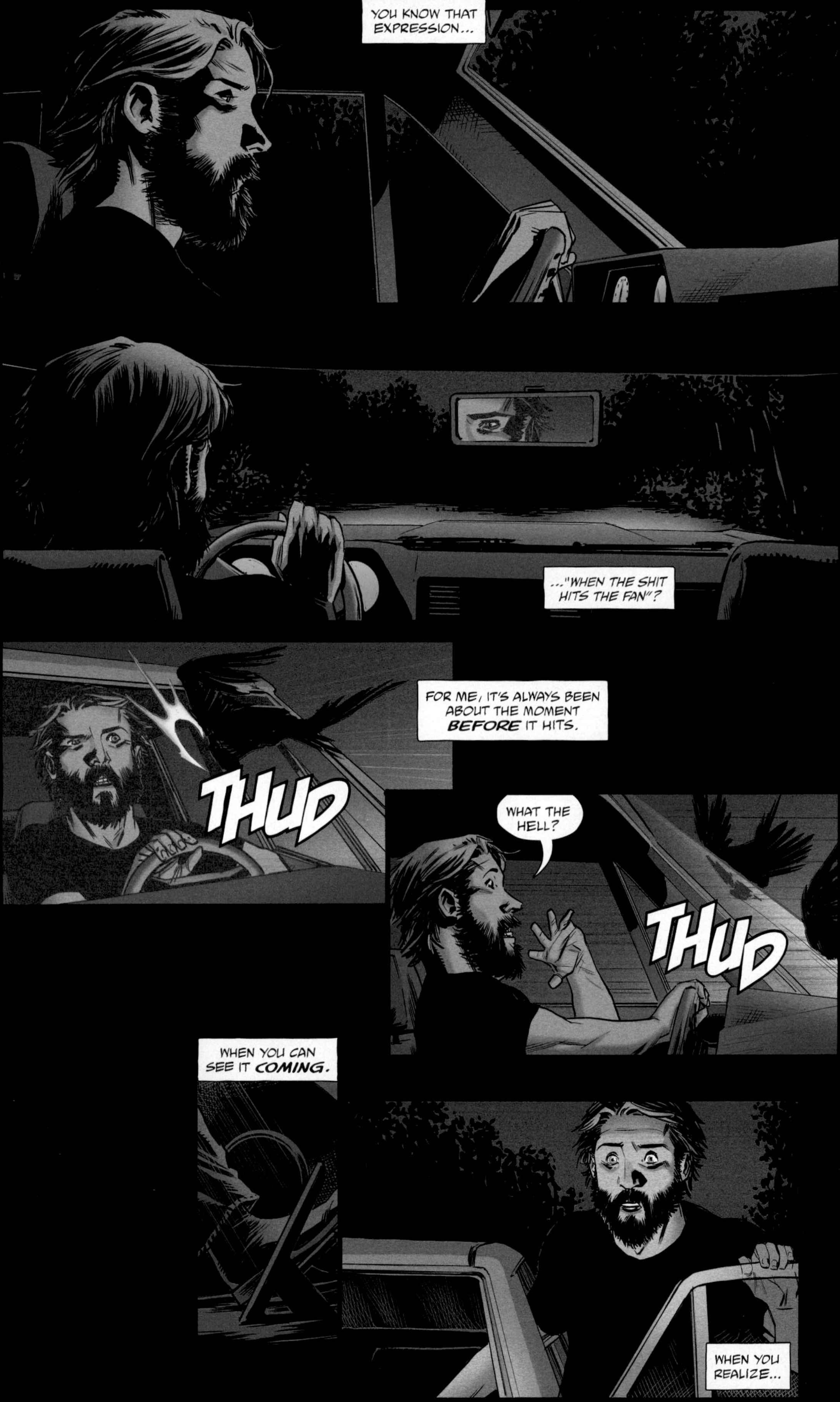
YOU KNOW THAT EXPRESSION...
..."WHEN THE SHIT HITS THE FAN"?
FOR ME, IT'S ALWAYS BEEN ABOUT THE MOMENT BEFORE IT HITS.
THUD
WHAT THE HELL?
THUD
WHEN YOU CAN SEE IT COMING.
WHEN YOU REALIZE...

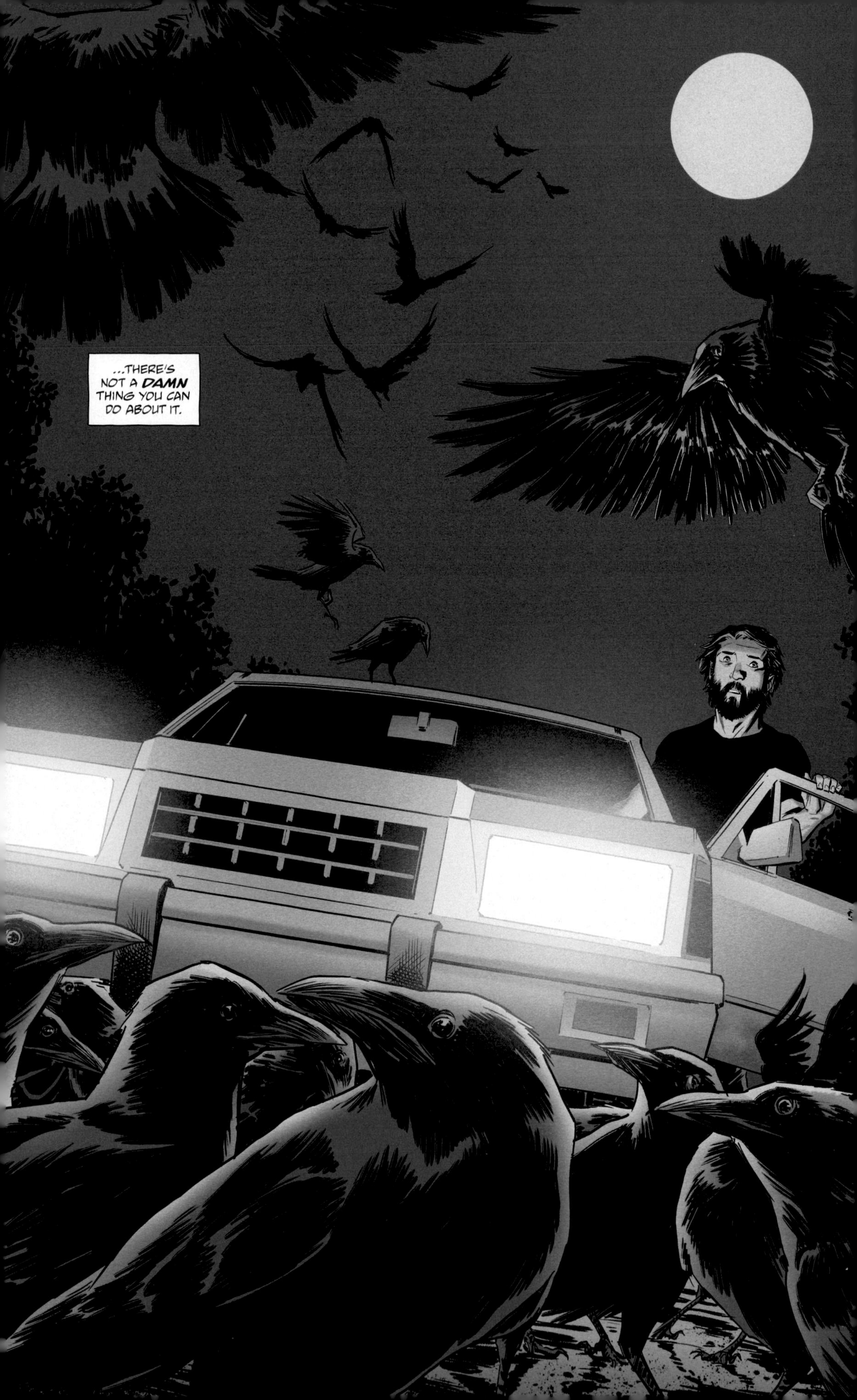
...THERE'S NOT A DAMN THING YOU CAN DO ABOUT IT.

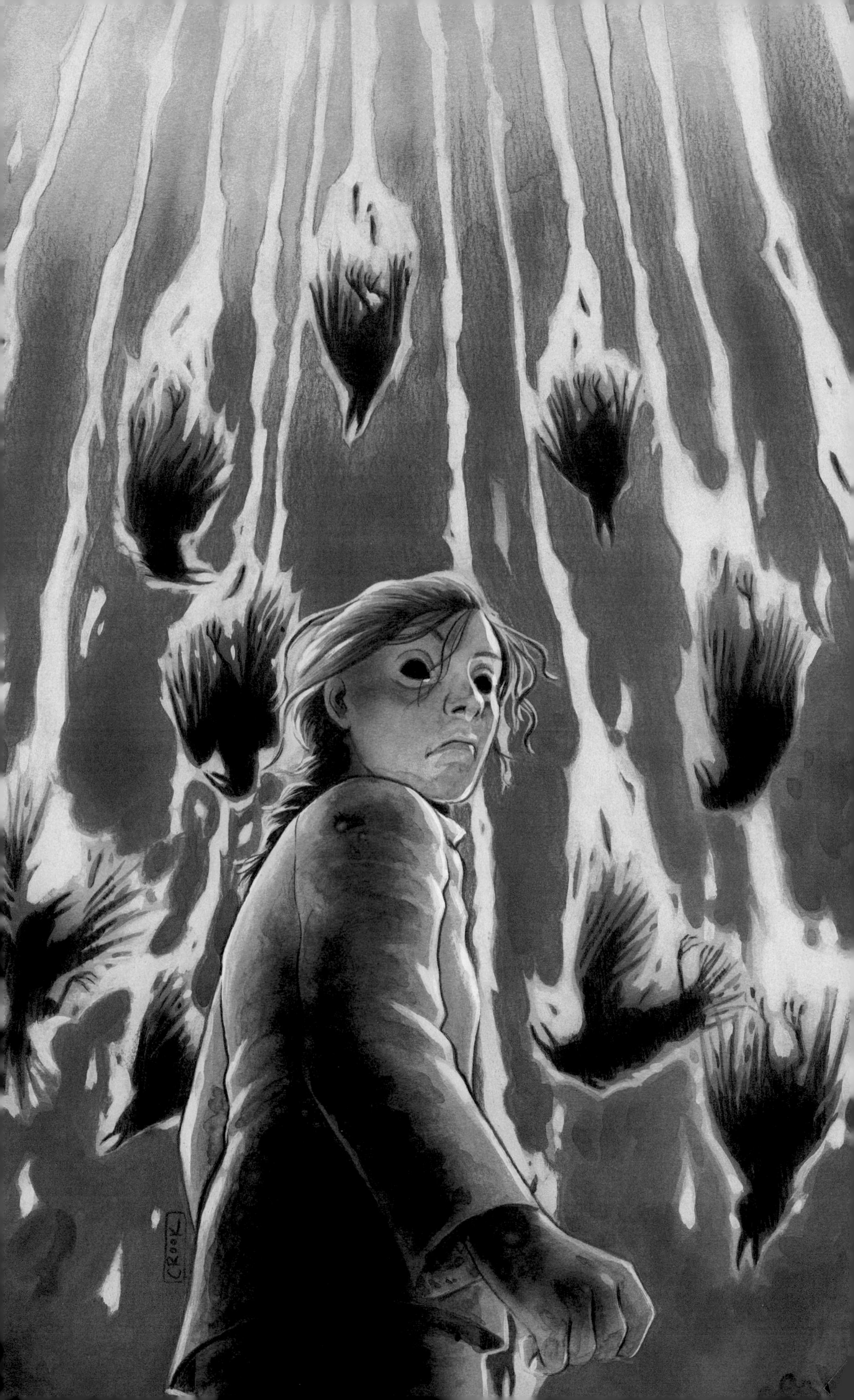
CROOK

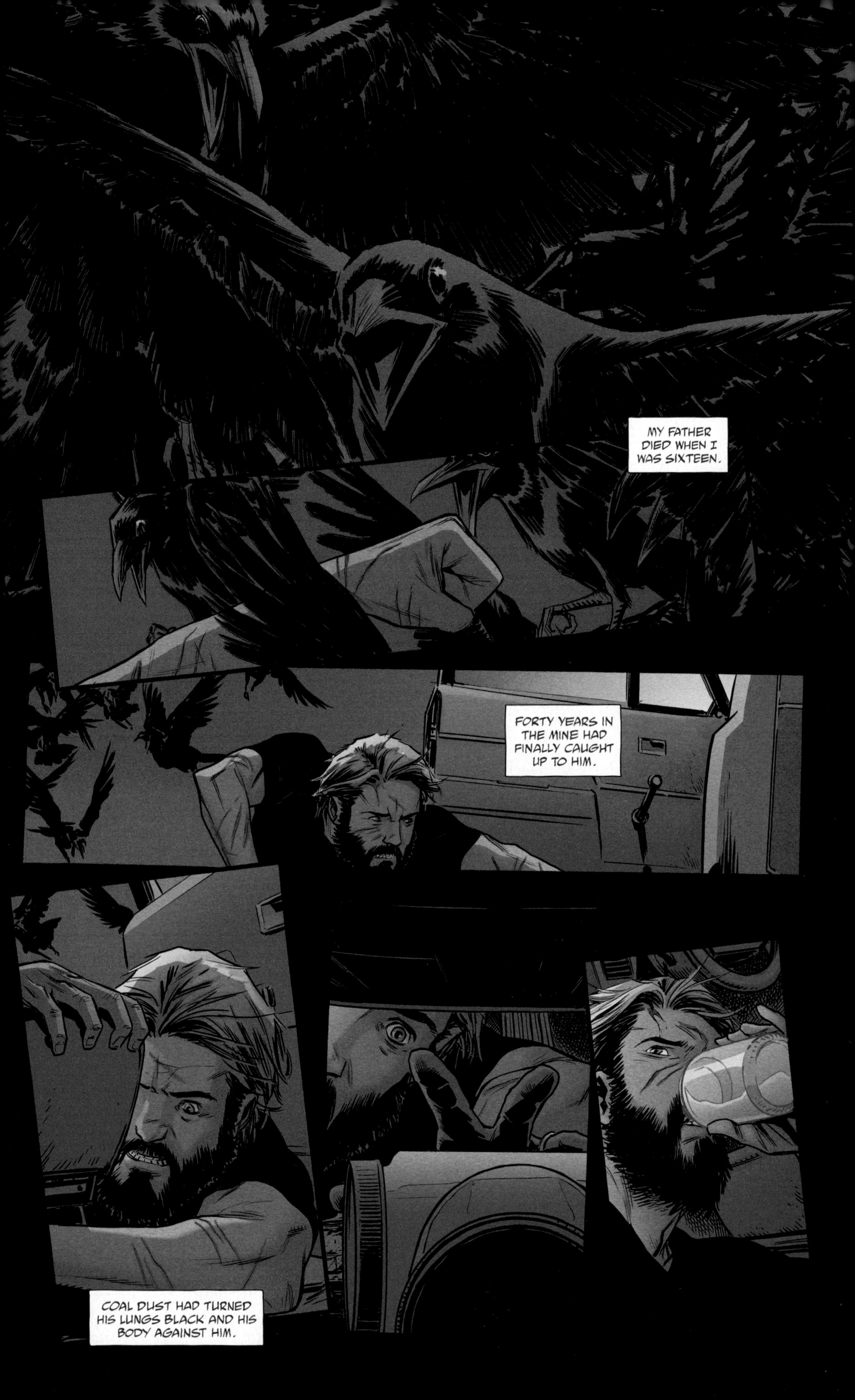
MY FATHER DIED WHEN I WAS SIXTEEN.
FORTY YEARS IN THE MINE HAD FINALLY CAUGHT UP TO HIM.
COAL DUST HAD TURNED HIS LUNGS BLACK AND HIS BODY AGAINST HIM.

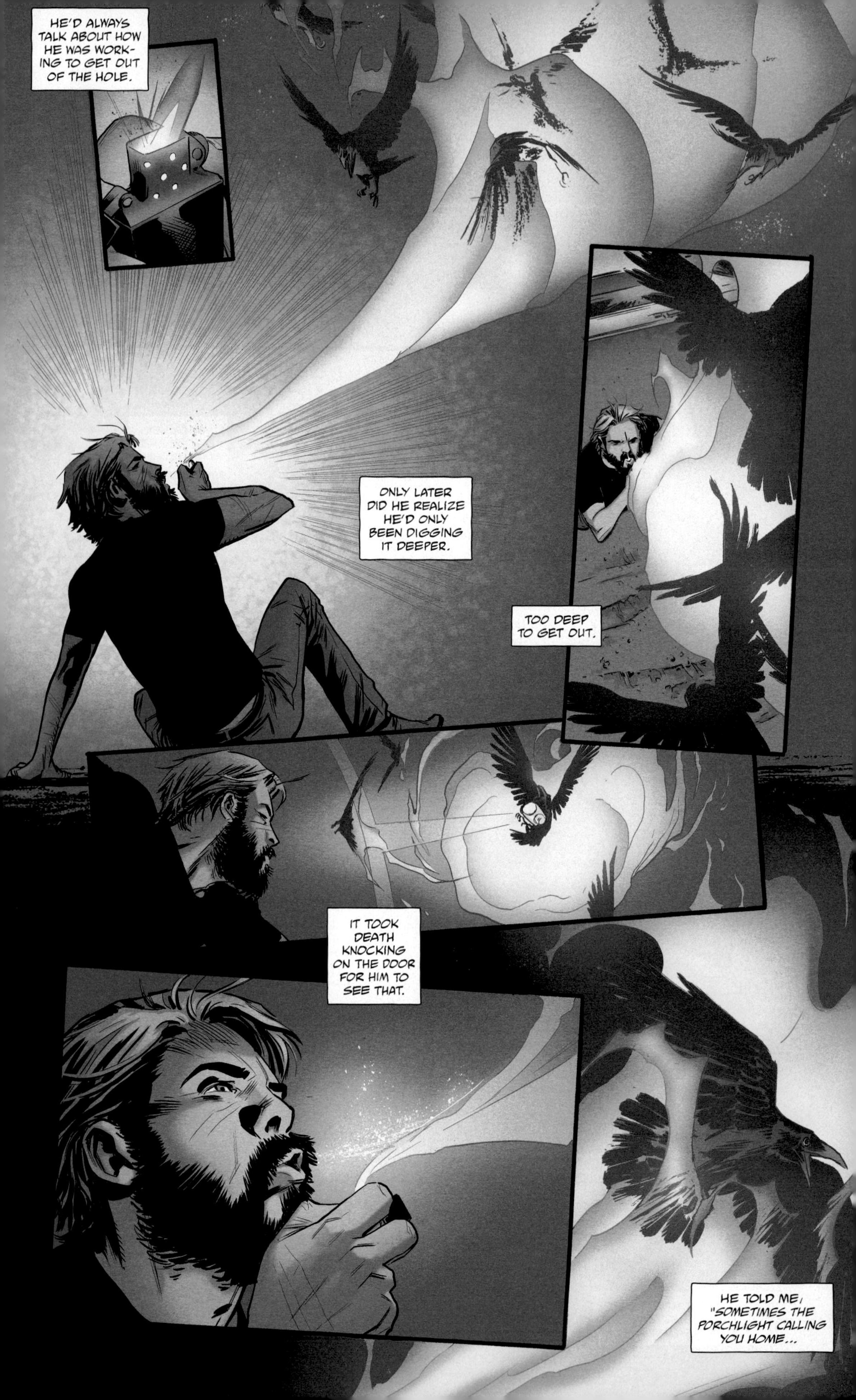
HE'D ALWAYS TALK ABOUT HOW HE WAS WORK-ING TO GET OUT OF THE HOLE.
ONLY LATER DID HE REALIZE HE'D ONLY BEEN DIGGING IT DEEPER.
TOO DEEP TO GET OUT.
IT TOOK DEATH KNOCKING ON THE DOOR FOR HIM TO SEE THAT.
HE TOLD ME, "SOMETIMES THE PORCHLIGHT CALLING YOU HOME...

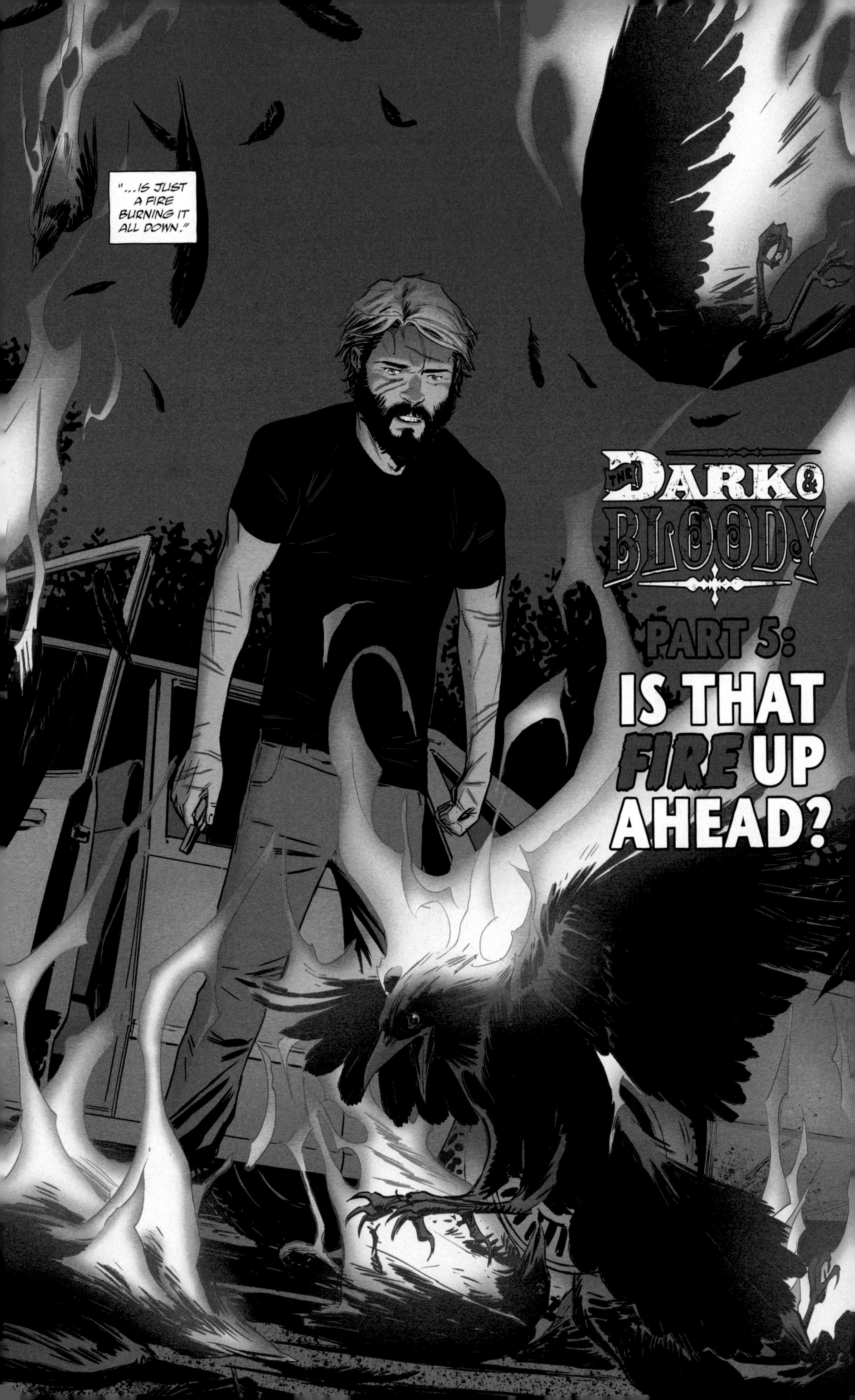
"...IS JUST A FIRE BURNING IT ALL DOWN."
THE DARK & BLOODY
PART 5:
IS THAT FIRE UP AHEAD?

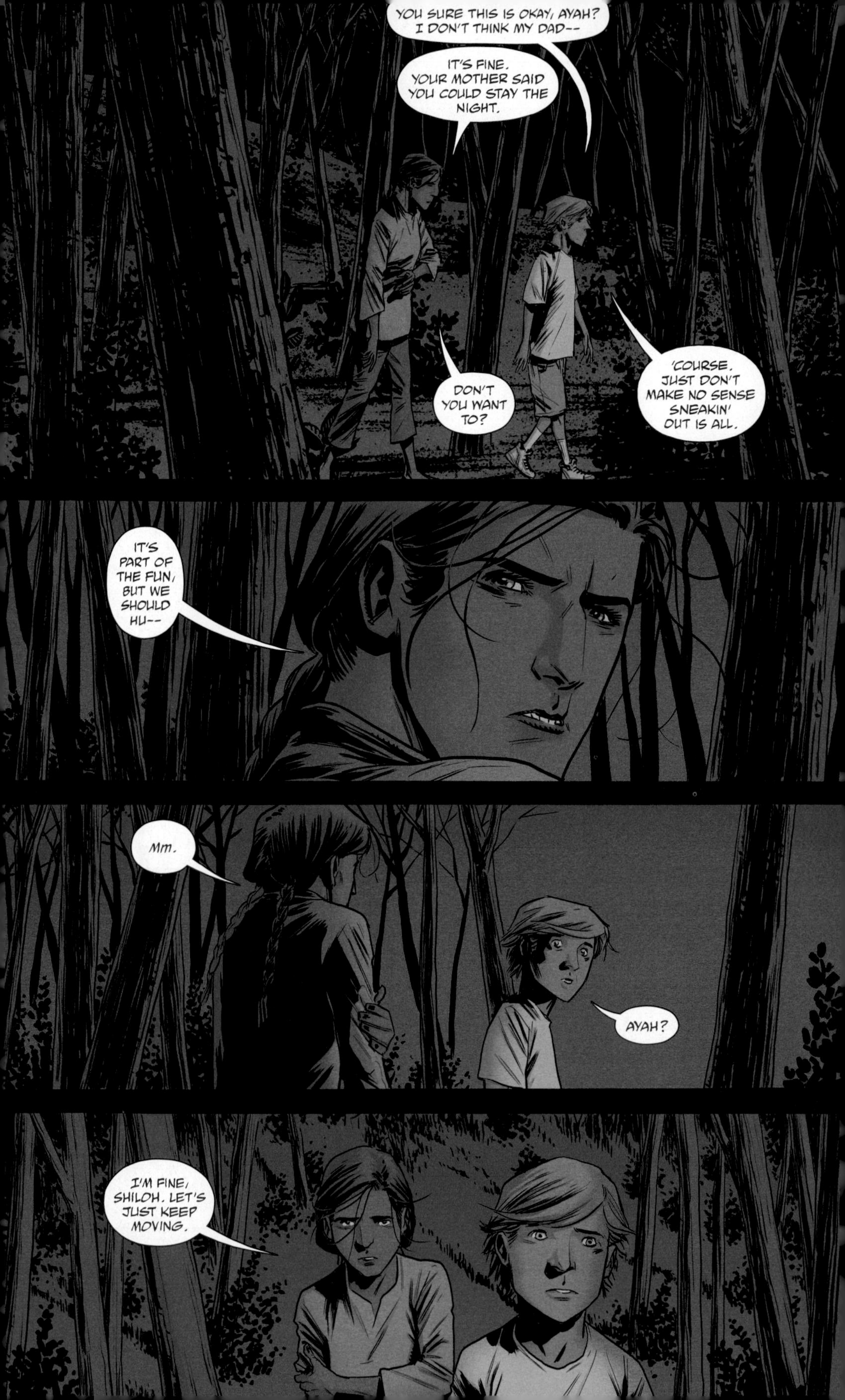
YOU SURE THIS IS OKAY, AYAH? I DON'T THINK MY DAD--
IT'S FINE. YOUR MOTHER SAID YOU COULD STAY THE NIGHT.
DON'T YOU WANT TO?
'COURSE. JUST DON'T MAKE NO SENSE SNEAKIN' OUT IS ALL.
IT'S PART OF THE FUN, BUT WE SHOULD HU--
Mm.
AYAH?
I'M FINE, SHILOH. LET'S JUST KEEP MOVING.

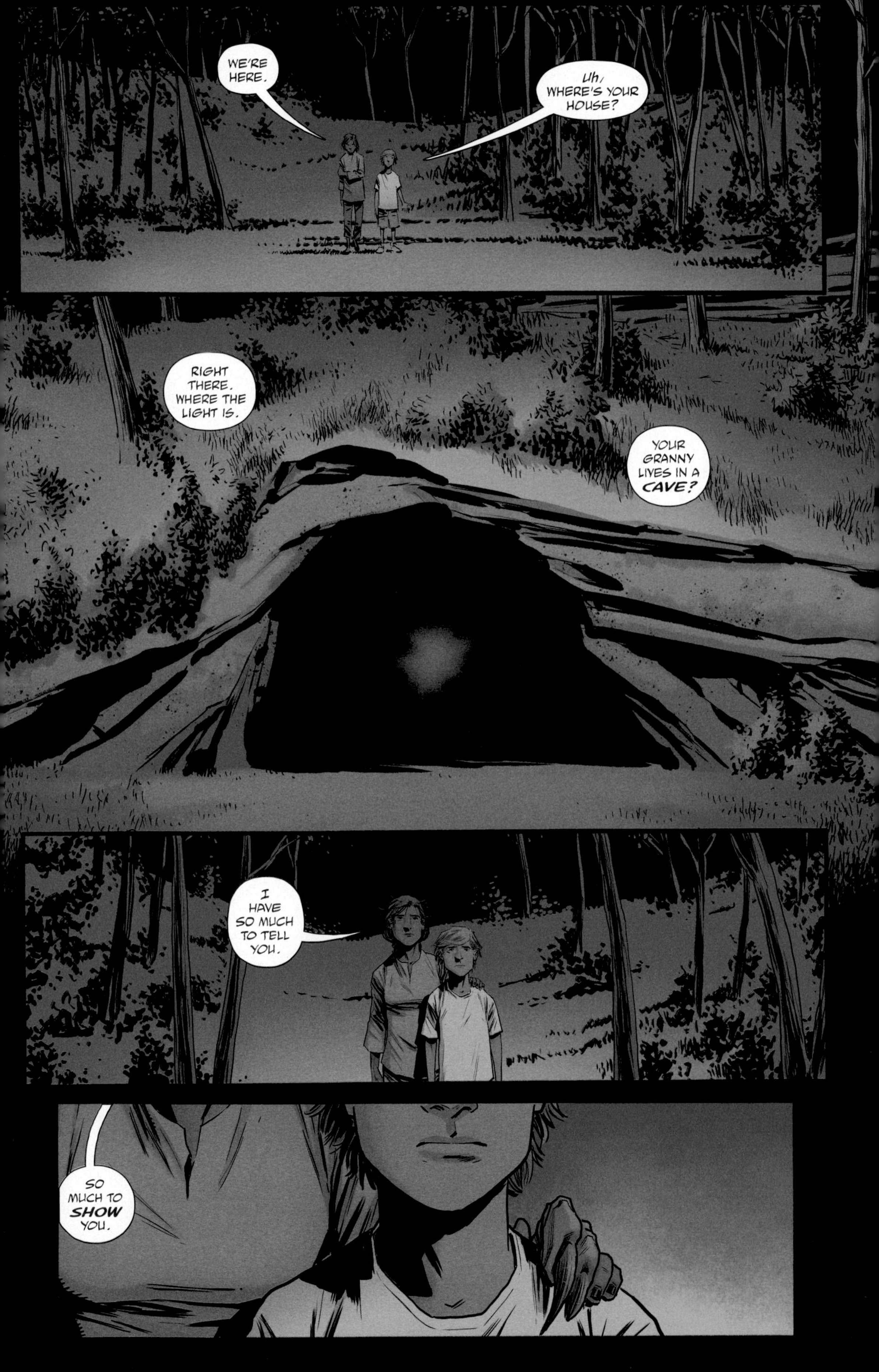
WE'RE HERE.
UH, WHERE'S YOUR HOUSE?
RIGHT THERE. WHERE THE LIGHT IS.
YOUR GRANNY LIVES IN A CAVE?
I HAVE SO MUCH TO TELL YOU.
SO MUCH TO SHOW YOU.

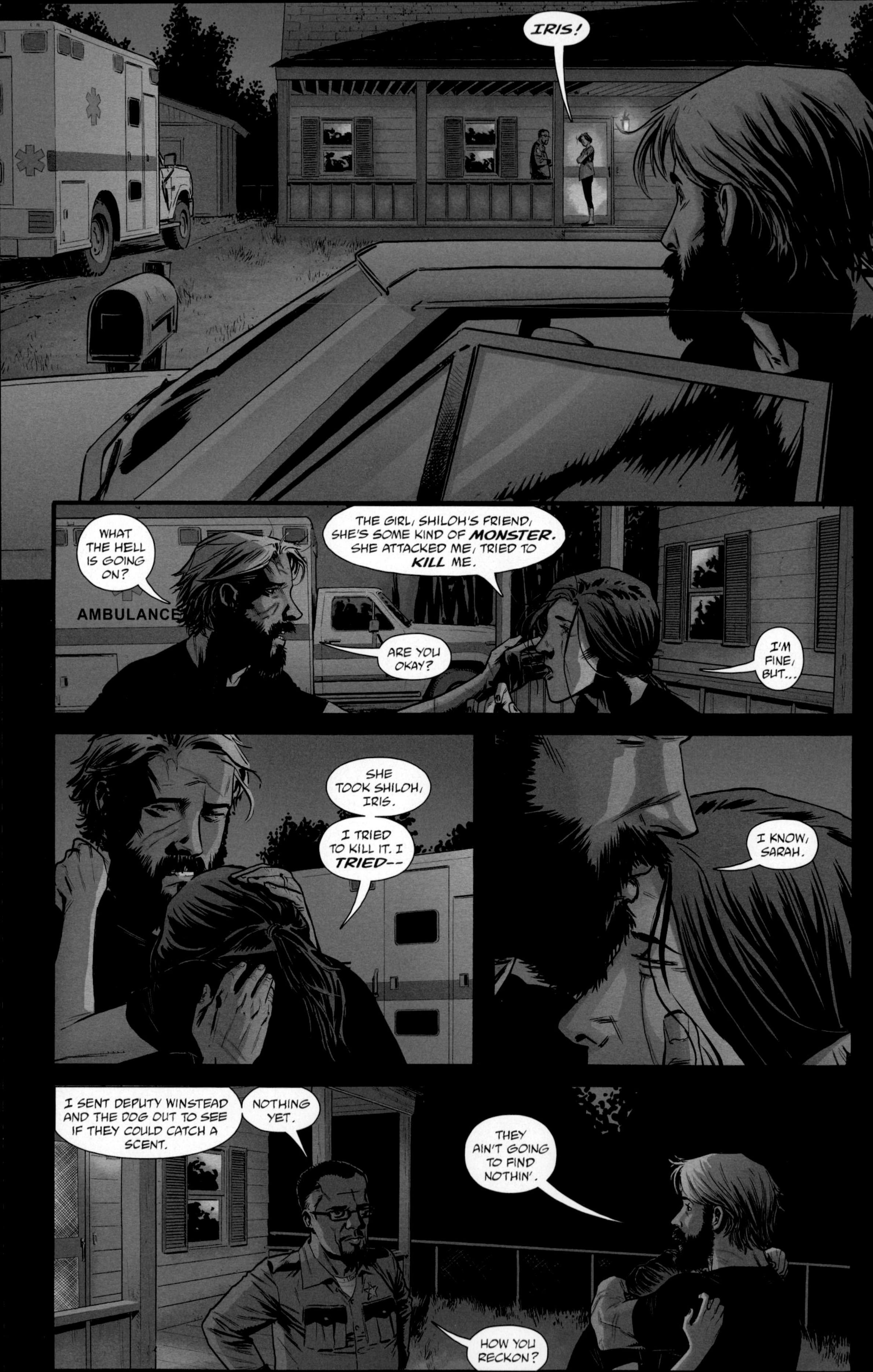
IRIS!
WHAT THE HELL IS GOING ON?
THE GIRL, SHILOH'S FRIEND, SHE'S SOME KIND OF **MONSTER.** SHE ATTACKED ME, TRIED TO **KILL** ME.
ARE YOU OKAY?
I'M FINE, BUT...
AMBULANCE
SHE TOOK SHILOH, IRIS.
I TRIED TO KILL IT. I **TRIED--**
I KNOW, SARAH.
I SENT DEPUTY WINSTEAD AND THE DOG OUT TO SEE IF THEY COULD CATCH A SCENT.
NOTHING YET.
THEY AIN'T GOING TO FIND NOTHIN'.
HOW YOU RECKON?

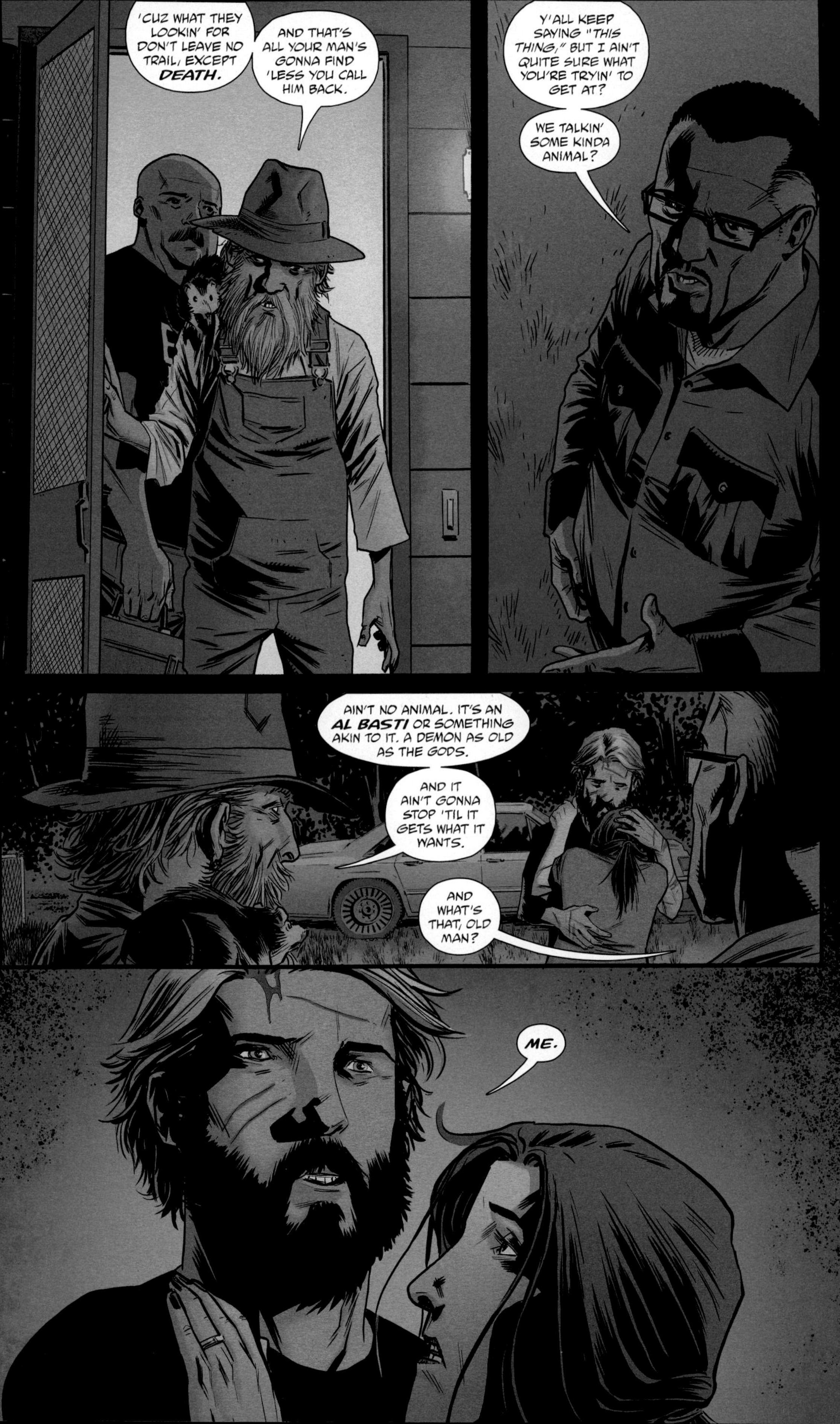
'CUZ WHAT THEY LOOKIN' FOR DON'T LEAVE NO TRAIL, EXCEPT **DEATH.**
AND THAT'S ALL YOUR MAN'S GONNA FIND 'LESS YOU CALL HIM BACK.
Y'ALL KEEP SAYING *"THIS THING,"* BUT I AIN'T QUITE SURE WHAT YOU'RE TRYIN' TO GET AT?
WE TALKIN' SOME KINDA ANIMAL?
AIN'T NO ANIMAL. IT'S AN ***AL BASTI*** OR SOMETHING AKIN TO IT. A DEMON AS OLD AS THE GODS.
AND IT AIN'T GONNA STOP 'TIL IT GETS WHAT IT WANTS.
AND WHAT'S THAT, OLD MAN?
***ME.***

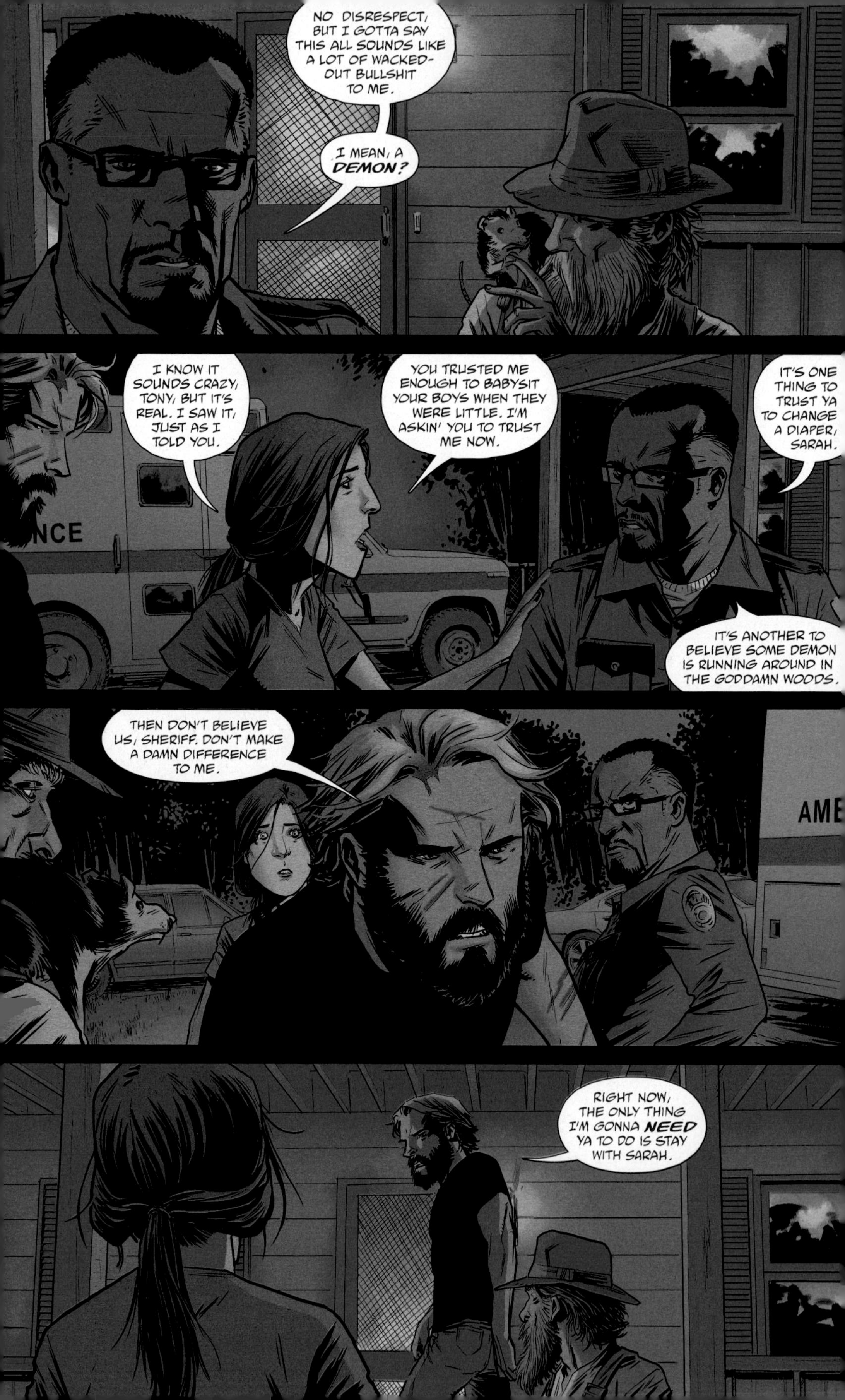
NO DISRESPECT, BUT I GOTTA SAY THIS ALL SOUNDS LIKE A LOT OF WACKED-OUT BULLSHIT TO ME.
I MEAN, A DEMON?
I KNOW IT SOUNDS CRAZY, TONY, BUT IT'S REAL. I SAW IT, JUST AS I TOLD YOU.
YOU TRUSTED ME ENOUGH TO BABYSIT YOUR BOYS WHEN THEY WERE LITTLE. I'M ASKIN' YOU TO TRUST ME NOW.
IT'S ONE THING TO TRUST YA TO CHANGE A DIAPER, SARAH.
IT'S ANOTHER TO BELIEVE SOME DEMON IS RUNNING AROUND IN THE GODDAMN WOODS.
NCE
THEN DON'T BELIEVE US, SHERIFF. DON'T MAKE A DAMN DIFFERENCE TO ME.
AME
RIGHT NOW, THE ONLY THING I'M GONNA NEED YA TO DO IS STAY WITH SARAH.

I START THINKIN' 'BOUT HOW MY FATHER DIED.

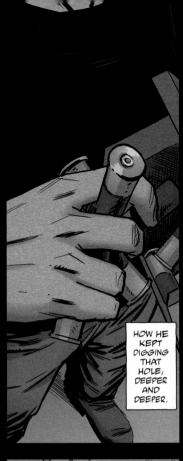

HOW HE KEPT DIGGING THAT HOLE, DEEPER AND DEEPER.

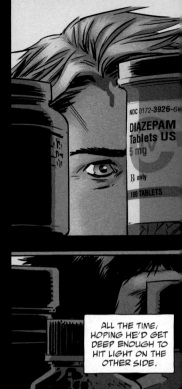

DIAZEPAM
Tablets US
5 mg

ALL THE TIME, HOPING HE'D GET DEEP ENOUGH TO HIT LIGHT ON THE OTHER SIDE.

ONLY TO GET EATEN UP BY THE DARKNESS.

I START THINKIN' I DON'T WANNA DIE LIKE THAT.

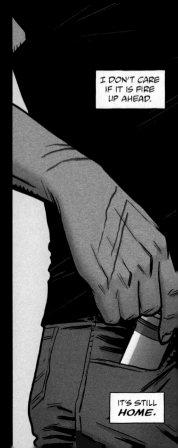

I DON'T CARE IF IT IS FIRE UP AHEAD.

IT'S STILL *HOME*.

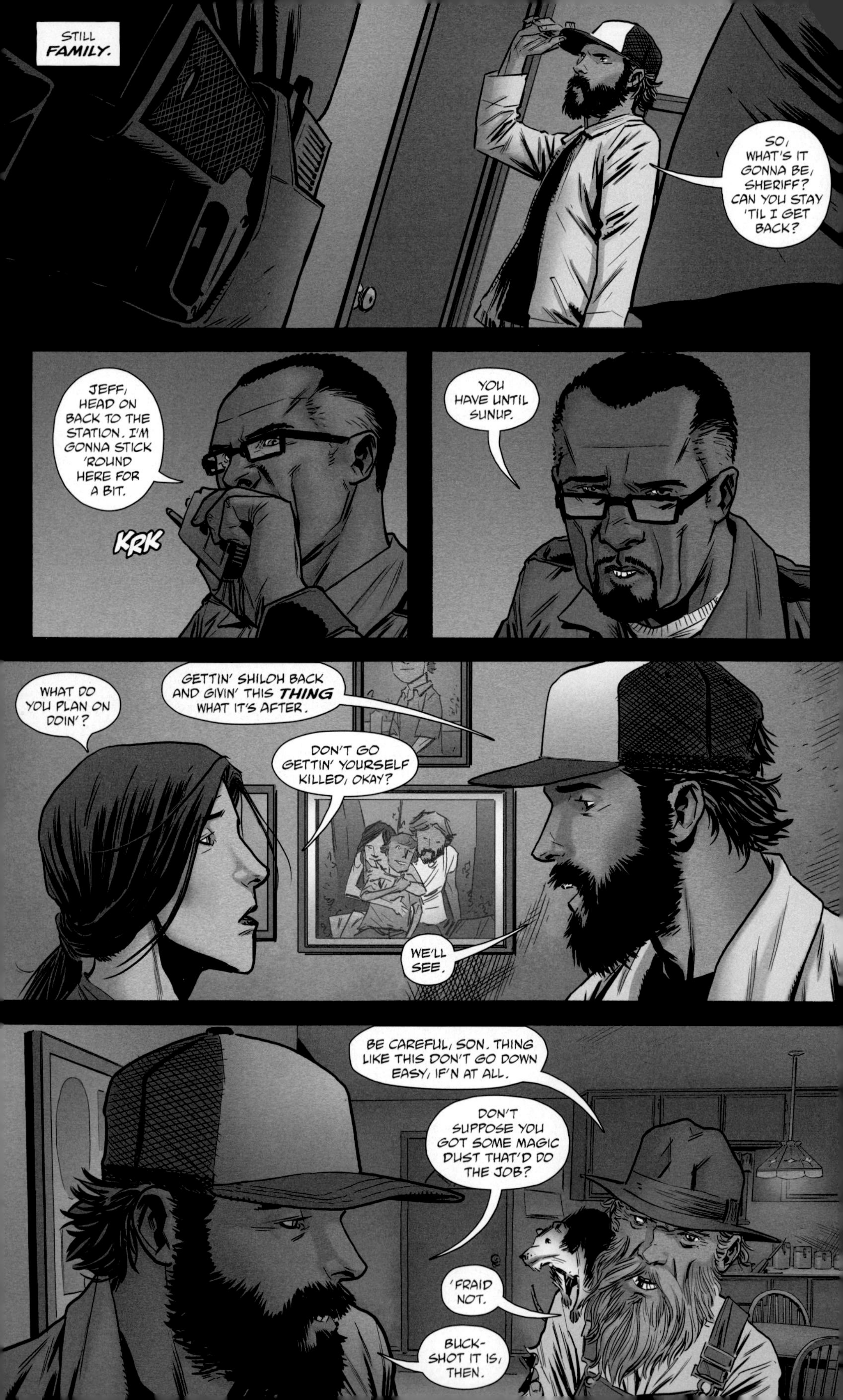
STILL FAMILY.
SO, WHAT'S IT GONNA BE, SHERIFF? CAN YOU STAY 'TIL I GET BACK?
JEFF, HEAD ON BACK TO THE STATION. I'M GONNA STICK 'ROUND HERE FOR A BIT.
KRK
YOU HAVE UNTIL SUNUP.
WHAT DO YOU PLAN ON DOIN'?
GETTIN' SHILOH BACK AND GIVIN' THIS THING WHAT IT'S AFTER.
DON'T GO GETTIN' YOURSELF KILLED, OKAY?
WE'LL SEE.
BE CAREFUL, SON. THING LIKE THIS DON'T GO DOWN EASY, IF'N AT ALL.
DON'T SUPPOSE YOU GOT SOME MAGIC DUST THAT'D DO THE JOB?
'FRAID NOT.
BUCK-SHOT IT IS, THEN.

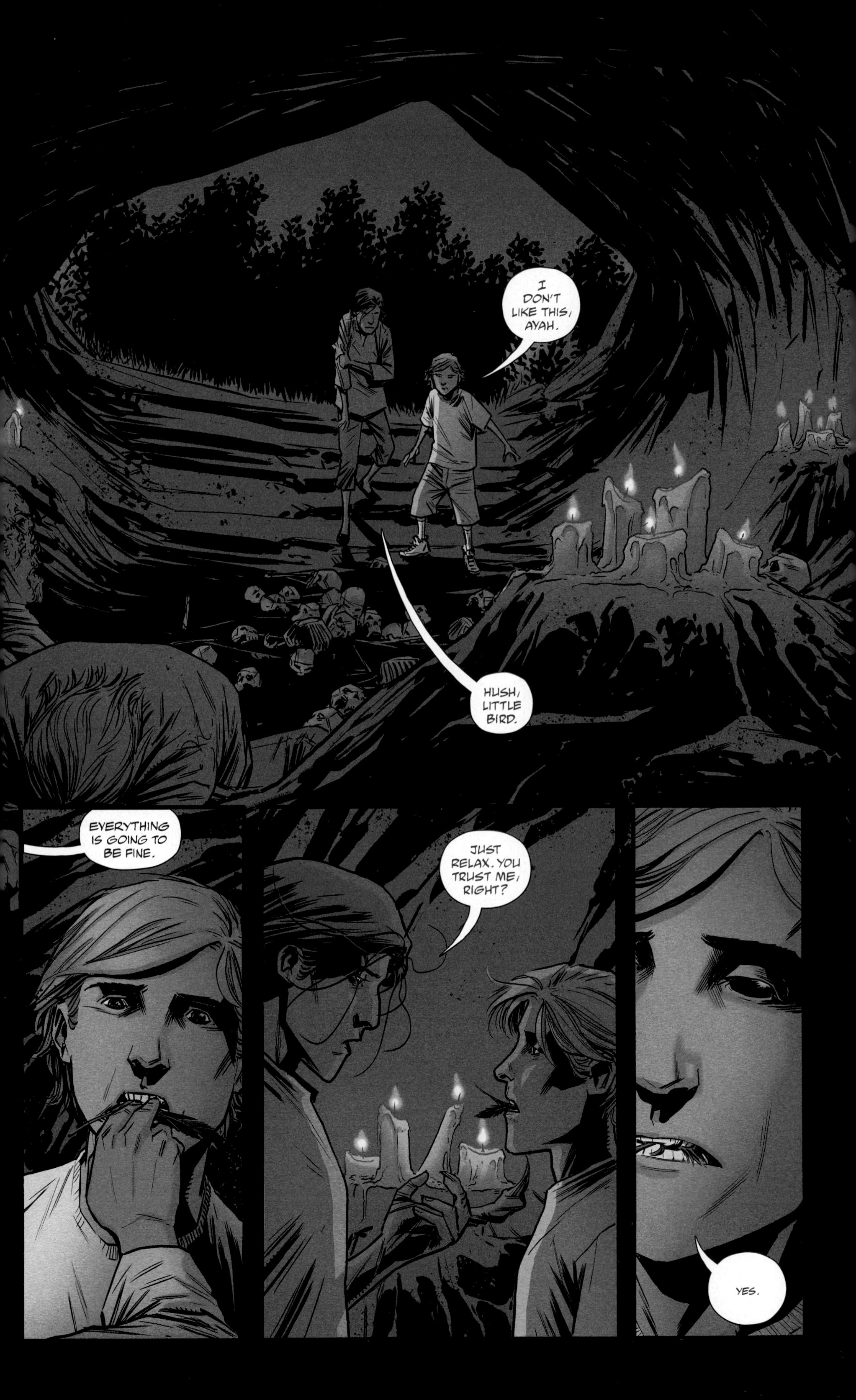
I DON'T LIKE THIS, AYAH.
HUSH, LITTLE BIRD.
EVERYTHING IS GOING TO BE FINE.
JUST RELAX. YOU TRUST ME, RIGHT?
YES.

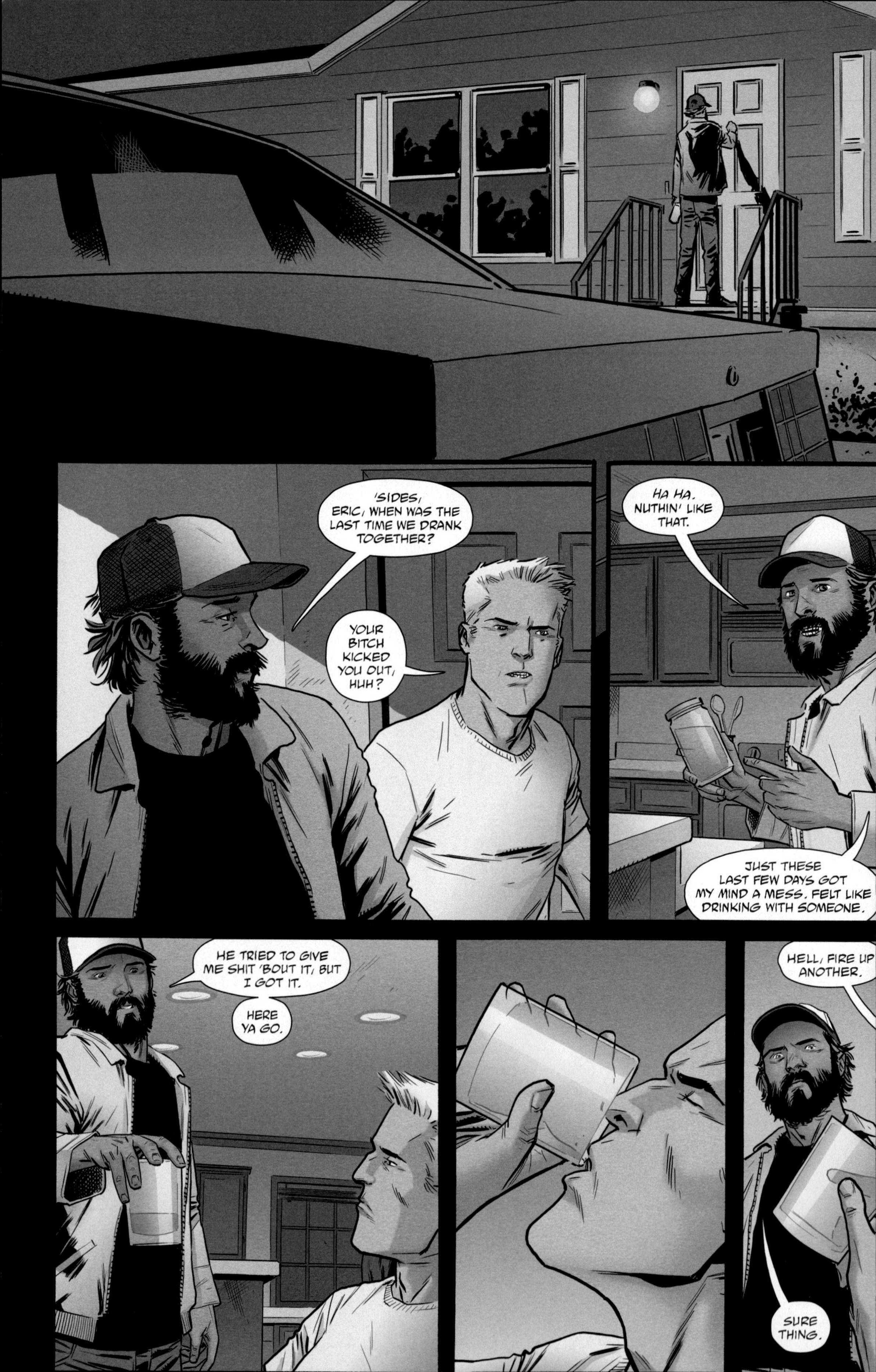
'SIDES, ERIC, WHEN WAS THE LAST TIME WE DRANK TOGETHER?
YOUR BITCH KICKED YOU OUT, HUH?
HA HA. NUTHIN' LIKE THAT.
JUST THESE LAST FEW DAYS GOT MY MIND A MESS. FELT LIKE DRINKING WITH SOMEONE.
HE TRIED TO GIVE ME SHIT 'BOUT IT, BUT I GOT IT.
HERE YA GO.
HELL, FIRE UP ANOTHER.
SURE THING.

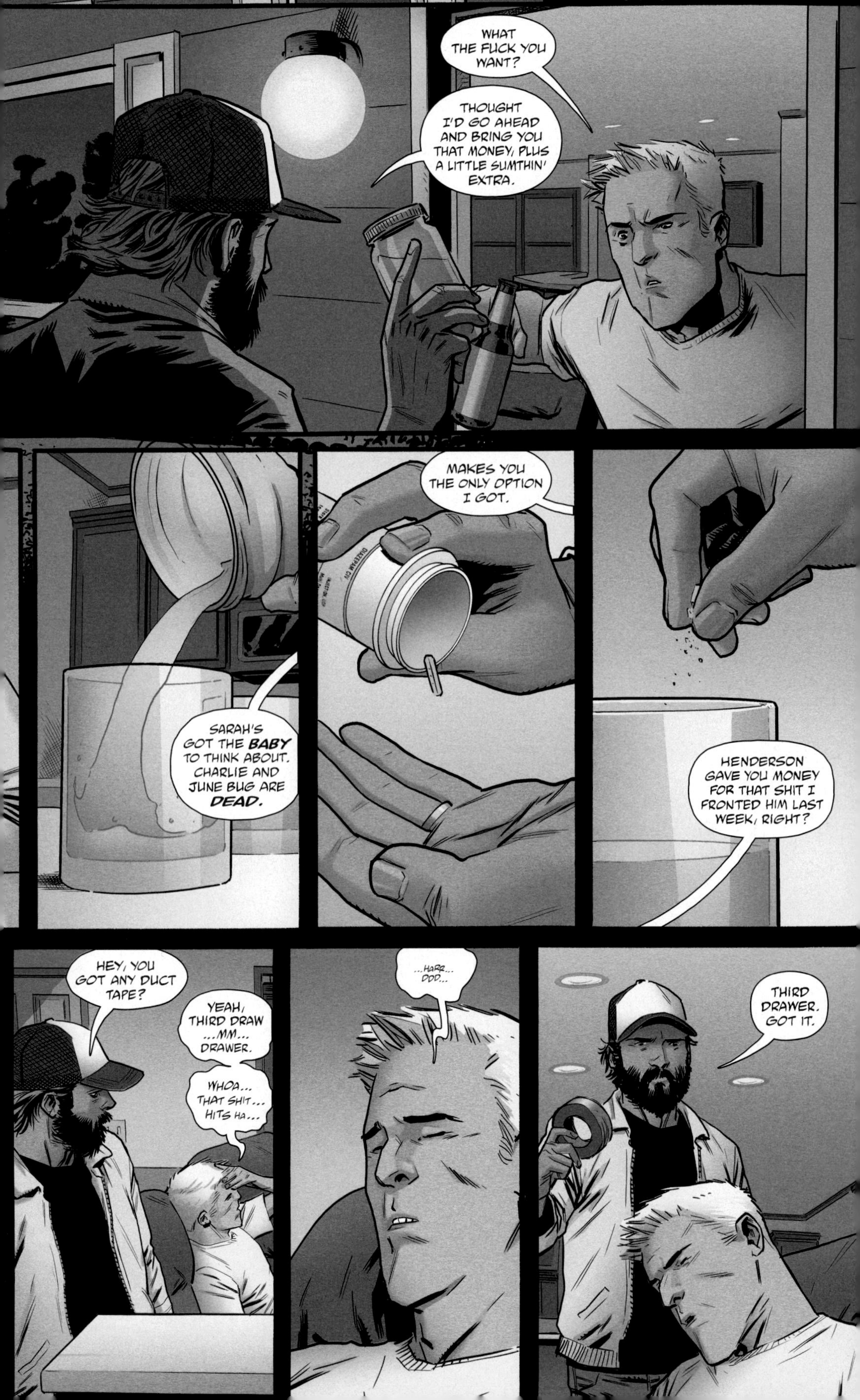
WHAT THE FUCK YOU WANT?
THOUGHT I'D GO AHEAD AND BRING YOU THAT MONEY, PLUS A LITTLE SUMTHIN' EXTRA.
MAKES YOU THE ONLY OPTION I GOT.
SARAH'S GOT THE BABY TO THINK ABOUT. CHARLIE AND JUNE BUG ARE DEAD.
HENDERSON GAVE YOU MONEY FOR THAT SHIT I FRONTED HIM LAST WEEK, RIGHT?
HEY, YOU GOT ANY DUCT TAPE?
YEAH, THIRD DRAW ...MM... DRAWER.
WHOA... THAT SHIT... HITS HA...
...HARR... DDD...
THIRD DRAWER. GOT IT.

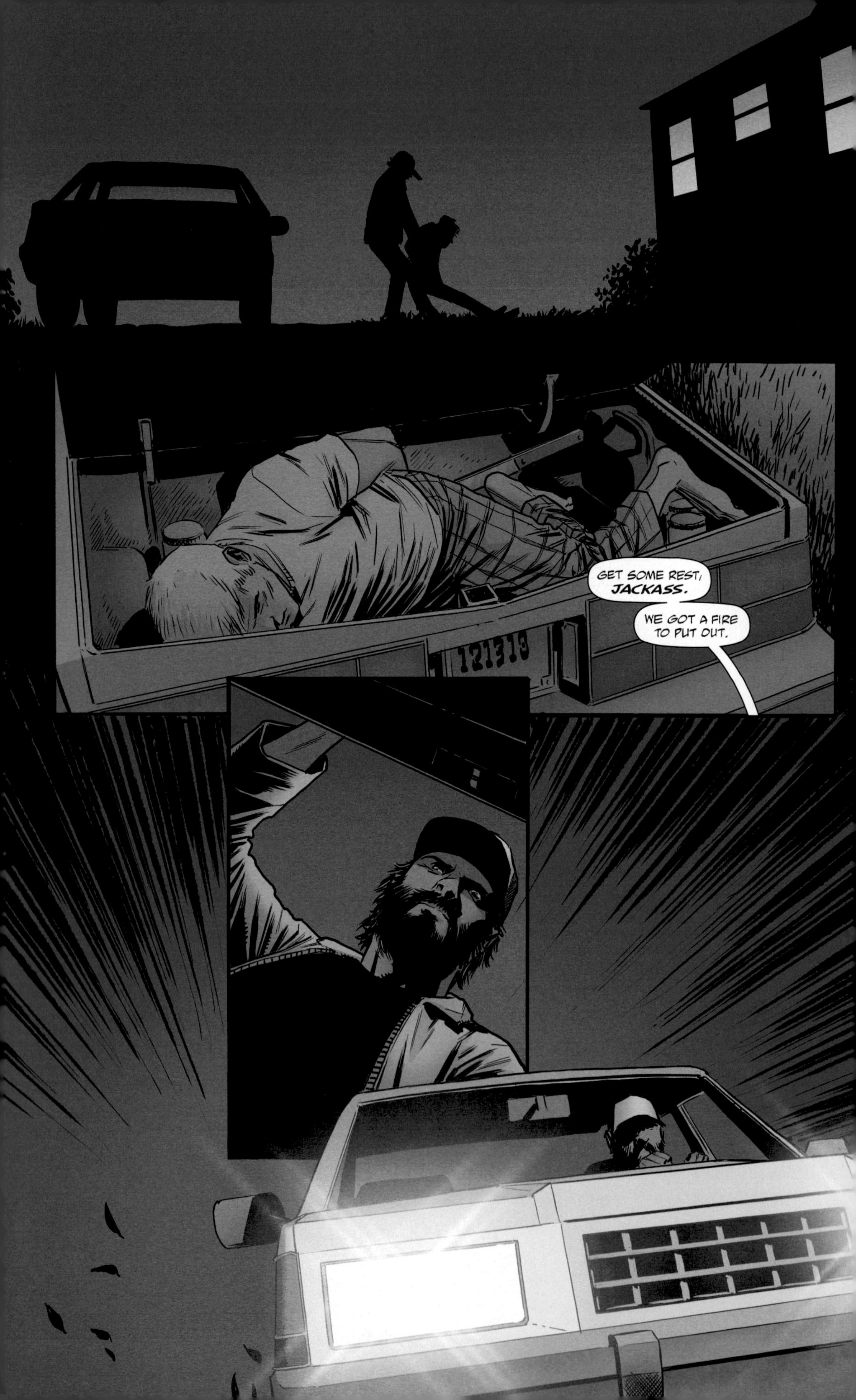
GET SOME REST, JACKASS.
WE GOT A FIRE TO PUT OUT.
121318

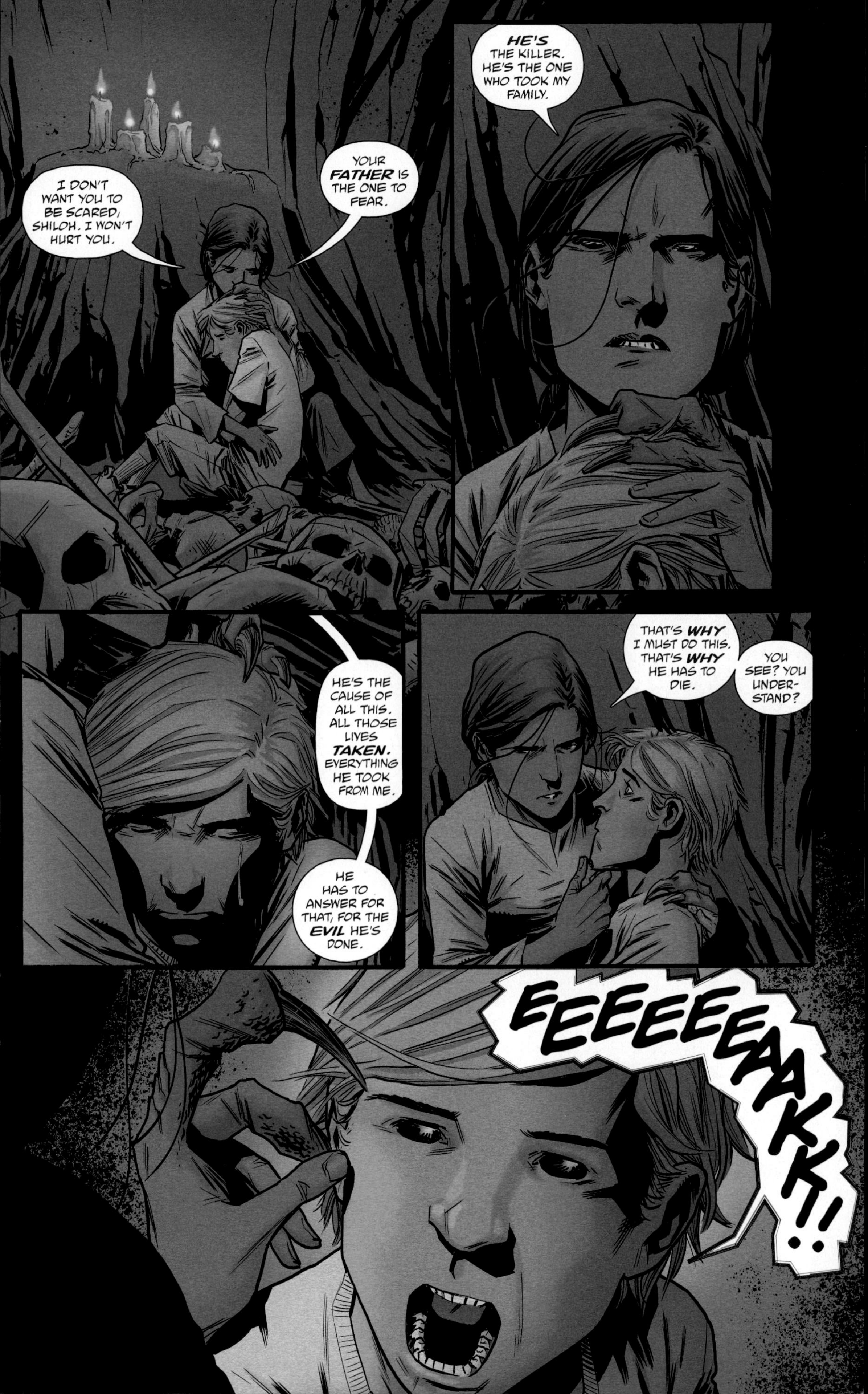
I DON'T WANT YOU TO BE SCARED, SHILOH. I WON'T HURT YOU.
YOUR FATHER IS THE ONE TO FEAR.
HE'S THE KILLER. HE'S THE ONE WHO TOOK MY FAMILY.
HE'S THE CAUSE OF ALL THIS. ALL THOSE LIVES TAKEN. EVERYTHING HE TOOK FROM ME.
HE HAS TO ANSWER FOR THAT, FOR THE EVIL HE'S DONE.
THAT'S WHY I MUST DO THIS. THAT'S WHY HE HAS TO DIE.
YOU SEE? YOU UNDERSTAND?
EEEEEEAAKK!!

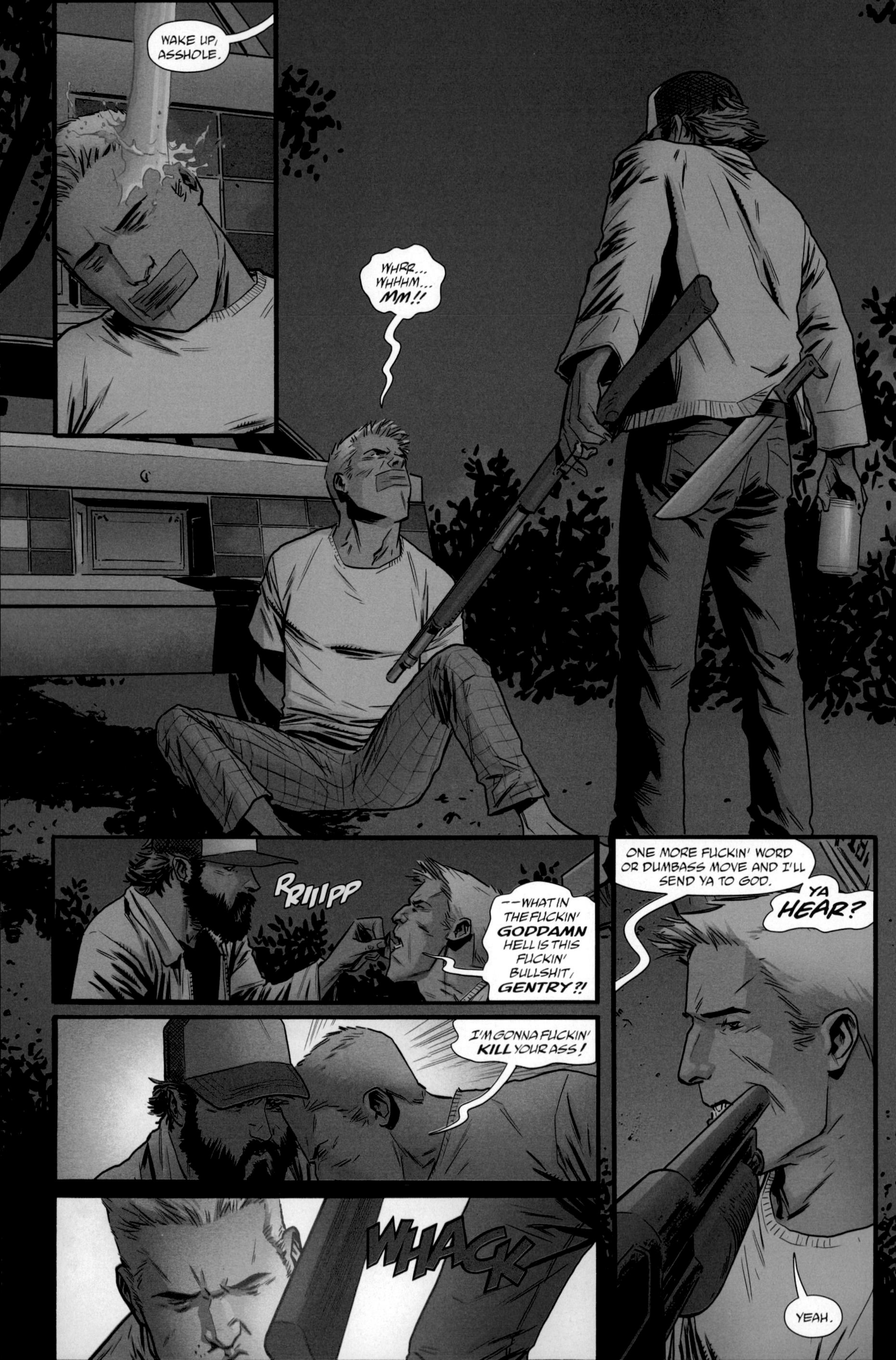
WAKE UP, ASSHOLE.
WHRR... WHHHM... MM!!
RRIIIPP
--WHAT IN THE FUCKIN' GODDAMN HELL IS THIS FUCKIN' BULLSHIT, GENTRY?!
I'M GONNA FUCKIN' KILL YOUR ASS!
WHACK
ONE MORE FUCKIN' WORD OR DUMBASS MOVE AND I'LL SEND YA TO GOD.
YA HEAR?
YEAH.

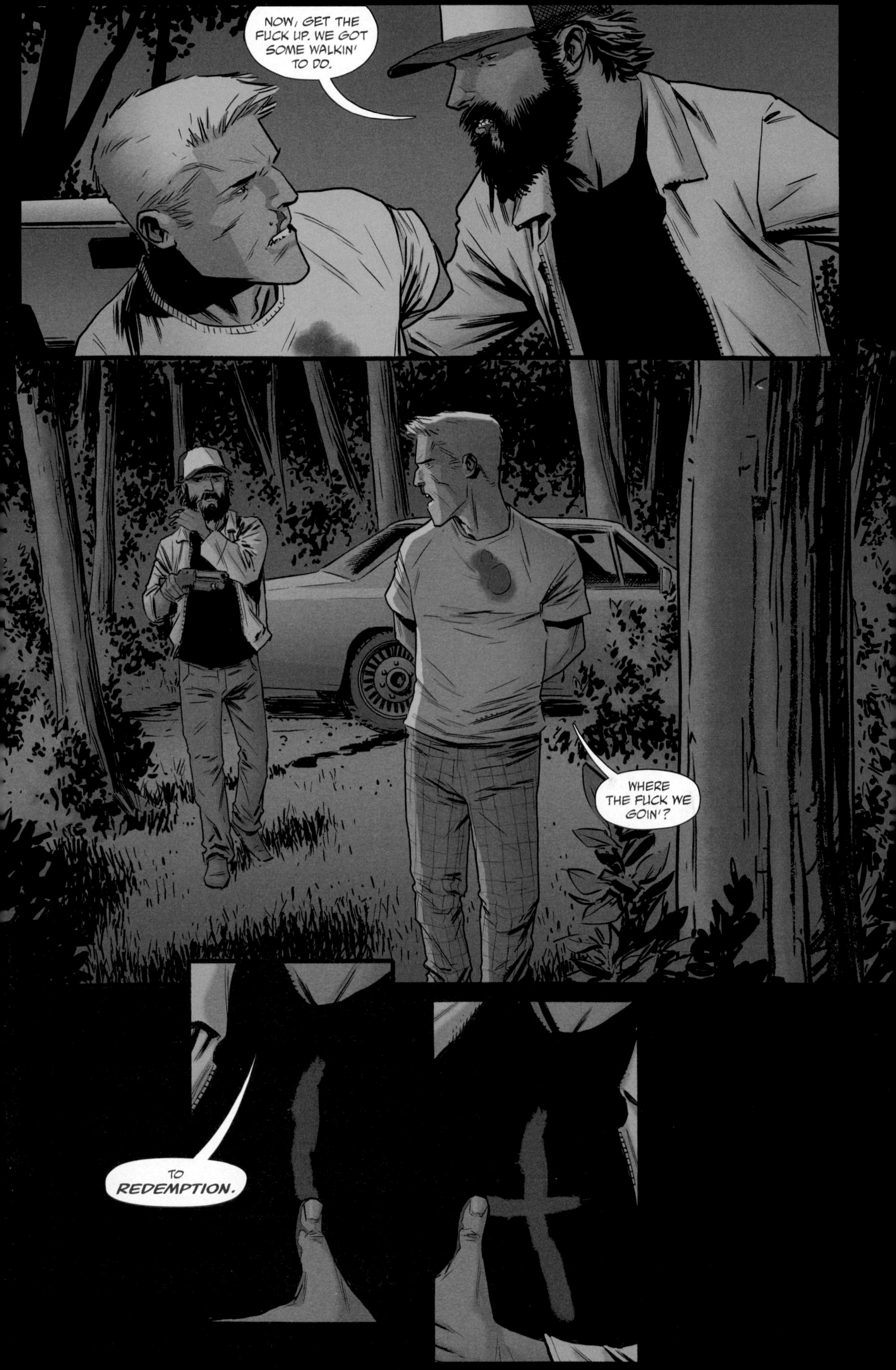
NOW, GET THE FUCK UP. WE GOT SOME WALKIN' TO DO.
WHERE THE FUCK WE GOIN'?
TO REDEMPTION.

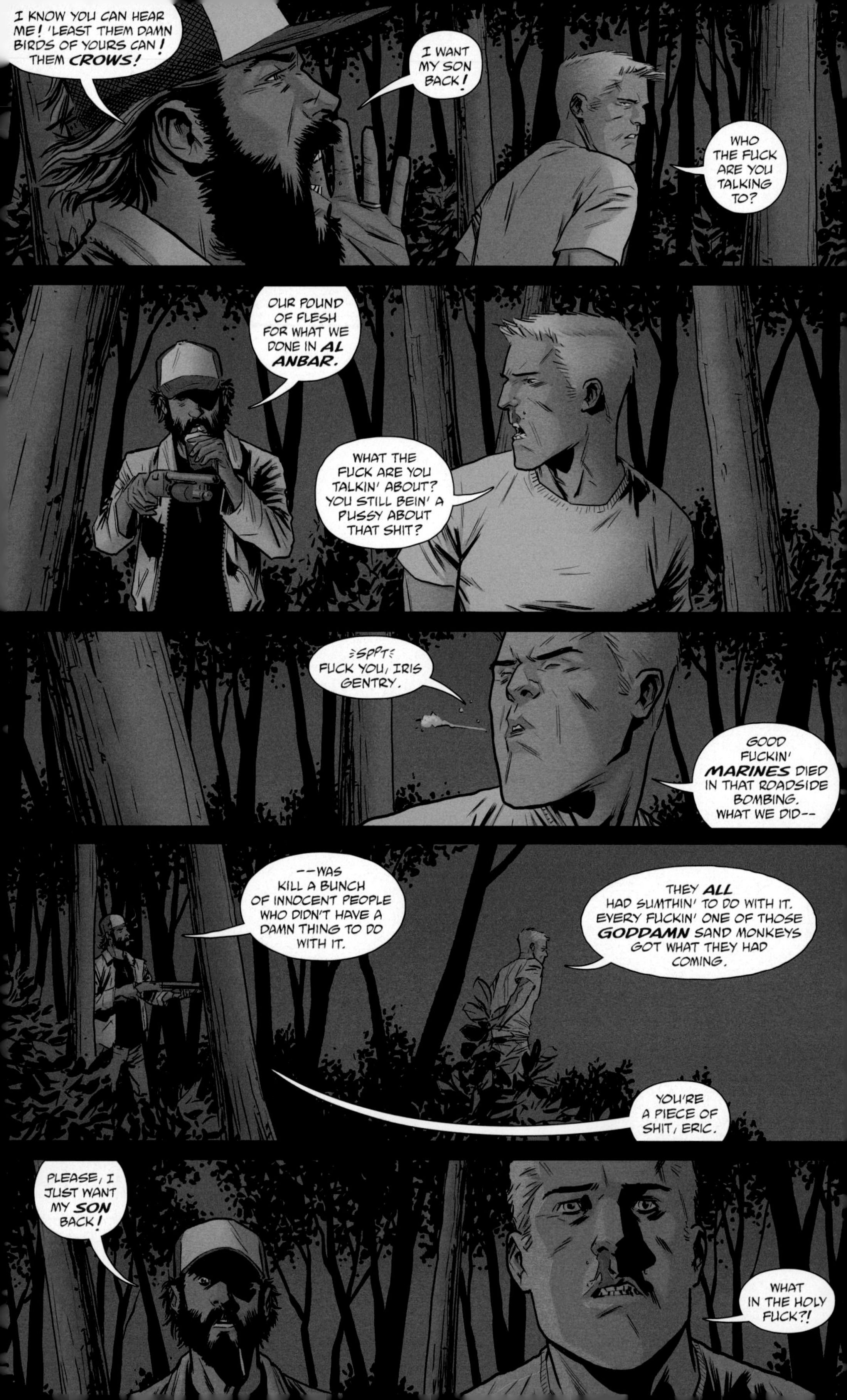
I KNOW YOU CAN HEAR ME! 'LEAST THEM DAMN BIRDS OF YOURS CAN! THEM CROWS!
I WANT MY SON BACK!
WHO THE FUCK ARE YOU TALKING TO?
OUR POUND OF FLESH FOR WHAT WE DONE IN AL ANBAR.
WHAT THE FUCK ARE YOU TALKIN' ABOUT? YOU STILL BEIN' A PUSSY ABOUT THAT SHIT?
SPPT
FUCK YOU, IRIS GENTRY.
GOOD FUCKIN' MARINES DIED IN THAT ROADSIDE BOMBING. WHAT WE DID--
--WAS KILL A BUNCH OF INNOCENT PEOPLE WHO DIDN'T HAVE A DAMN THING TO DO WITH IT.
THEY ALL HAD SUMTHIN' TO DO WITH IT. EVERY FUCKIN' ONE OF THOSE GODDAMN SAND MONKEYS GOT WHAT THEY HAD COMING.
YOU'RE A PIECE OF SHIT, ERIC.
PLEASE, I JUST WANT MY SON BACK!
WHAT IN THE HOLY FUCK?!

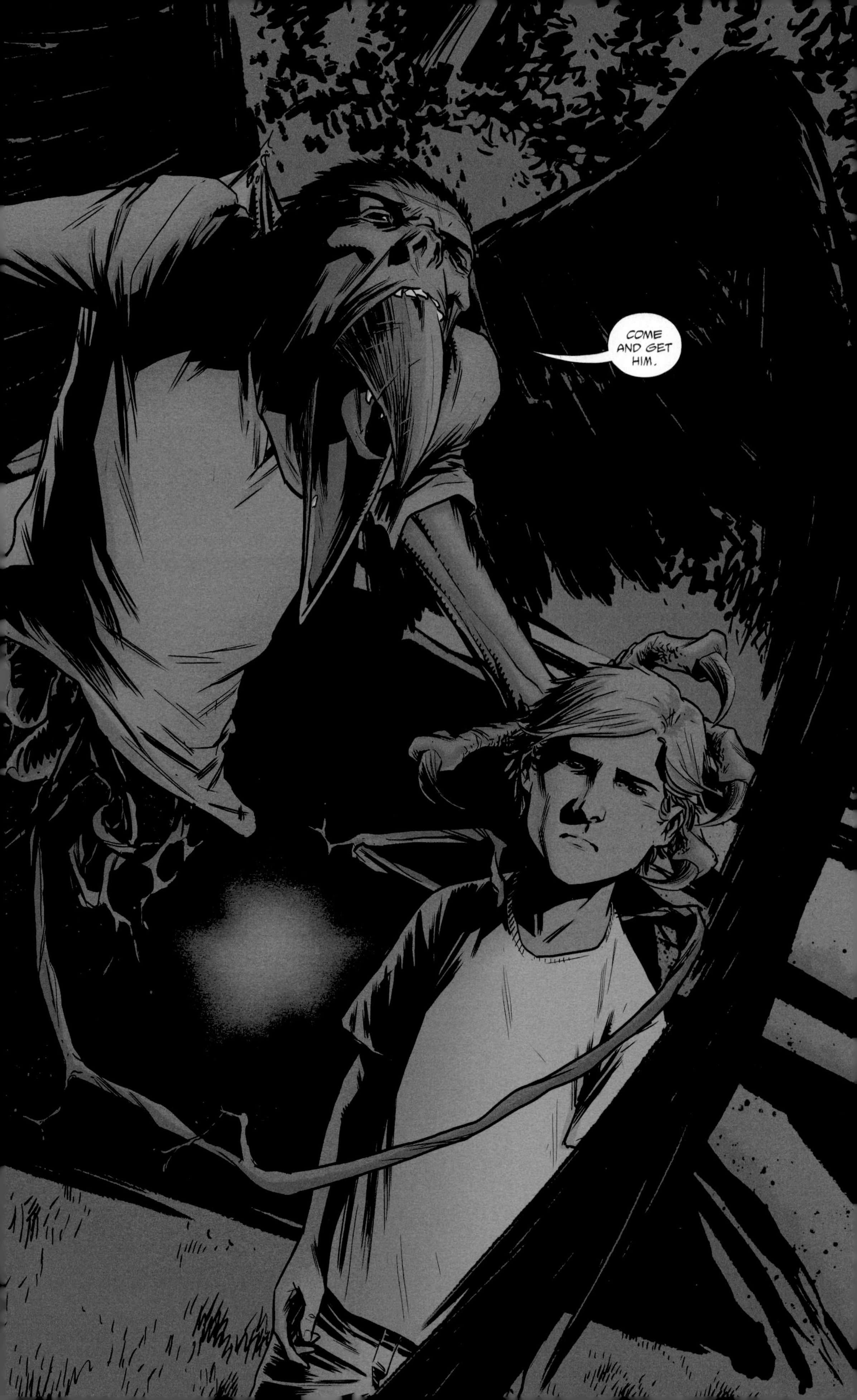
COME AND GET HIM.

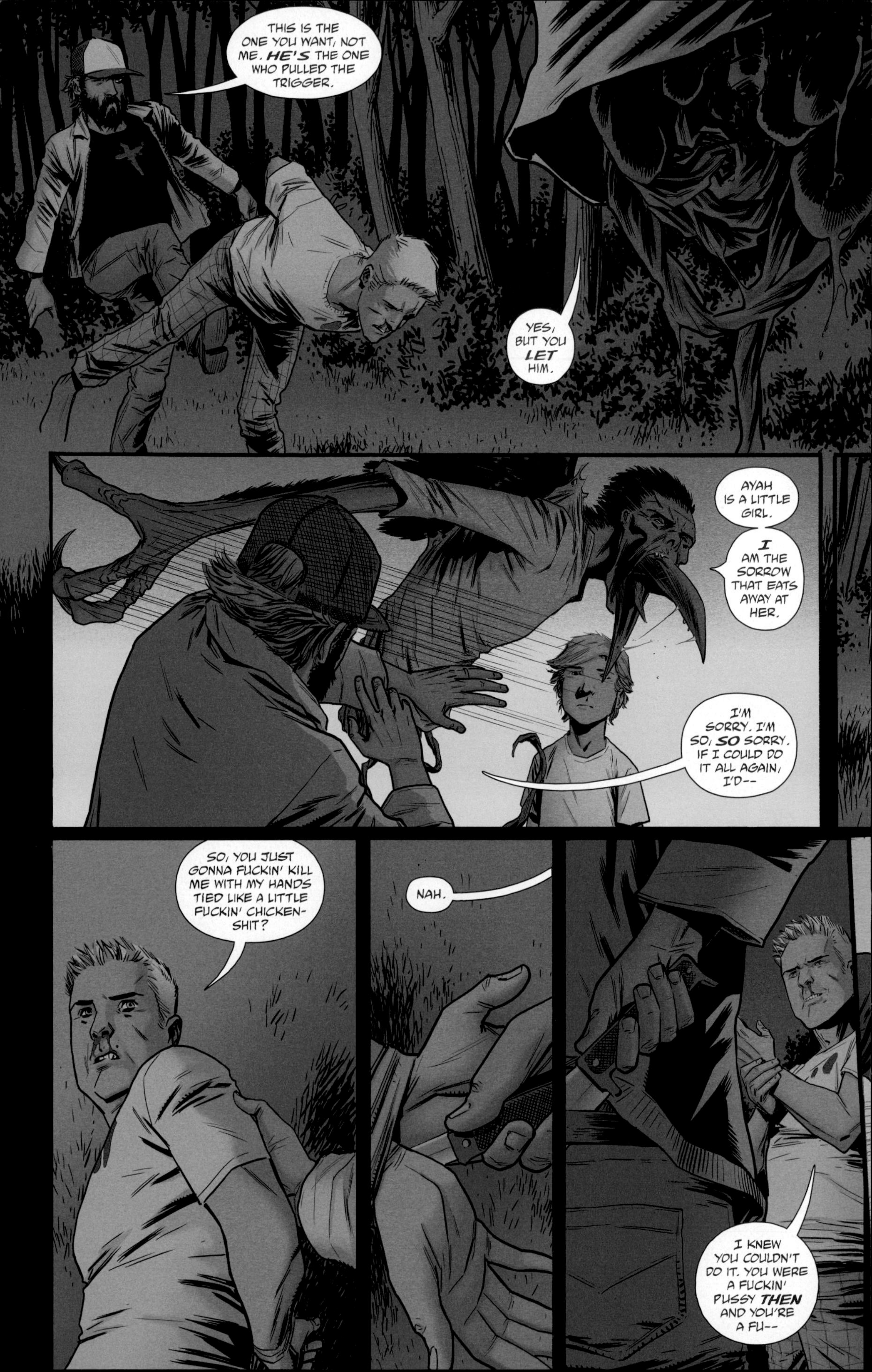
THIS IS THE ONE YOU WANT, NOT ME. HE'S THE ONE WHO PULLED THE TRIGGER.
YES, BUT YOU LET HIM.
AYAH IS A LITTLE GIRL.
I AM THE SORROW THAT EATS AWAY AT HER.
I'M SORRY. I'M SO, SO SORRY. IF I COULD DO IT ALL AGAIN, I'D--
SO, YOU JUST GONNA FUCKIN' KILL ME WITH MY HANDS TIED LIKE A LITTLE FUCKIN' CHICKEN-SHIT?
NAH.
I KNEW YOU COULDN'T DO IT. YOU WERE A FUCKIN' PUSSY THEN AND YOU'RE A FU--

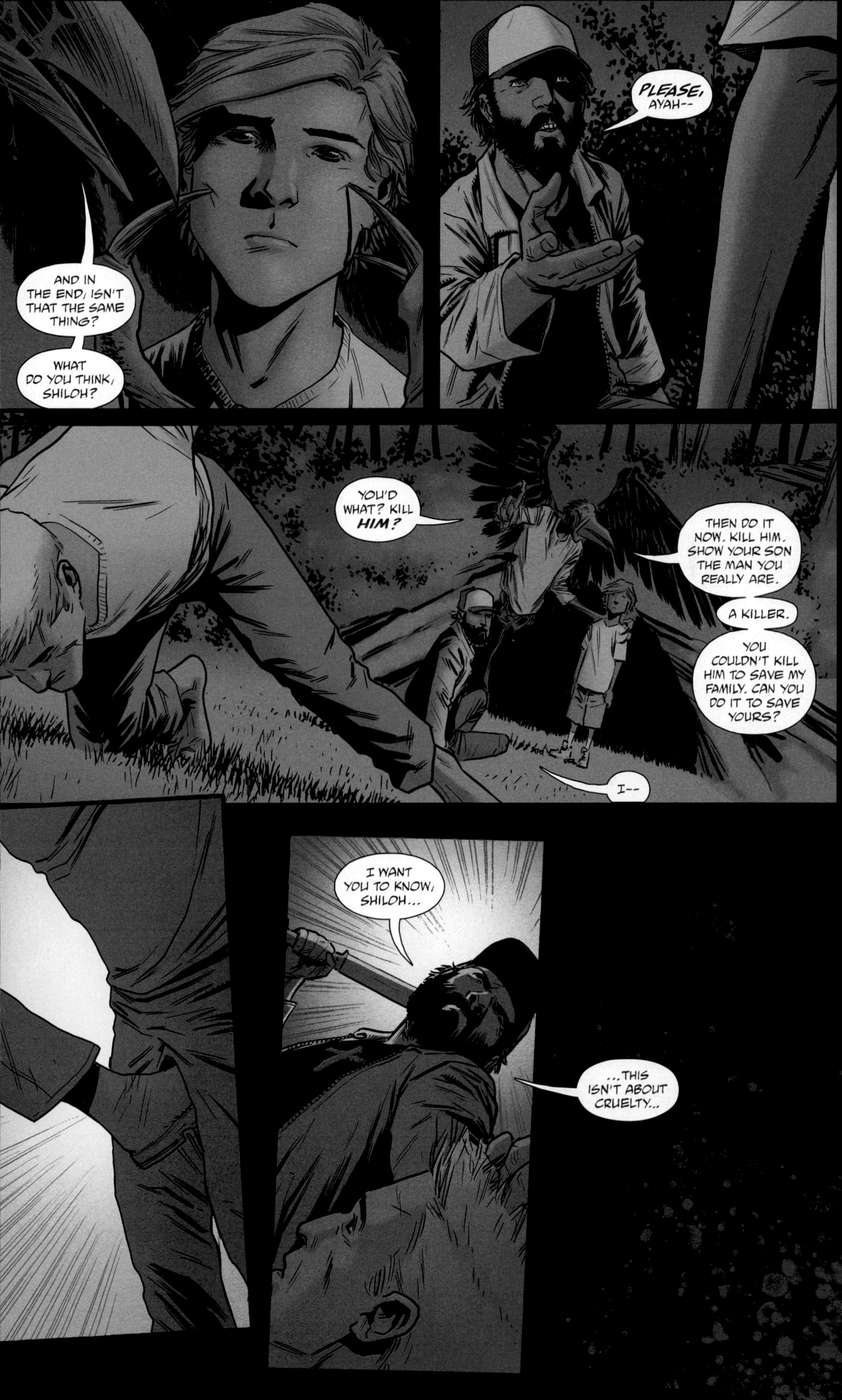
AND IN THE END, ISN'T THAT THE SAME THING?
WHAT DO YOU THINK, SHILOH?
PLEASE, AYAH--
YOU'D WHAT? KILL HIM?
THEN DO IT NOW. KILL HIM. SHOW YOUR SON THE MAN YOU REALLY ARE.
A KILLER.
YOU COULDN'T KILL HIM TO SAVE MY FAMILY. CAN YOU DO IT TO SAVE YOURS?
I--
I WANT YOU TO KNOW, SHILOH...
...THIS ISN'T ABOUT CRUELTY...

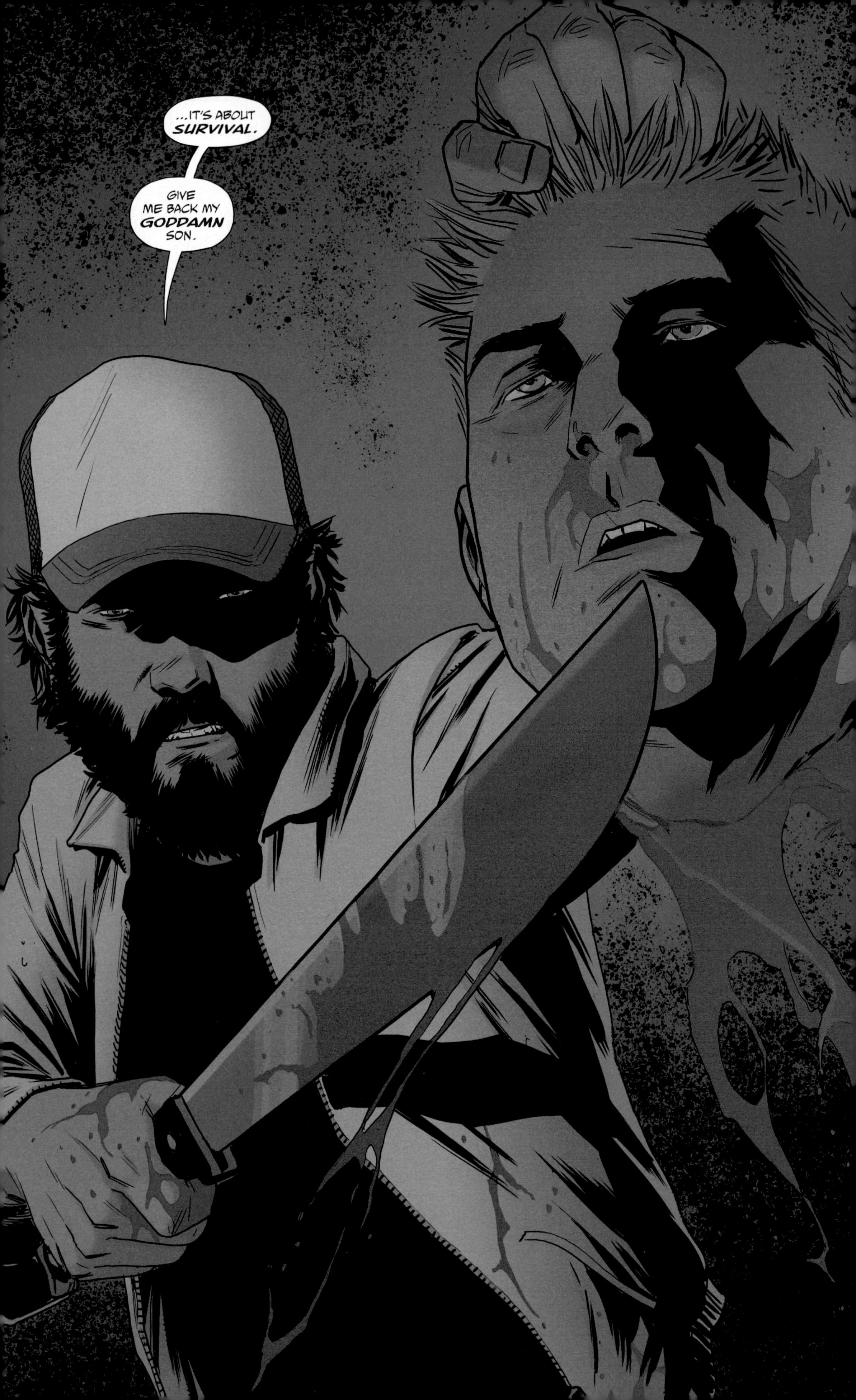
...IT'S ABOUT SURVIVAL.
GIVE ME BACK MY GODDAMN SON.

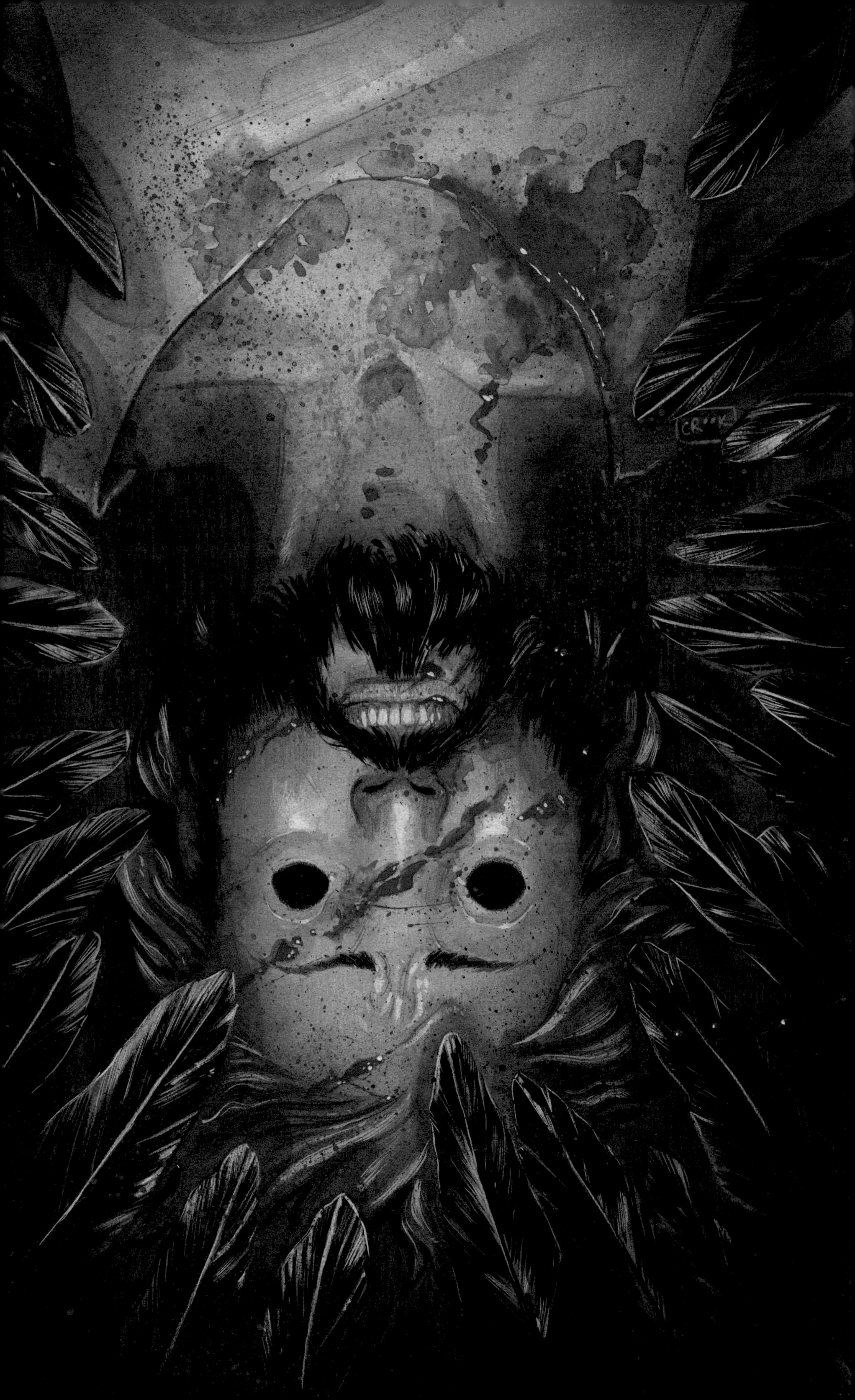

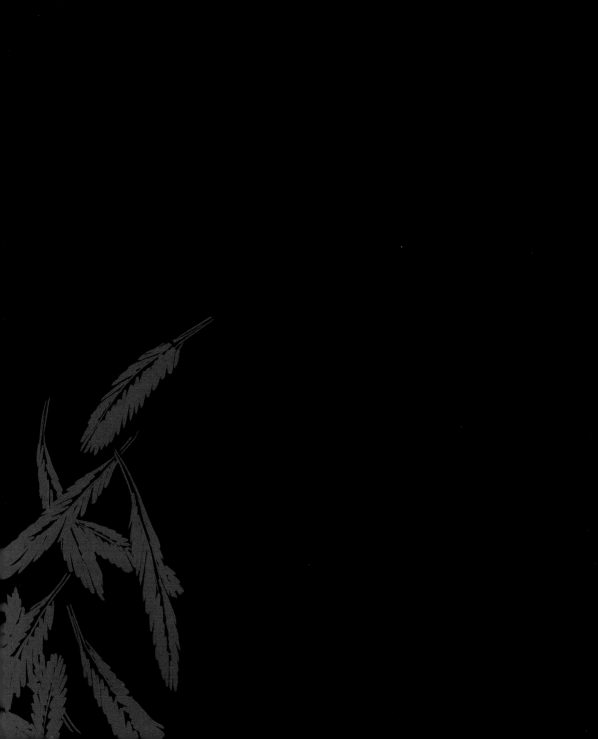

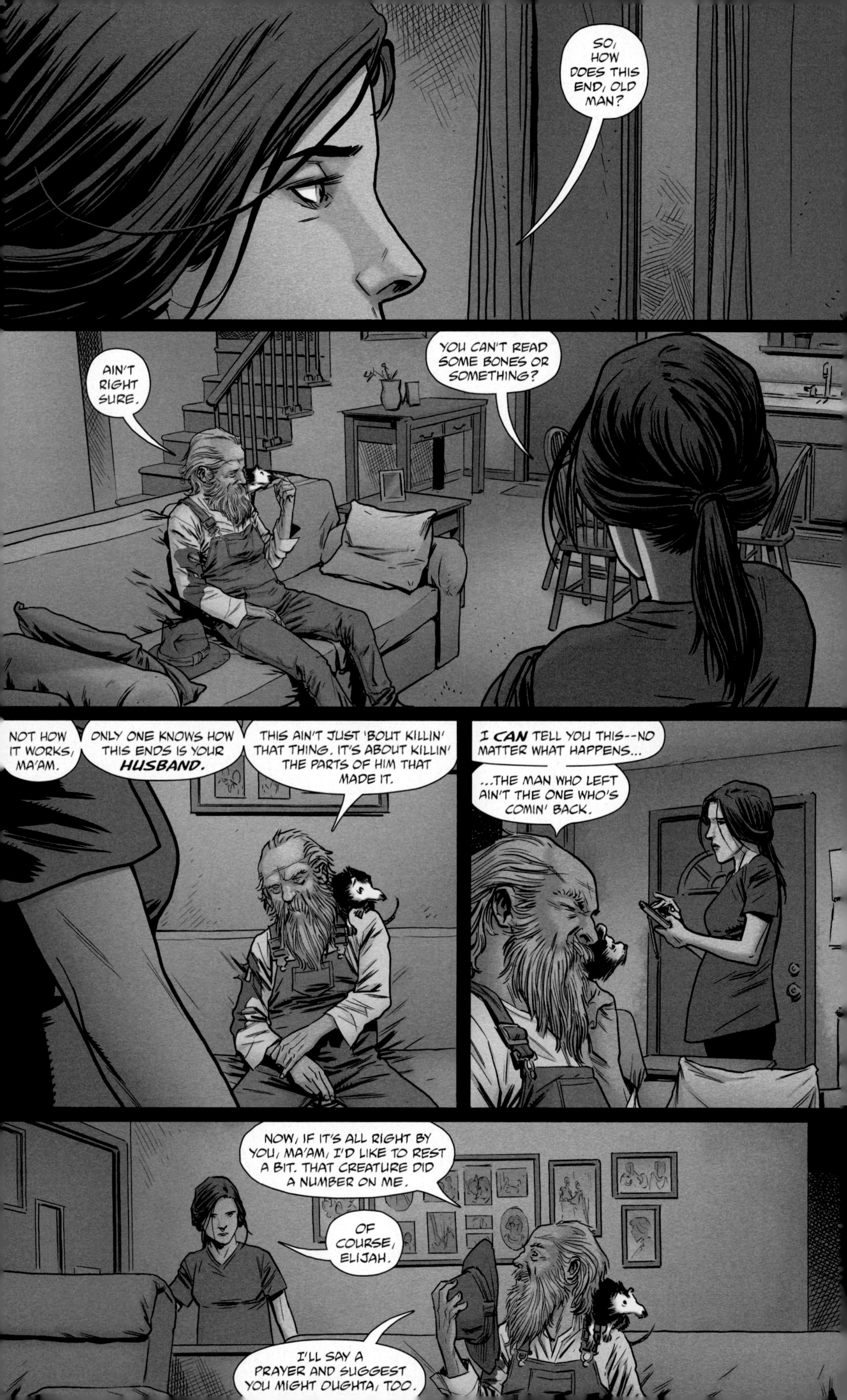
SO, HOW DOES THIS END, OLD MAN?
AIN'T RIGHT SURE.
YOU CAN'T READ SOME BONES OR SOMETHING?
NOT HOW IT WORKS, MA'AM.
ONLY ONE KNOWS HOW THIS ENDS IS YOUR HUSBAND.
THIS AIN'T JUST 'BOUT KILLIN' THAT THING. IT'S ABOUT KILLIN' THE PARTS OF HIM THAT MADE IT.
I CAN TELL YOU THIS--NO MATTER WHAT HAPPENS...
...THE MAN WHO LEFT AIN'T THE ONE WHO'S COMIN' BACK.
NOW, IF IT'S ALL RIGHT BY YOU, MA'AM, I'D LIKE TO REST A BIT. THAT CREATURE DID A NUMBER ON ME.
OF COURSE, ELIJAH.
I'LL SAY A PRAYER AND SUGGEST YOU MIGHT OUGHTA, TOO.

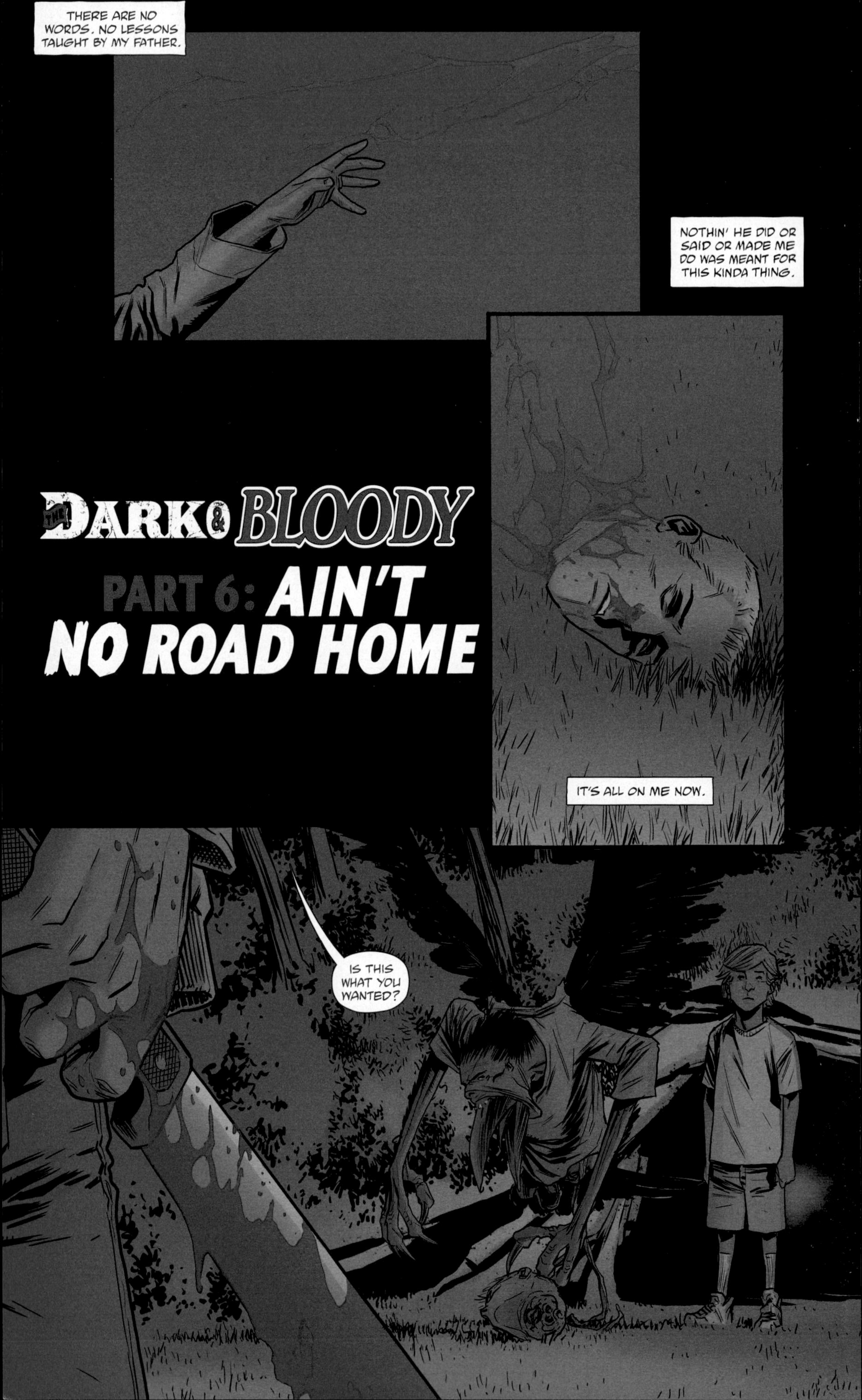

THERE ARE NO WORDS. NO LESSONS TAUGHT BY MY FATHER.
NOTHIN' HE DID OR SAID OR MADE ME DO WAS MEANT FOR THIS KINDA THING.
THE DARK & BLOODY
PART 6: AIN'T NO ROAD HOME
IT'S ALL ON ME NOW.
IS THIS WHAT YOU WANTED?

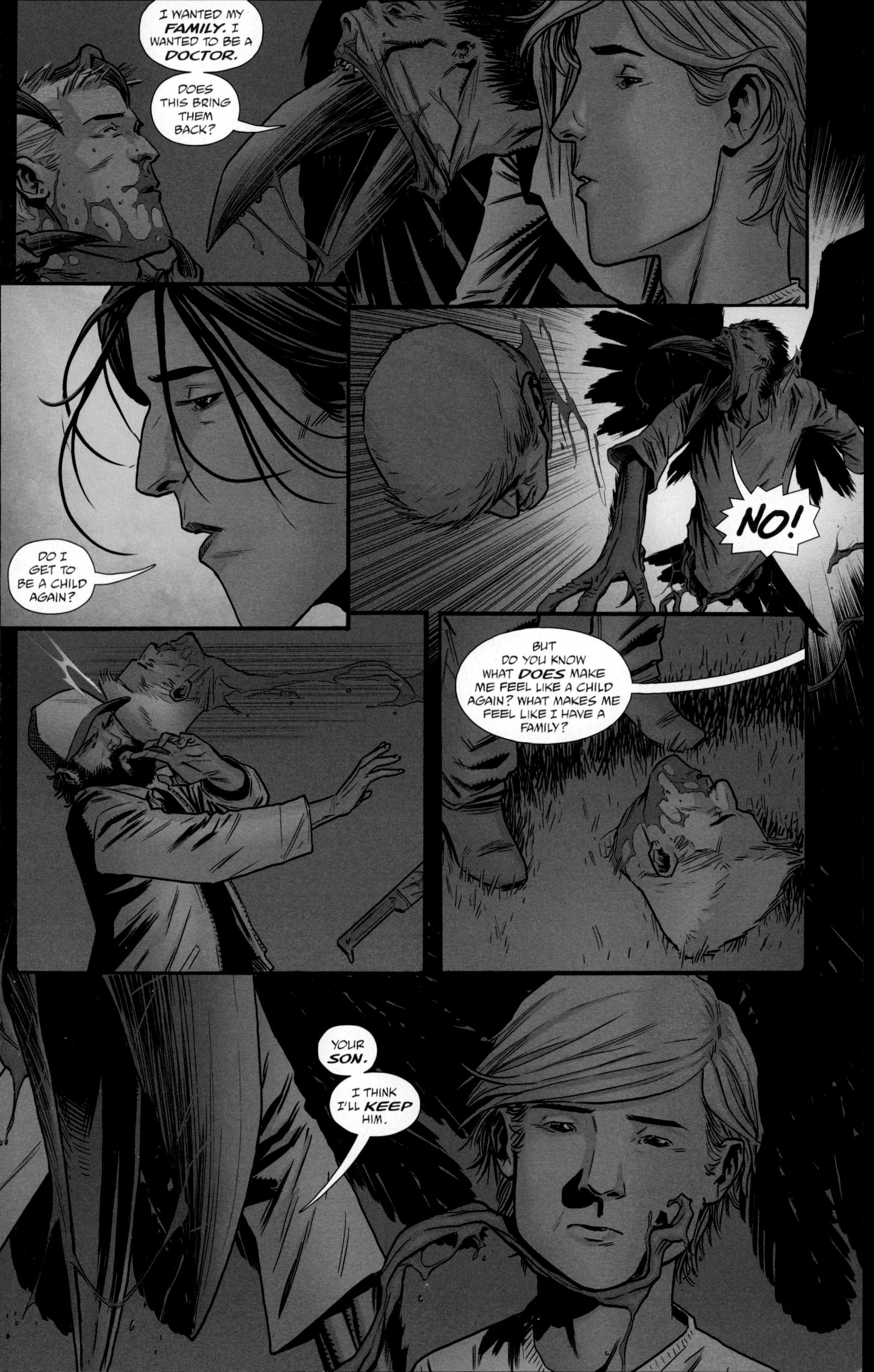
I WANTED MY **FAMILY.** I WANTED TO BE A **DOCTOR.**
DOES THIS BRING THEM BACK?
DO I GET TO BE A CHILD AGAIN?
NO!
BUT DO YOU KNOW WHAT **DOES** MAKE ME FEEL LIKE A CHILD AGAIN? WHAT MAKES ME FEEL LIKE I HAVE A FAMILY?
YOUR **SON.**
I THINK I'LL **KEEP** HIM.

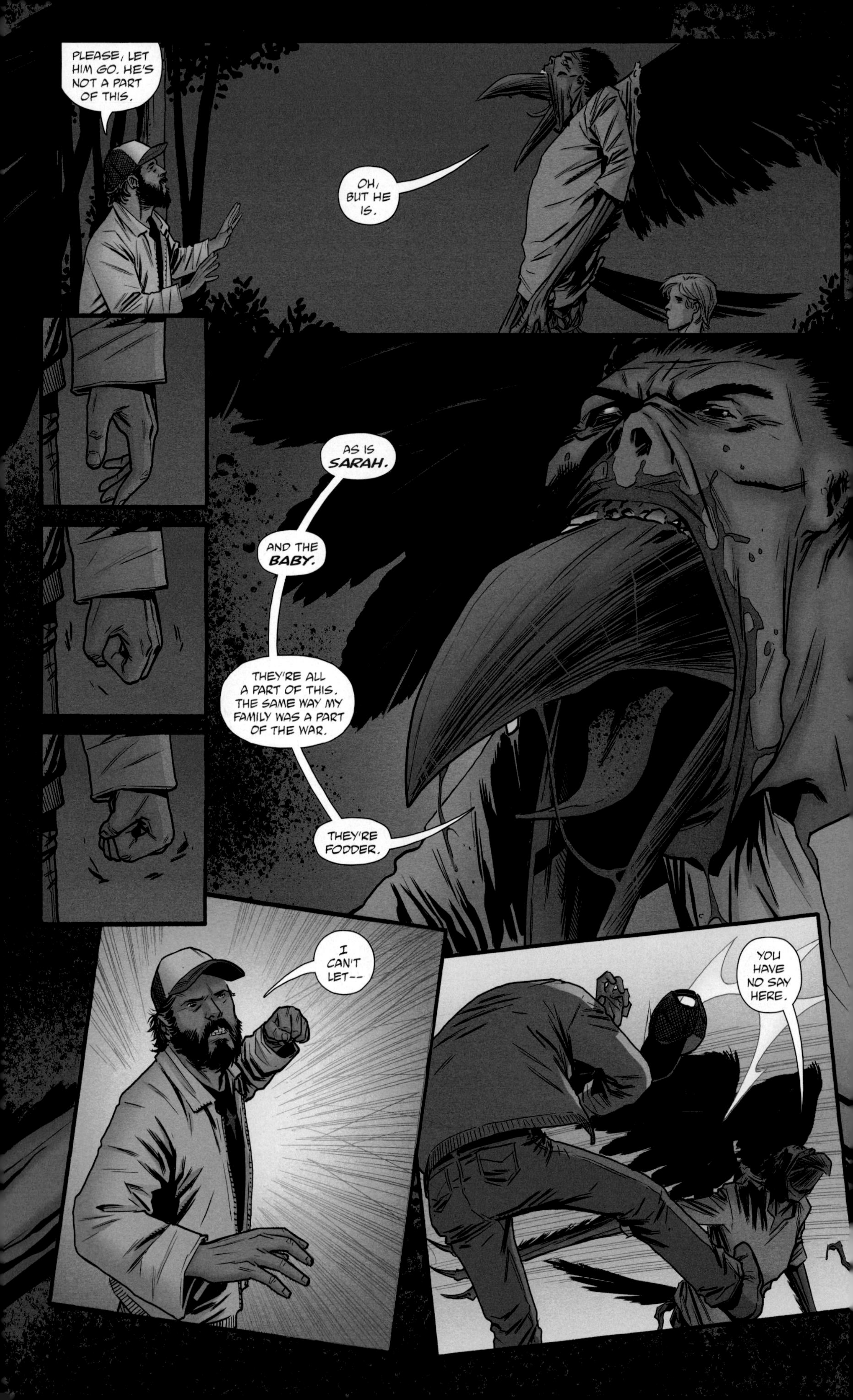
PLEASE, LET HIM GO. HE'S NOT A PART OF THIS.
OH, BUT HE IS.
AS IS SARAH.
AND THE BABY.
THEY'RE ALL A PART OF THIS. THE SAME WAY MY FAMILY WAS A PART OF THE WAR.
THEY'RE FODDER.
I CAN'T LET--
YOU HAVE NO SAY HERE.

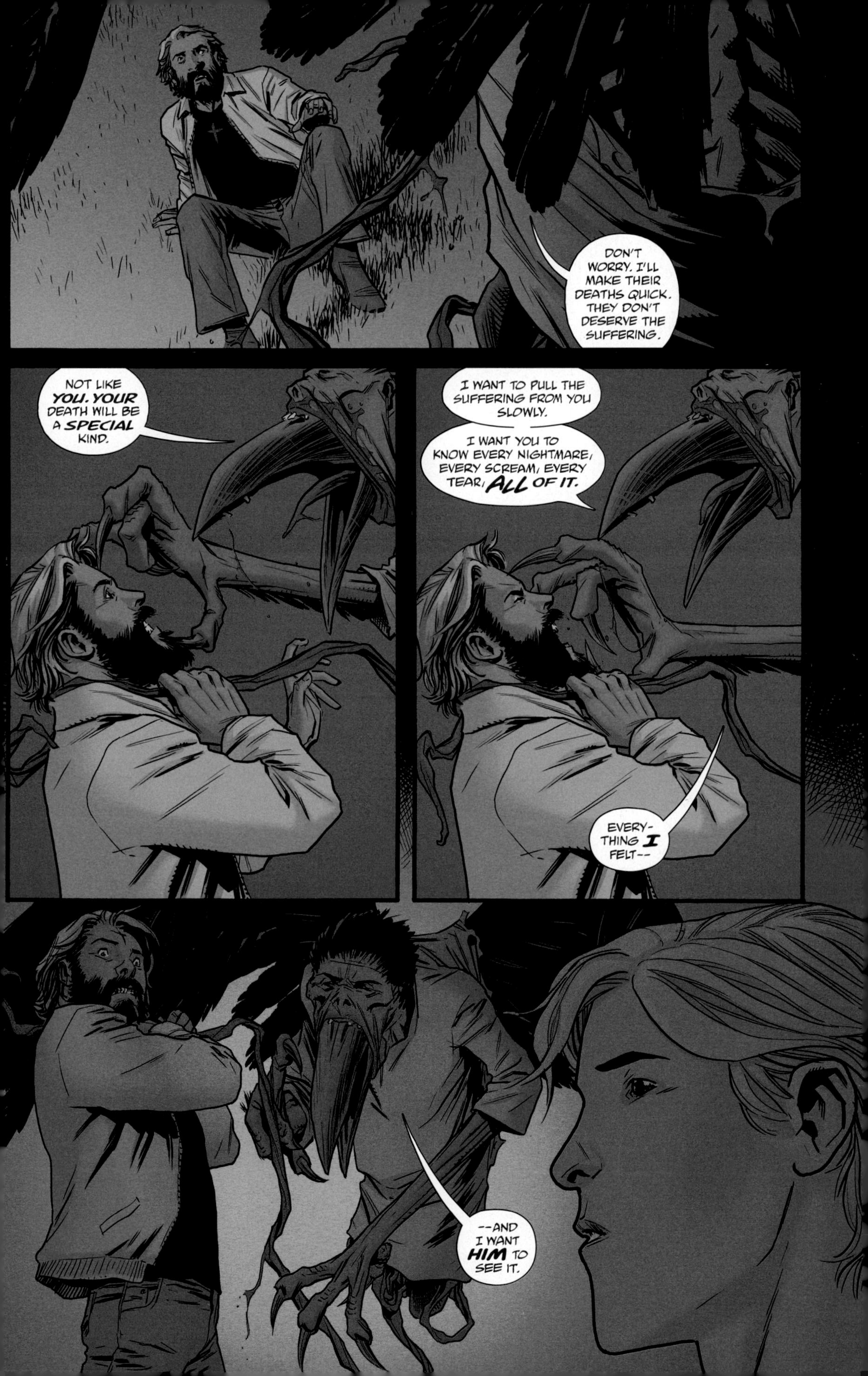
DON'T WORRY. I'LL MAKE THEIR DEATHS QUICK. THEY DON'T DESERVE THE SUFFERING.
NOT LIKE **YOU. YOUR** DEATH WILL BE A **SPECIAL** KIND.
I WANT TO PULL THE SUFFERING FROM YOU SLOWLY.
I WANT YOU TO KNOW EVERY NIGHTMARE, EVERY SCREAM, EVERY TEAR, **ALL** OF IT.
EVERY-THING **I** FELT--
--AND I WANT **HIM** TO SEE IT.

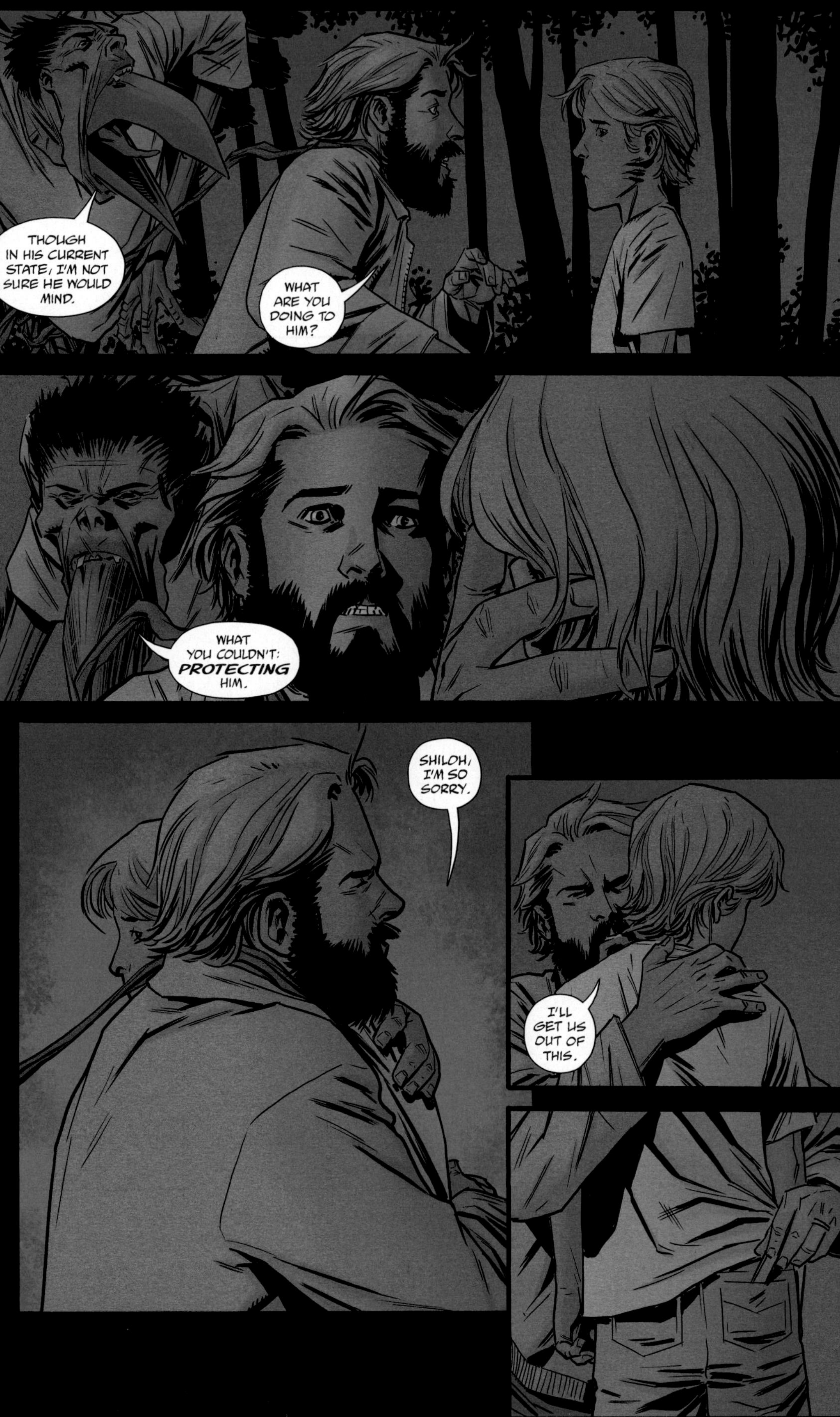
THOUGH IN HIS CURRENT STATE, I'M NOT SURE HE WOULD MIND.
WHAT ARE YOU DOING TO HIM?
WHAT YOU COULDN'T: **PROTECTING** HIM.
SHILOH, I'M SO SORRY.
I'LL GET US OUT OF THIS.

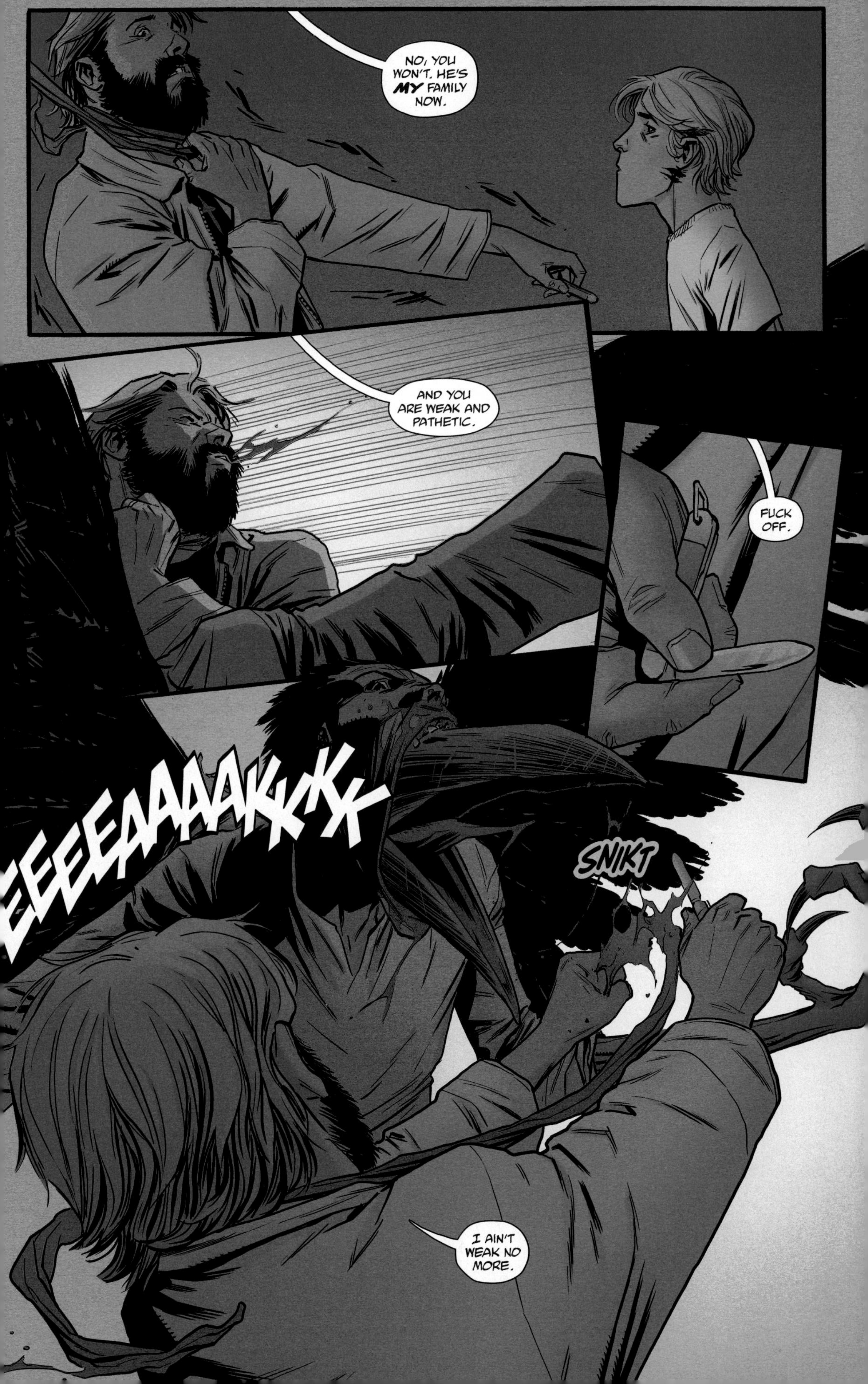
NO, YOU WON'T. HE'S MY FAMILY NOW.
AND YOU ARE WEAK AND PATHETIC.
FUCK OFF.
EEEEAAAAKKKK
SNIKT
I AIN'T WEAK NO MORE.

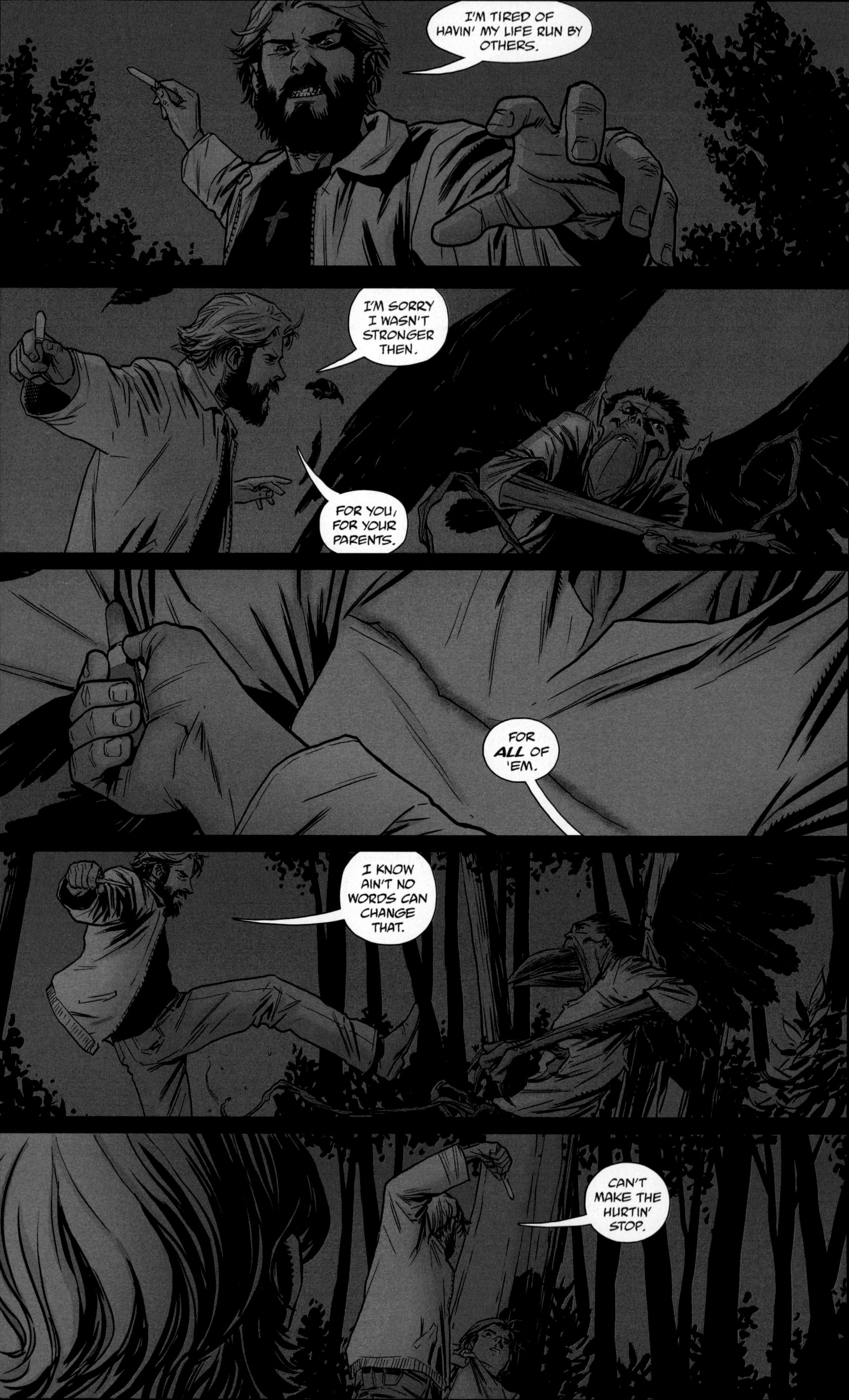
I'M TIRED OF HAVIN' MY LIFE RUN BY OTHERS.
I'M SORRY I WASN'T STRONGER THEN.
FOR YOU, FOR YOUR PARENTS.
FOR ALL OF 'EM.
I KNOW AIN'T NO WORDS CAN CHANGE THAT.
CAN'T MAKE THE HURTIN' STOP.

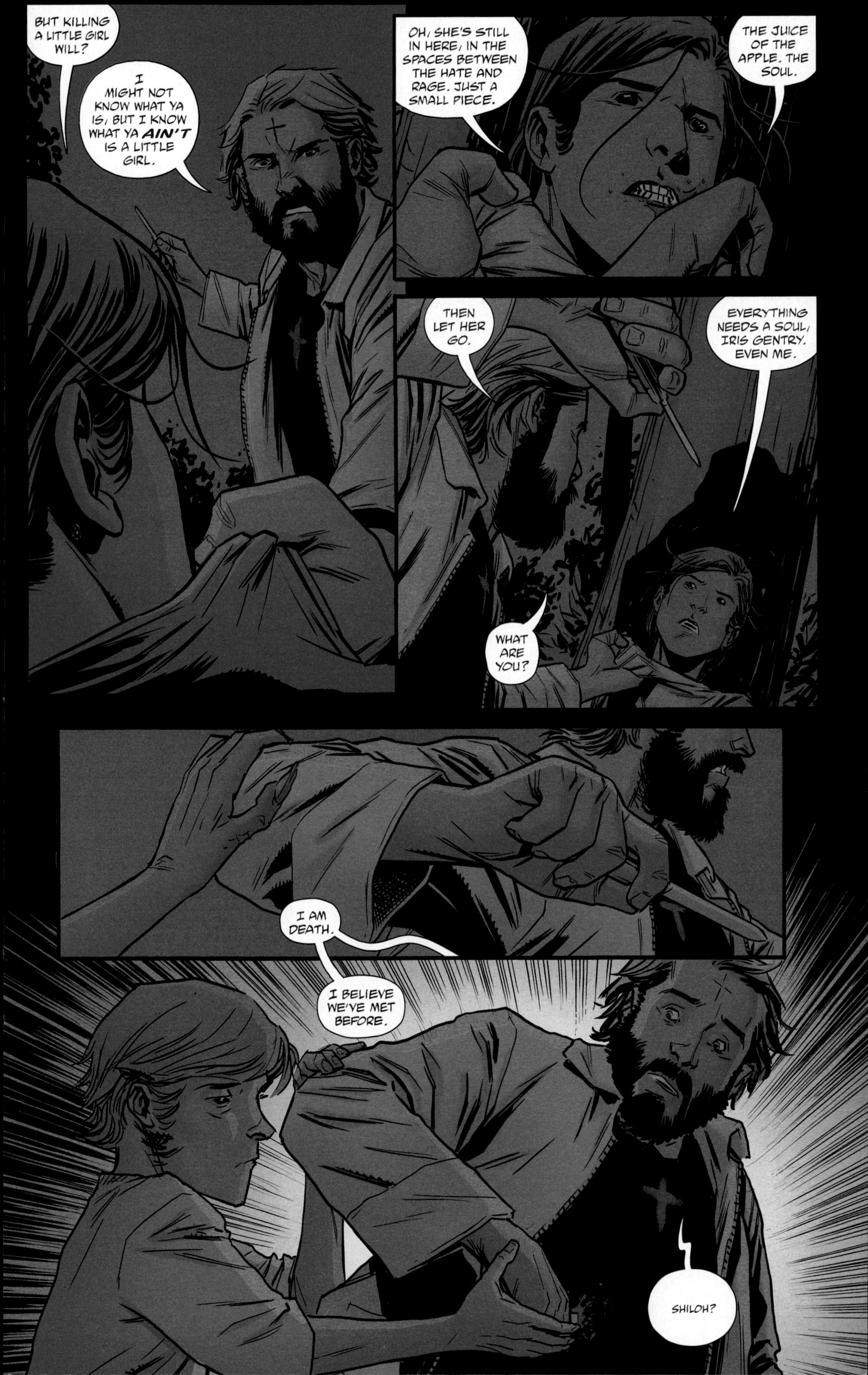
BUT KILLING A LITTLE GIRL WILL?
I MIGHT NOT KNOW WHAT YA IS, BUT I KNOW WHAT YA AIN'T IS A LITTLE GIRL.
OH, SHE'S STILL IN HERE, IN THE SPACES BETWEEN THE HATE AND RAGE. JUST A SMALL PIECE.
THE JUICE OF THE APPLE. THE SOUL.
THEN LET HER GO.
EVERYTHING NEEDS A SOUL, IRIS GENTRY. EVEN ME.
WHAT ARE YOU?
I AM DEATH.
I BELIEVE WE'VE MET BEFORE.
SHILOH?

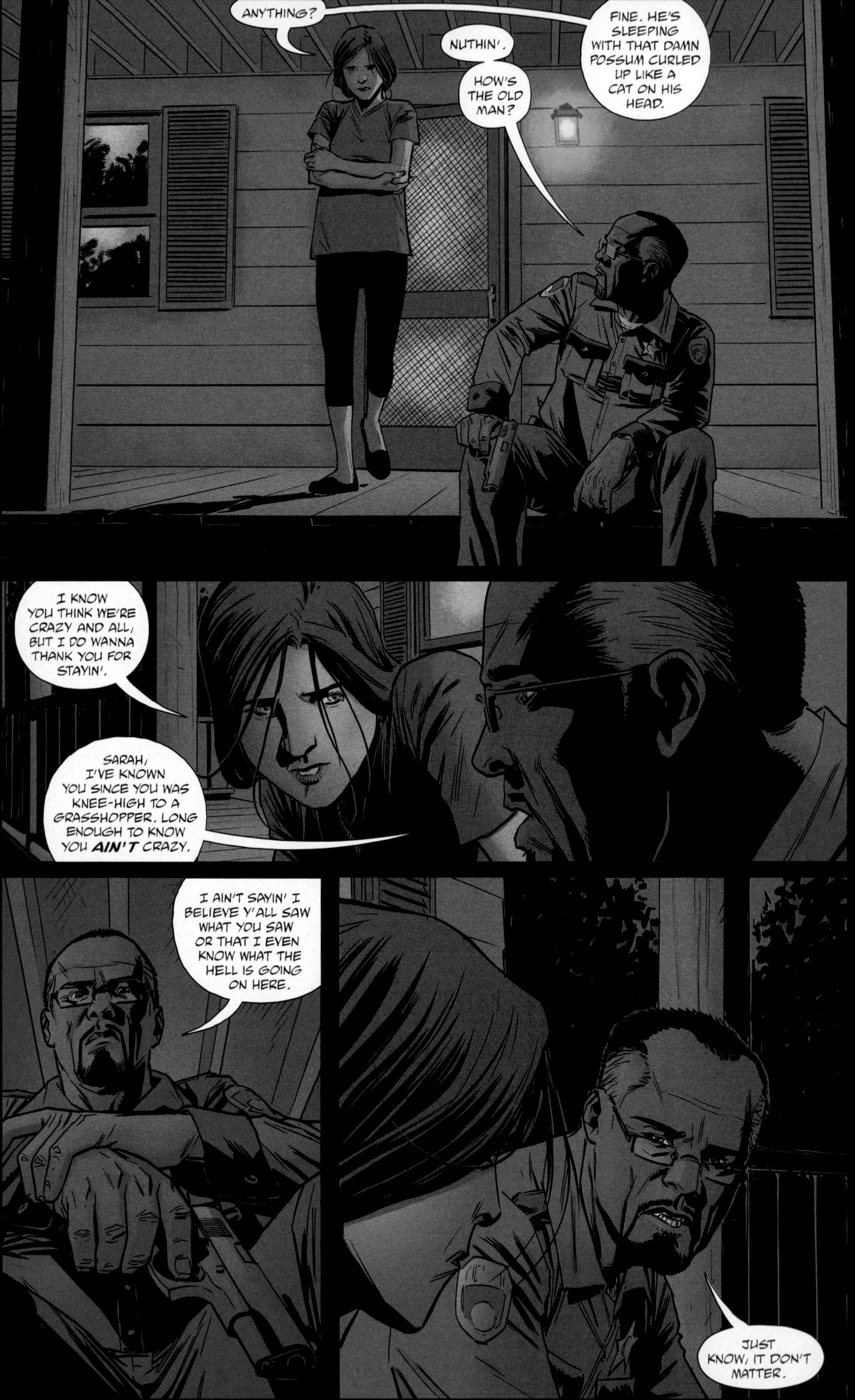
ANYTHING?
NUTHIN'.
HOW'S THE OLD MAN?
FINE. HE'S SLEEPING WITH THAT DAMN POSSUM CURLED UP LIKE A CAT ON HIS HEAD.
I KNOW YOU THINK WE'RE CRAZY AND ALL, BUT I DO WANNA THANK YOU FOR STAYIN'.
SARAH, I'VE KNOWN YOU SINCE YOU WAS KNEE-HIGH TO A GRASSHOPPER. LONG ENOUGH TO KNOW YOU **AIN'T** CRAZY.
I AIN'T SAYIN' I BELIEVE Y'ALL SAW WHAT YOU SAW OR THAT I EVEN KNOW WHAT THE HELL IS GOING ON HERE.
JUST KNOW, IT DON'T MATTER.

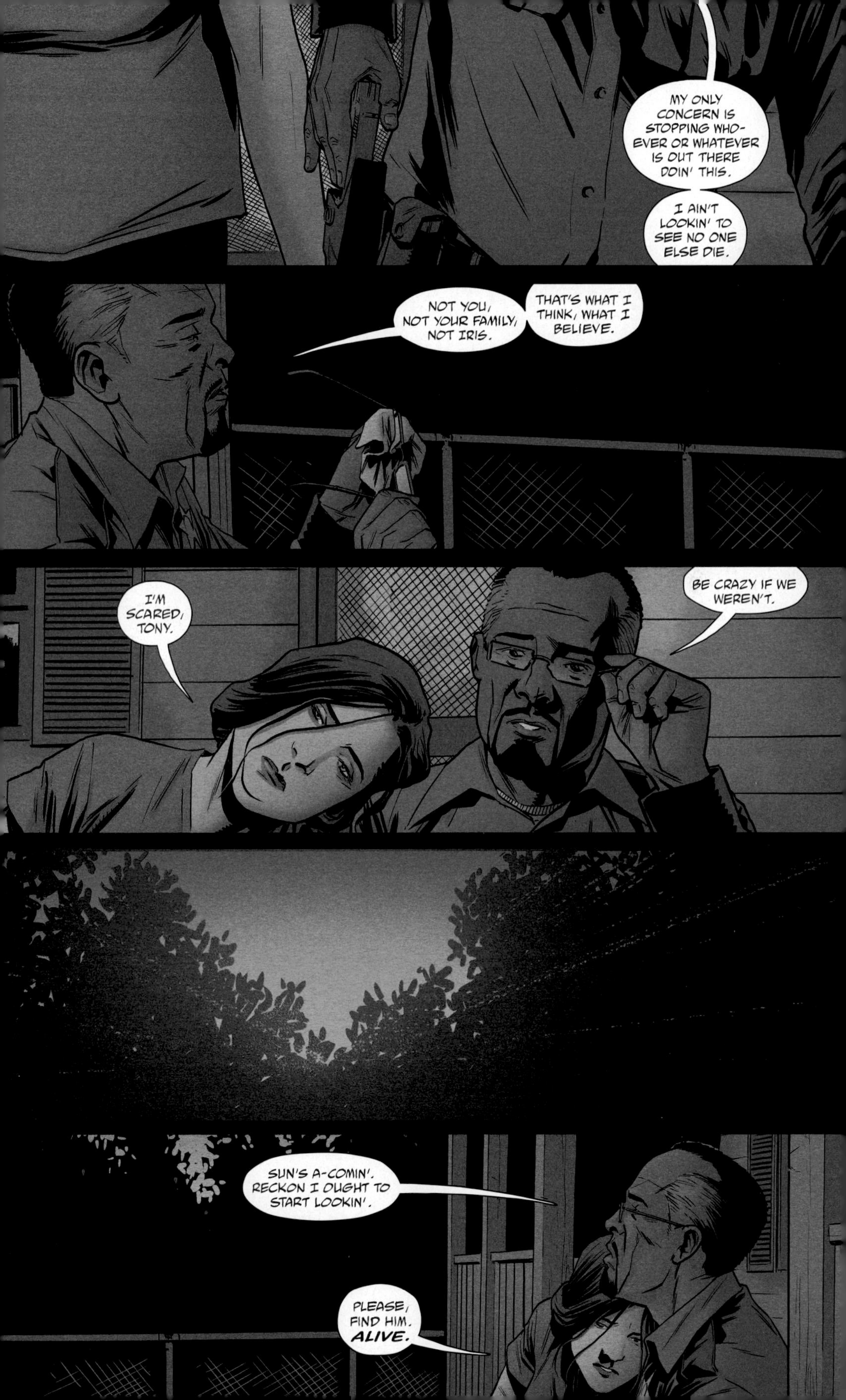
MY ONLY CONCERN IS STOPPING WHOEVER OR WHATEVER IS OUT THERE DOIN' THIS.
I AIN'T LOOKIN' TO SEE NO ONE ELSE DIE.
NOT YOU, NOT YOUR FAMILY, NOT IRIS.
THAT'S WHAT I THINK, WHAT I BELIEVE.
I'M SCARED, TONY.
BE CRAZY IF WE WEREN'T.
SUN'S A-COMIN'. RECKON I OUGHT TO START LOOKIN'.
PLEASE, FIND HIM. ALIVE.

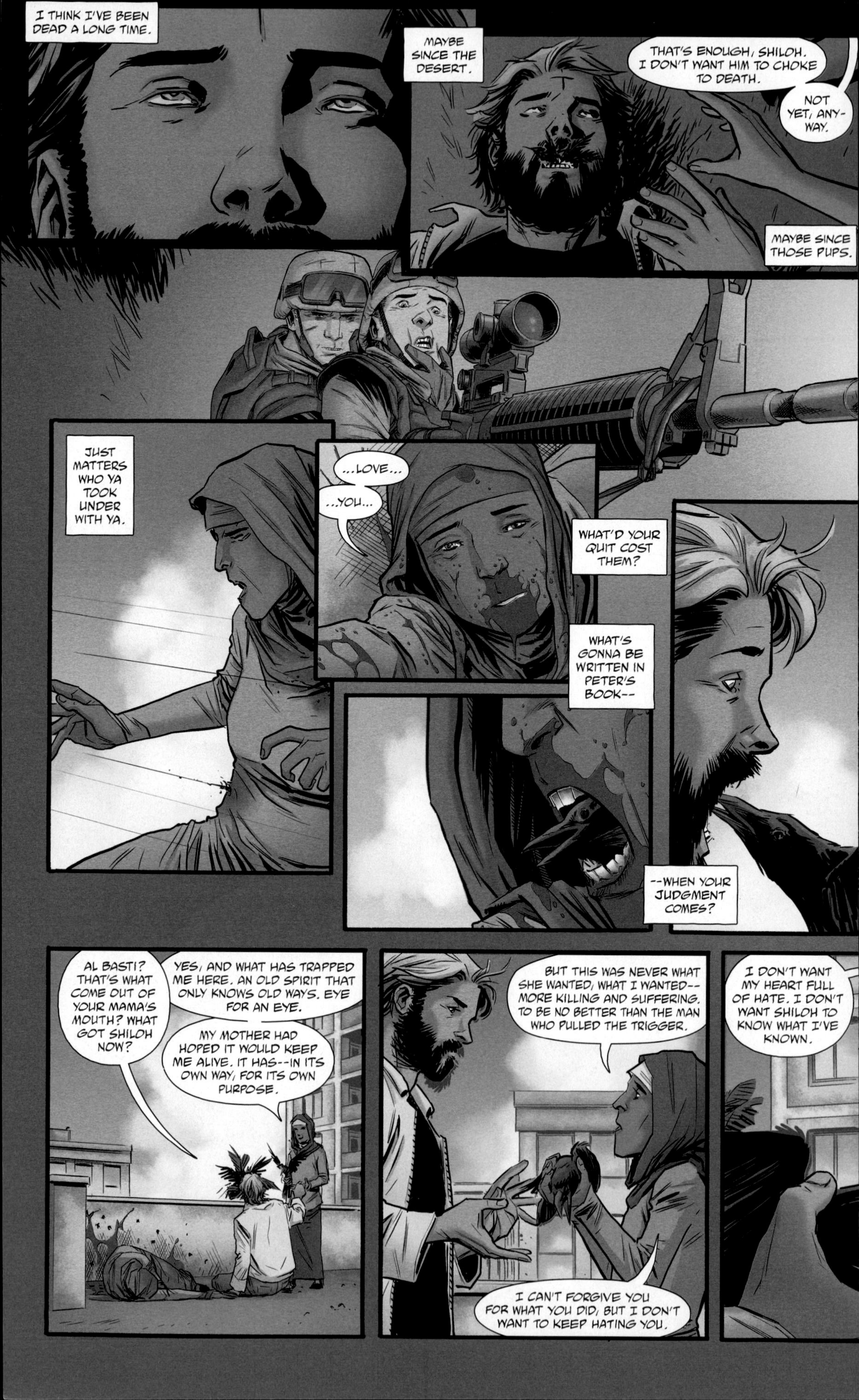

I THINK I'VE BEEN DEAD A LONG TIME.
MAYBE SINCE THE DESERT.
THAT'S ENOUGH, SHILOH. I DON'T WANT HIM TO CHOKE TO DEATH.
NOT YET, ANY-WAY.
MAYBE SINCE THOSE PUPS.
JUST MATTERS WHO YA TOOK UNDER WITH YA.
...LOVE...
...YOU...
WHAT'D YOUR QUIT COST THEM?
WHAT'S GONNA BE WRITTEN IN PETER'S BOOK--
--WHEN YOUR JUDGMENT COMES?
AL BASTI? THAT'S WHAT COME OUT OF YOUR MAMA'S MOUTH? WHAT GOT SHILOH NOW?
YES, AND WHAT HAS TRAPPED ME HERE. AN OLD SPIRIT THAT ONLY KNOWS OLD WAYS. EYE FOR AN EYE.
MY MOTHER HAD HOPED IT WOULD KEEP ME ALIVE. IT HAS--IN ITS OWN WAY, FOR ITS OWN PURPOSE.
BUT THIS WAS NEVER WHAT SHE WANTED, WHAT I WANTED-- MORE KILLING AND SUFFERING. TO BE NO BETTER THAN THE MAN WHO PULLED THE TRIGGER.
I CAN'T FORGIVE YOU FOR WHAT YOU DID, BUT I DON'T WANT TO KEEP HATING YOU.
I DON'T WANT MY HEART FULL OF HATE. I DON'T WANT SHILOH TO KNOW WHAT I'VE KNOWN.

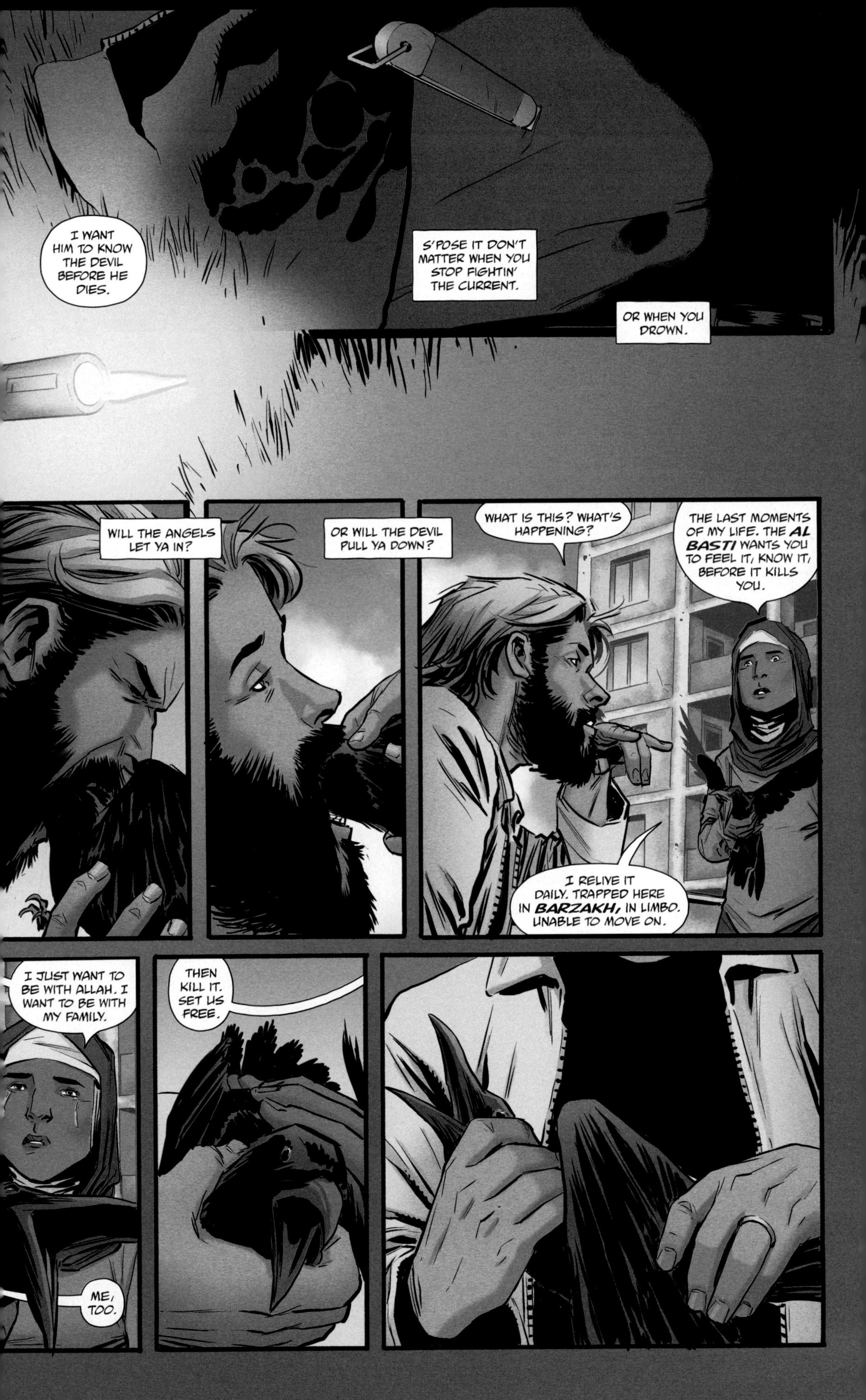
I WANT HIM TO KNOW THE DEVIL BEFORE HE DIES.
S'POSE IT DON'T MATTER WHEN YOU STOP FIGHTIN' THE CURRENT.
OR WHEN YOU DROWN.
WILL THE ANGELS LET YA IN?
OR WILL THE DEVIL PULL YA DOWN?
WHAT IS THIS? WHAT'S HAPPENING?
THE LAST MOMENTS OF MY LIFE. THE AL BASTI WANTS YOU TO FEEL IT, KNOW IT, BEFORE IT KILLS YOU.
I RELIVE IT DAILY. TRAPPED HERE IN BARZAKH, IN LIMBO. UNABLE TO MOVE ON.
I JUST WANT TO BE WITH ALLAH. I WANT TO BE WITH MY FAMILY.
THEN KILL IT. SET US FREE.
ME, TOO.

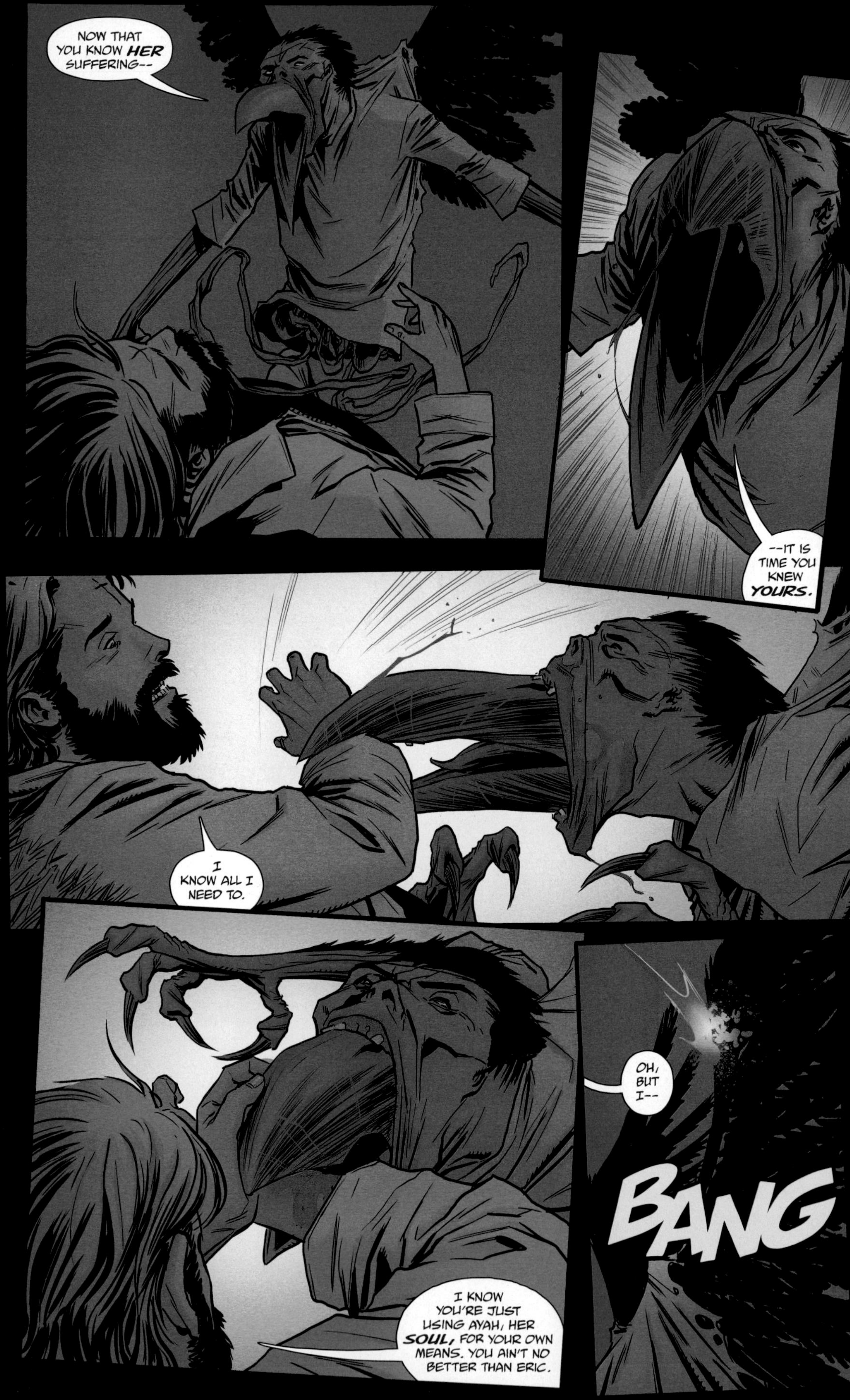
NOW THAT YOU KNOW **HER** SUFFERING--
--IT IS TIME YOU KNEW **YOURS.**
I KNOW ALL I NEED TO.
I KNOW YOU'RE JUST USING AYAH, HER **SOUL,** FOR YOUR OWN MEANS. YOU AIN'T NO BETTER THAN ERIC.
OH, BUT I--
BANG

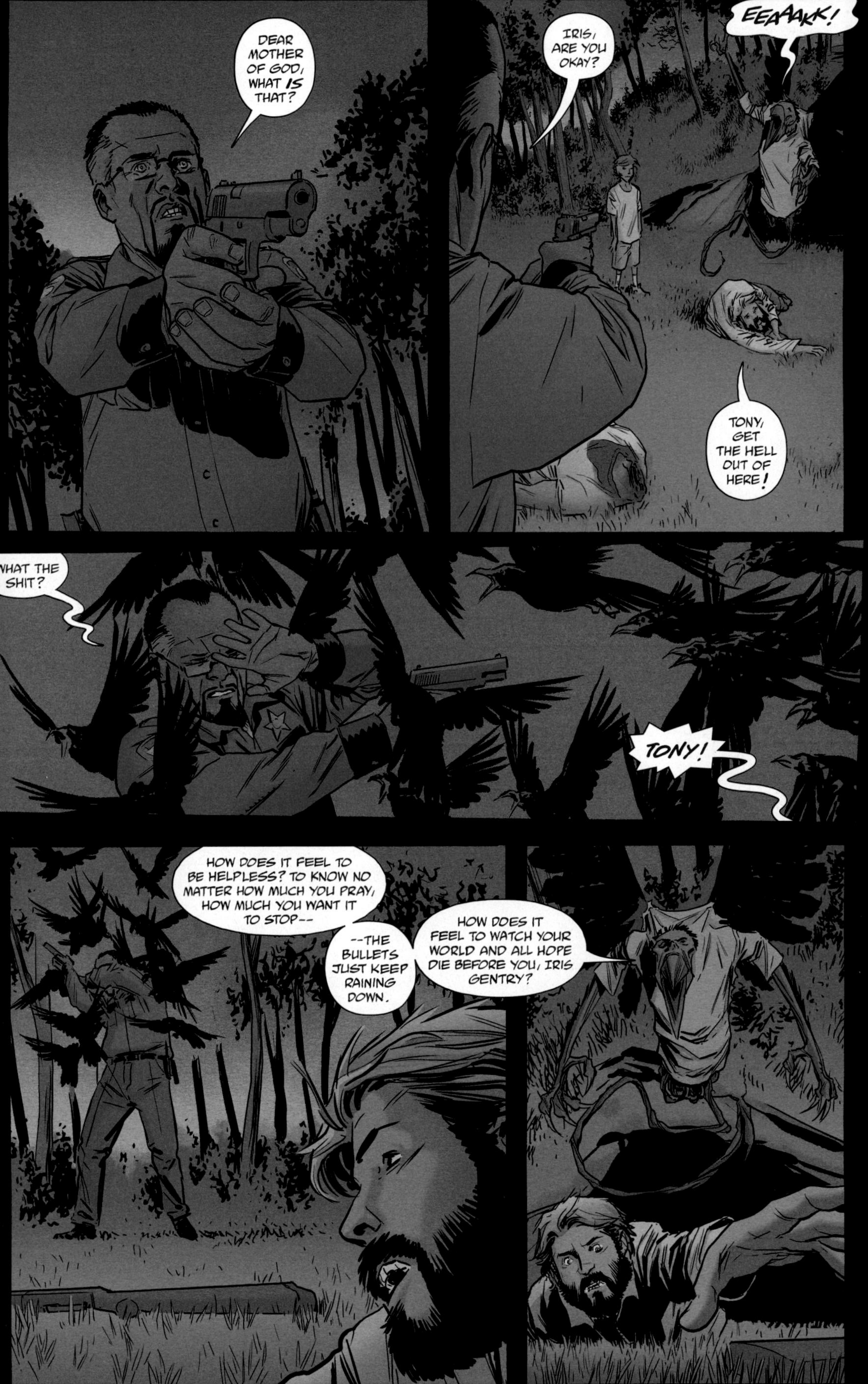
DEAR MOTHER OF GOD, WHAT **IS** THAT?
IRIS, ARE YOU OKAY?
EEAAAKK!
TONY, GET THE HELL OUT OF HERE!
WHAT THE SHIT?
TONY!
HOW DOES IT FEEL TO BE HELPLESS? TO KNOW NO MATTER HOW MUCH YOU PRAY, HOW MUCH YOU WANT IT TO STOP--
--THE BULLETS JUST KEEP RAINING DOWN.
HOW DOES IT FEEL TO WATCH YOUR WORLD AND ALL HOPE DIE BEFORE YOU, IRIS GENTRY?

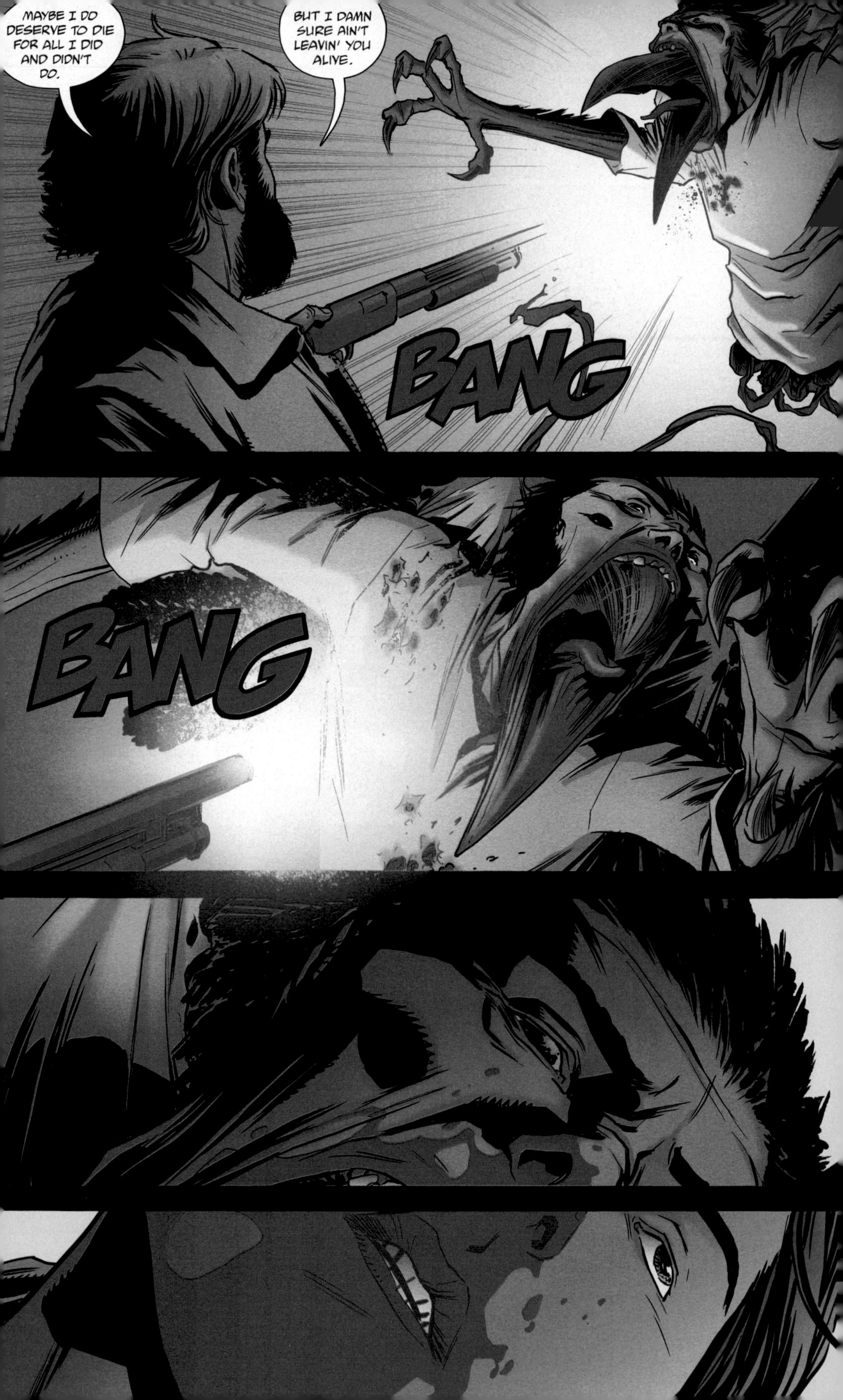

MAYBE I DO DESERVE TO DIE FOR ALL I DID AND DIDN'T DO.
BUT I DAMN SURE AIN'T LEAVIN' YOU ALIVE.
BANG
BANG

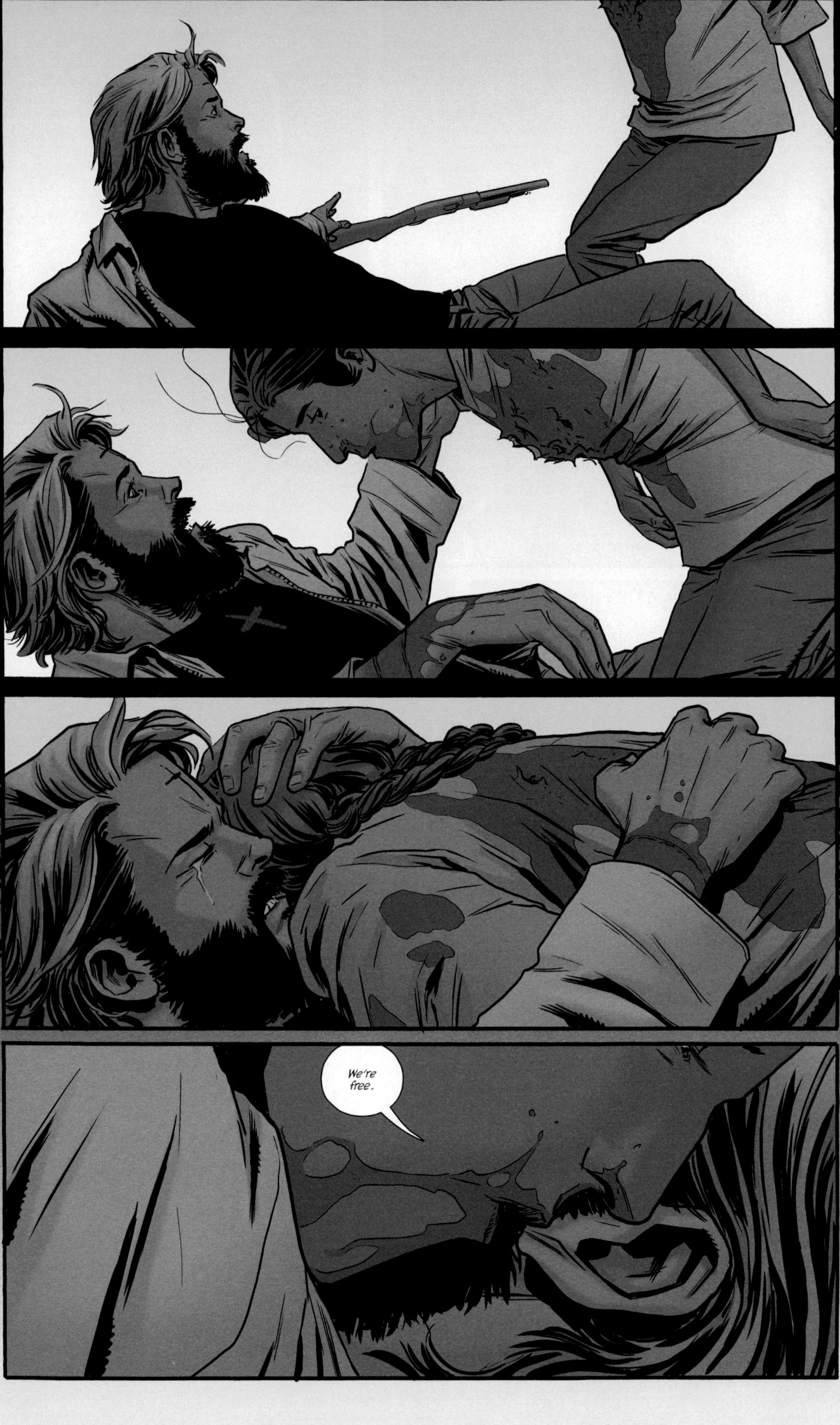
We're free.

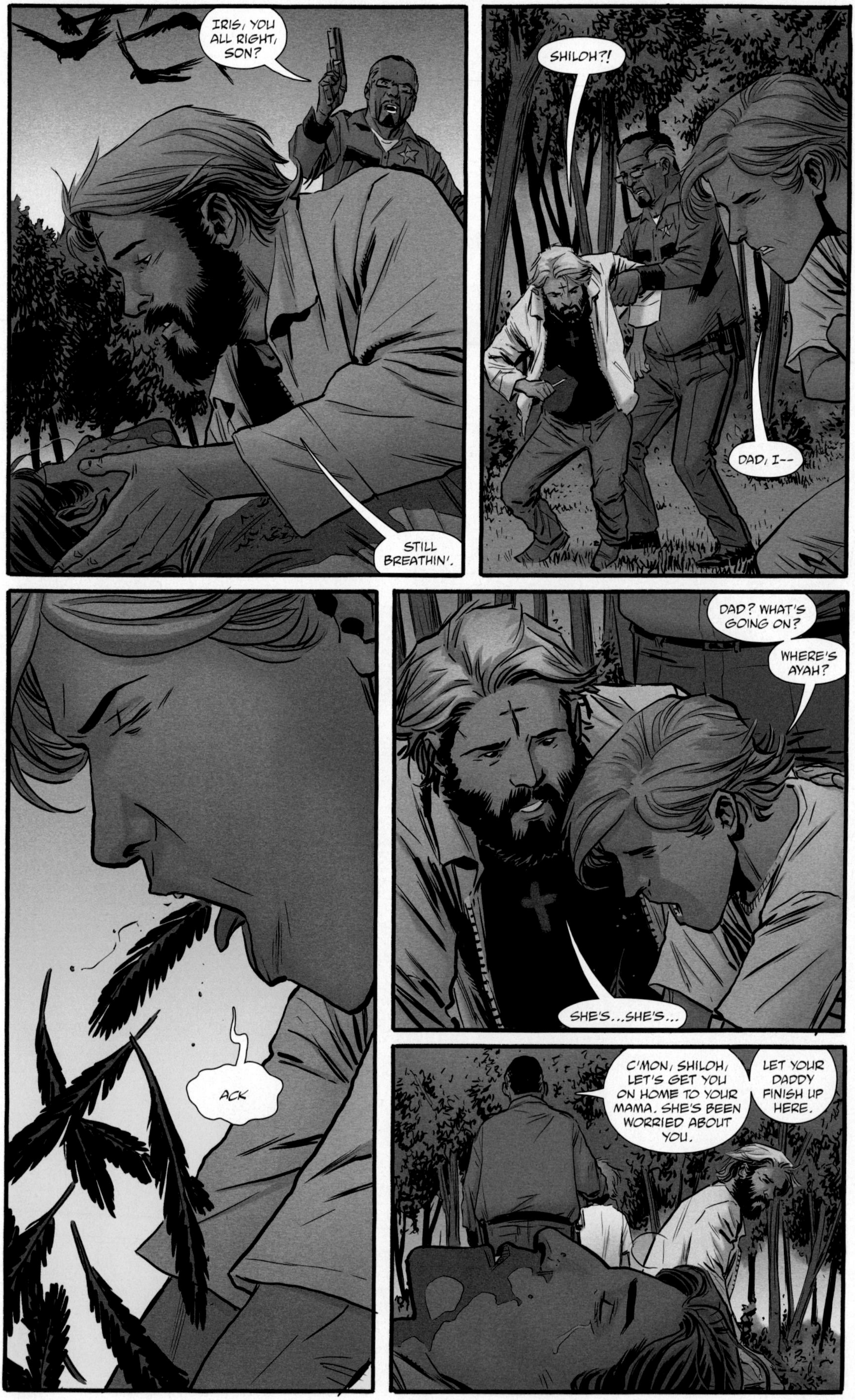
IRIS, YOU ALL RIGHT, SON?
STILL BREATHIN'.
SHILOH?!
DAD, I--
ACK
DAD? WHAT'S GOING ON?
WHERE'S AYAH?
SHE'S...SHE'S...
C'MON, SHILOH, LET'S GET YOU ON HOME TO YOUR MAMA. SHE'S BEEN WORRIED ABOUT YOU.
LET YOUR DADDY FINISH UP HERE.

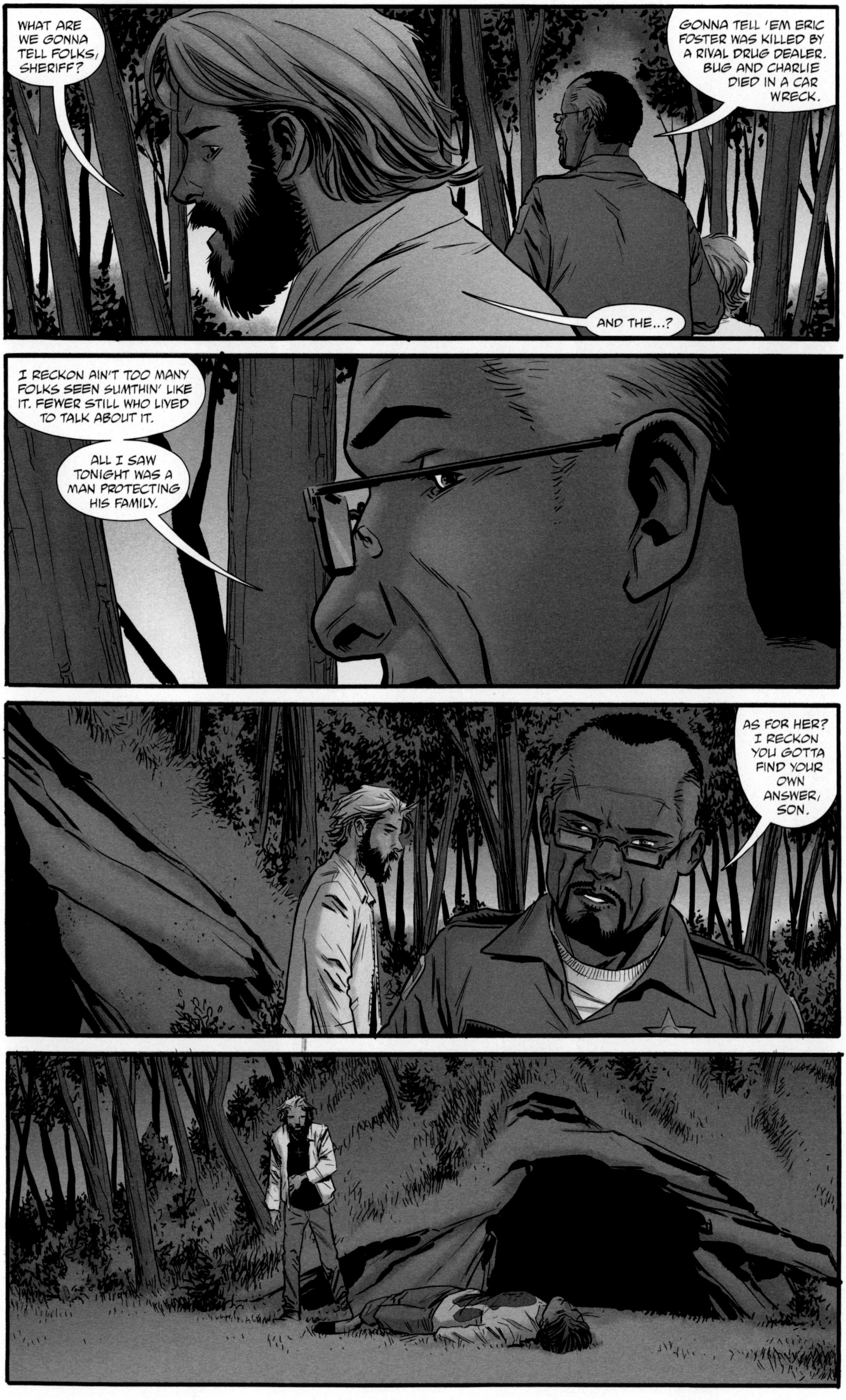
WHAT ARE WE GONNA TELL FOLKS, SHERIFF?
GONNA TELL 'EM ERIC FOSTER WAS KILLED BY A RIVAL DRUG DEALER. BUG AND CHARLIE DIED IN A CAR WRECK.
AND THE...?
I RECKON AIN'T TOO MANY FOLKS SEEN SUMTHIN' LIKE IT. FEWER STILL WHO LIVED TO TALK ABOUT IT.
ALL I SAW TONIGHT WAS A MAN PROTECTING HIS FAMILY.
AS FOR HER? I RECKON YOU GOTTA FIND YOUR OWN ANSWER, SON.

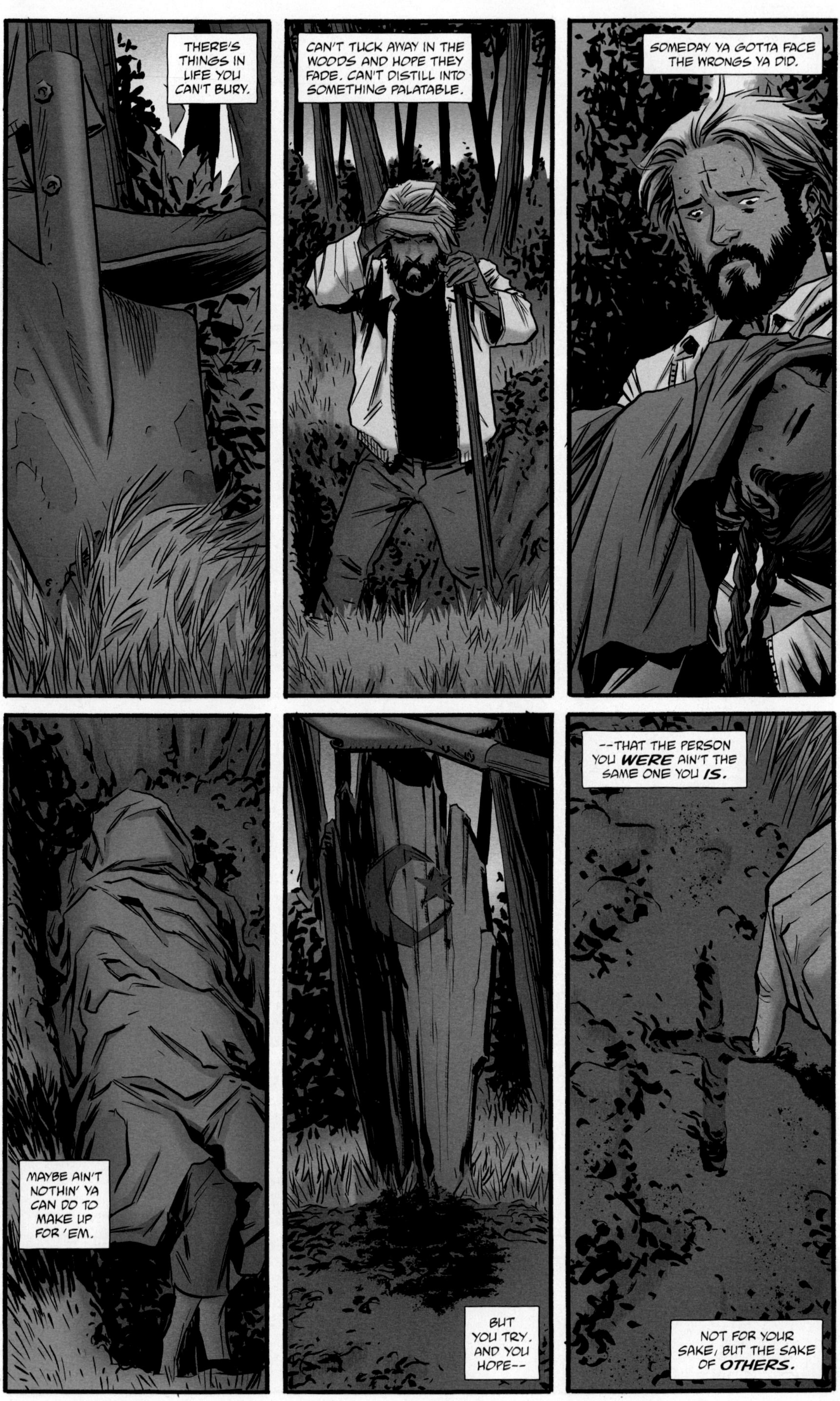
THERE'S THINGS IN LIFE YOU CAN'T BURY.
CAN'T TUCK AWAY IN THE WOODS AND HOPE THEY FADE. CAN'T DISTILL INTO SOMETHING PALATABLE.
SOMEDAY YA GOTTA FACE THE WRONGS YA DID.
MAYBE AIN'T NOTHIN' YA CAN DO TO MAKE UP FOR 'EM.
BUT YOU TRY. AND YOU HOPE--
--THAT THE PERSON YOU WERE AIN'T THE SAME ONE YOU IS.
NOT FOR YOUR SAKE, BUT THE SAKE OF OTHERS.

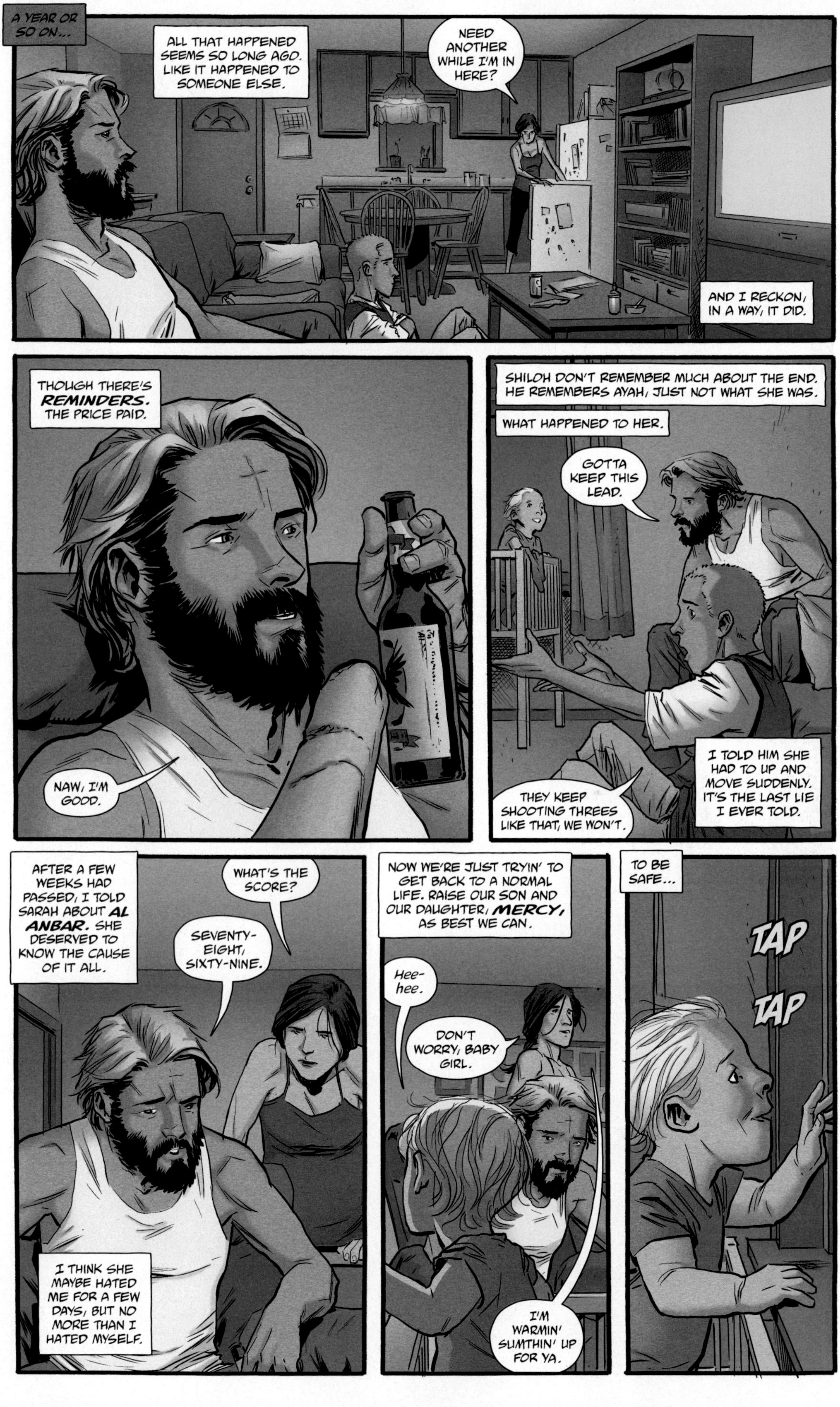
A YEAR OR SO ON...
ALL THAT HAPPENED SEEMS SO LONG AGO. LIKE IT HAPPENED TO SOMEONE ELSE.
NEED ANOTHER WHILE I'M IN HERE?
AND I RECKON, IN A WAY, IT DID.
THOUGH THERE'S **REMINDERS.** THE PRICE PAID.
NAW, I'M GOOD.
SHILOH DON'T REMEMBER MUCH ABOUT THE END. HE REMEMBERS AYAH, JUST NOT WHAT SHE WAS.
WHAT HAPPENED TO HER.
GOTTA KEEP THIS LEAD.
THEY KEEP SHOOTING THREES LIKE THAT, WE WON'T.
I TOLD HIM SHE HAD TO UP AND MOVE SUDDENLY. IT'S THE LAST LIE I EVER TOLD.
AFTER A FEW WEEKS HAD PASSED, I TOLD SARAH ABOUT **AL ANBAR.** SHE DESERVED TO KNOW THE CAUSE OF IT ALL.
WHAT'S THE SCORE?
SEVENTY-EIGHT, SIXTY-NINE.
I THINK SHE MAYBE HATED ME FOR A FEW DAYS, BUT NO MORE THAN I HATED MYSELF.
NOW WE'RE JUST TRYIN' TO GET BACK TO A NORMAL LIFE. RAISE OUR SON AND OUR DAUGHTER, **MERCY,** AS BEST WE CAN.
Hee-hee.
DON'T WORRY, BABY GIRL.
I'M WARMIN' SUMTHIN' UP FOR YA.
TO BE SAFE...
TAP
TAP

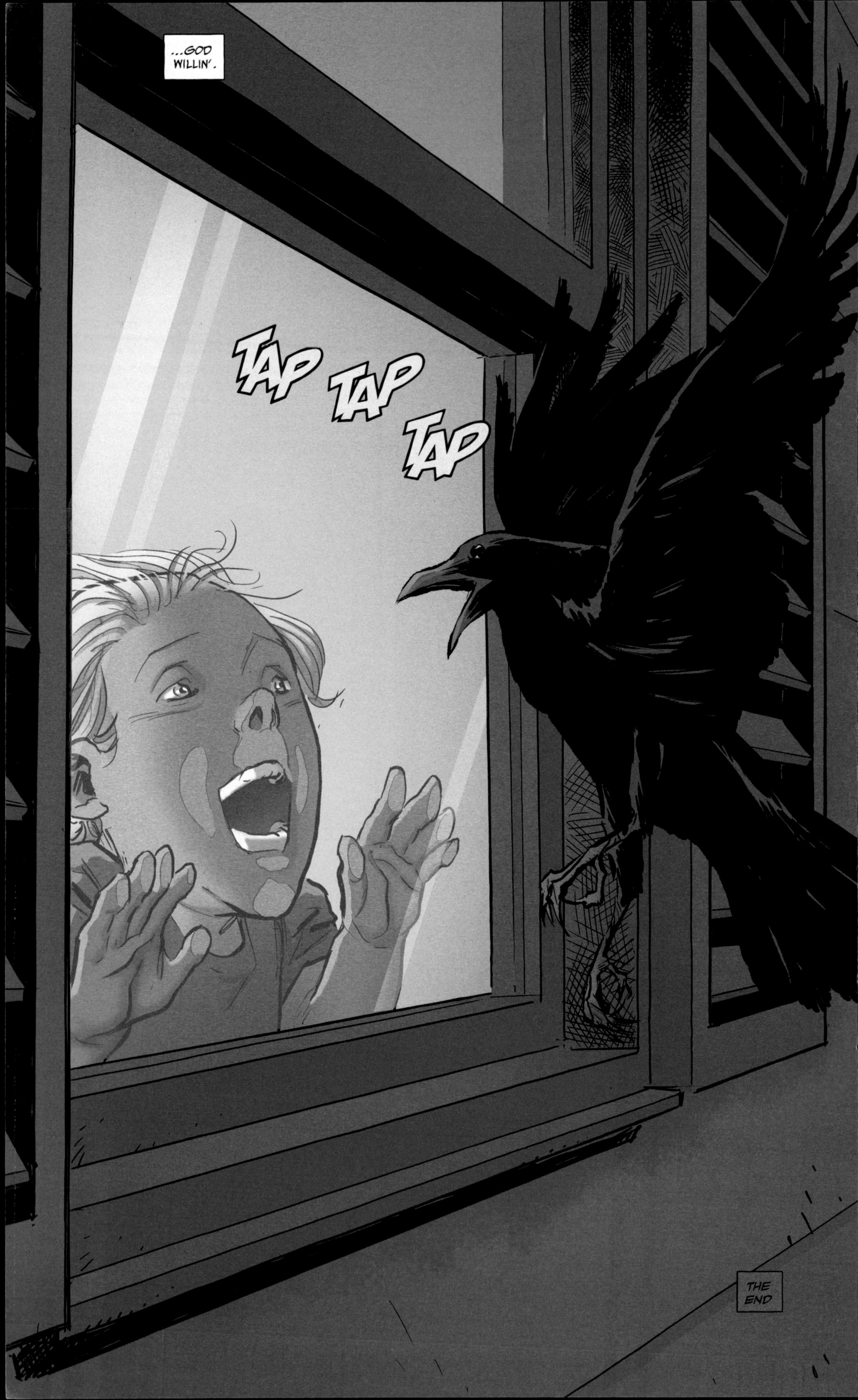
...GOD WILLIN'.
TAP TAP TAP
THE END

Promotional art for the series by
**Scott Godlewski**

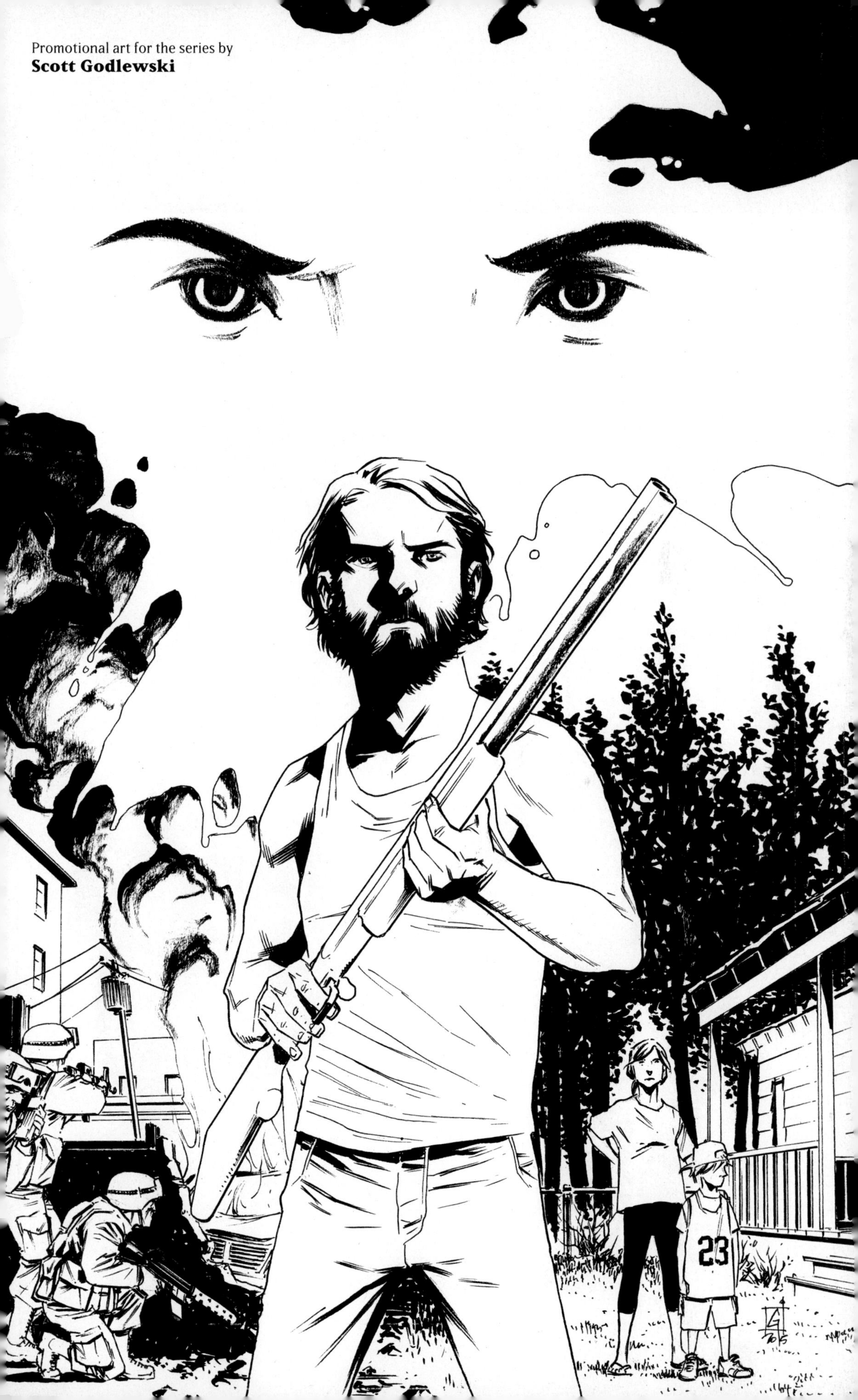
23

# THE CROW'S NEST

Character designs by **Scott Godlewski**

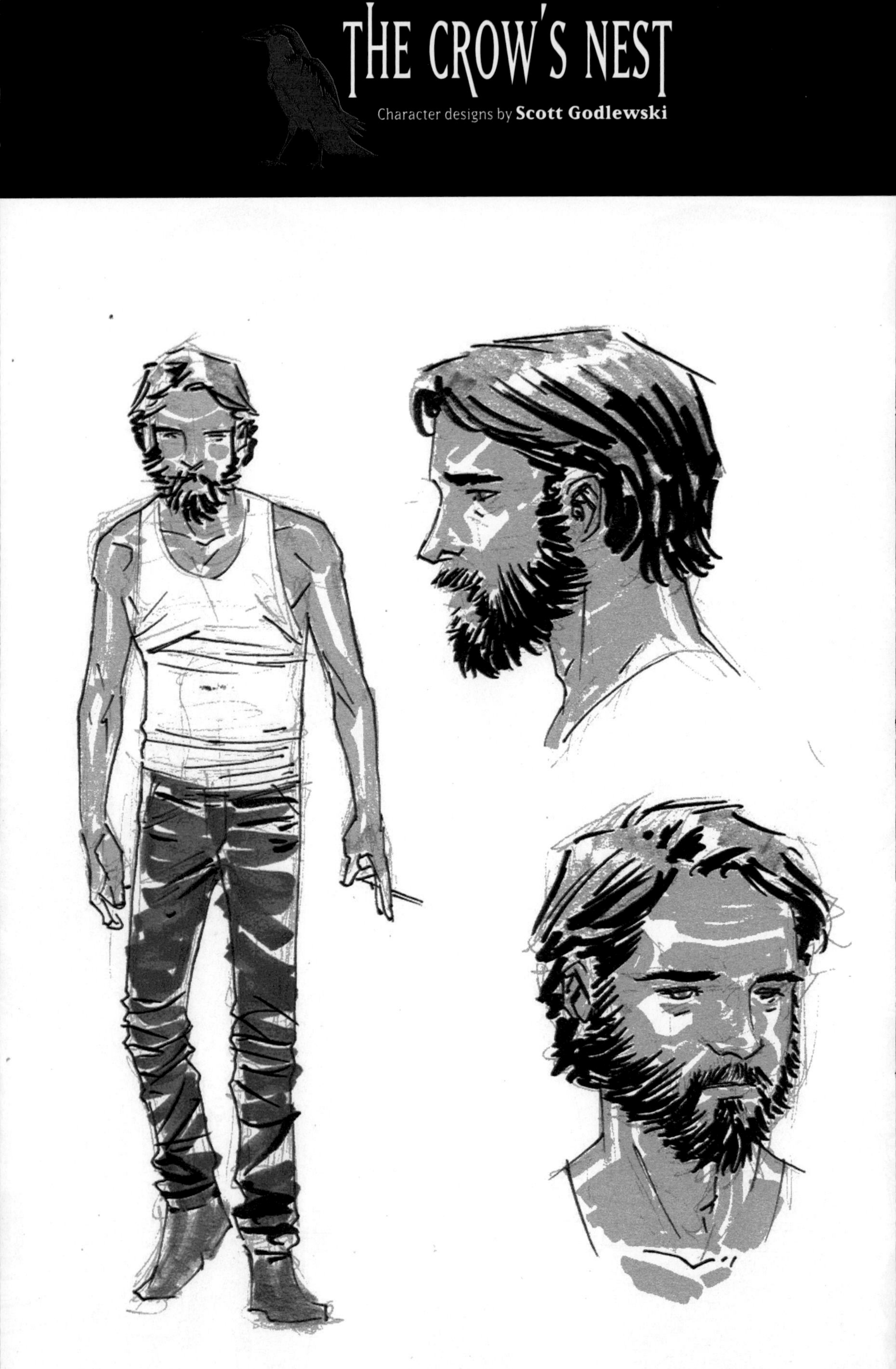

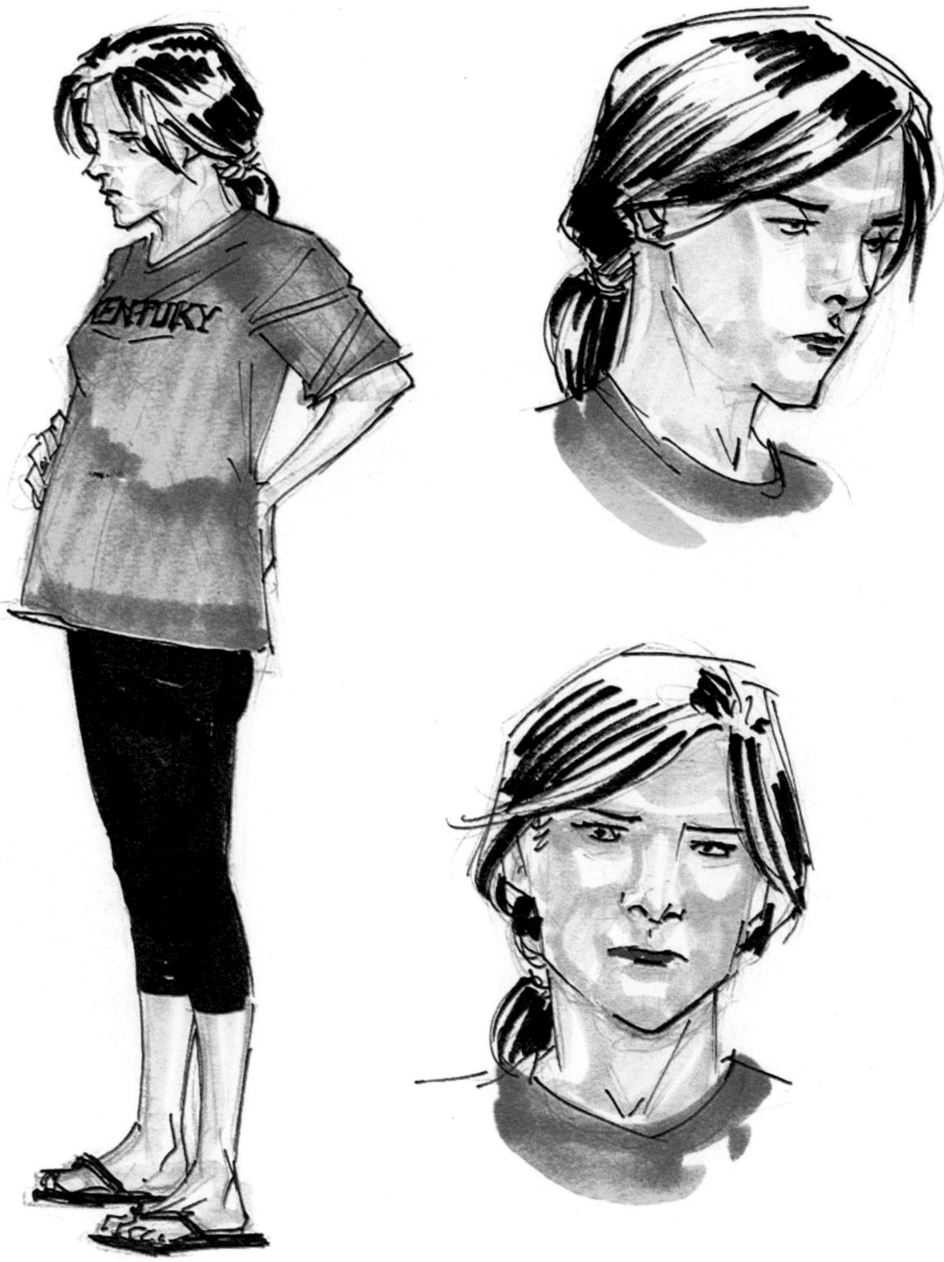

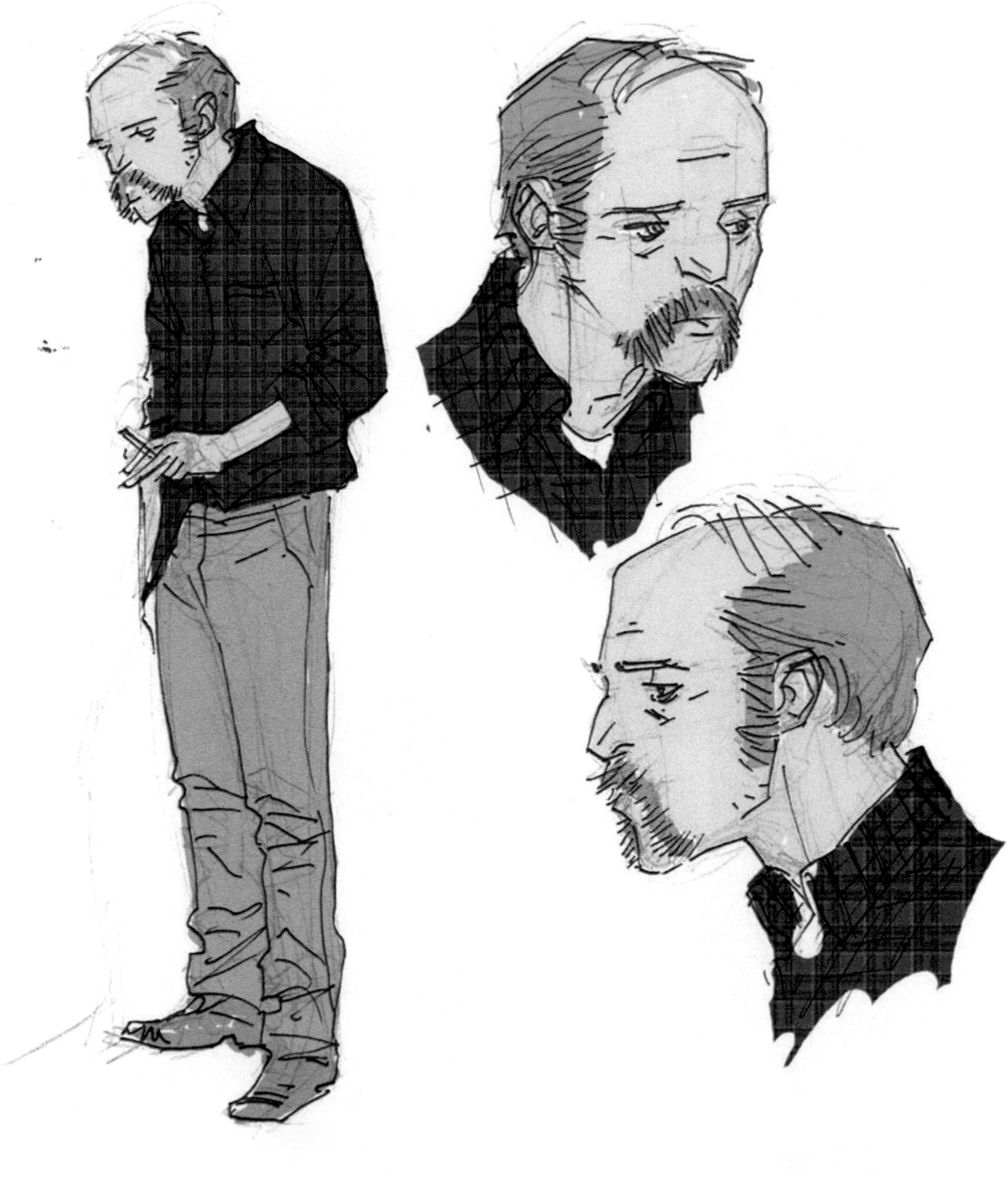

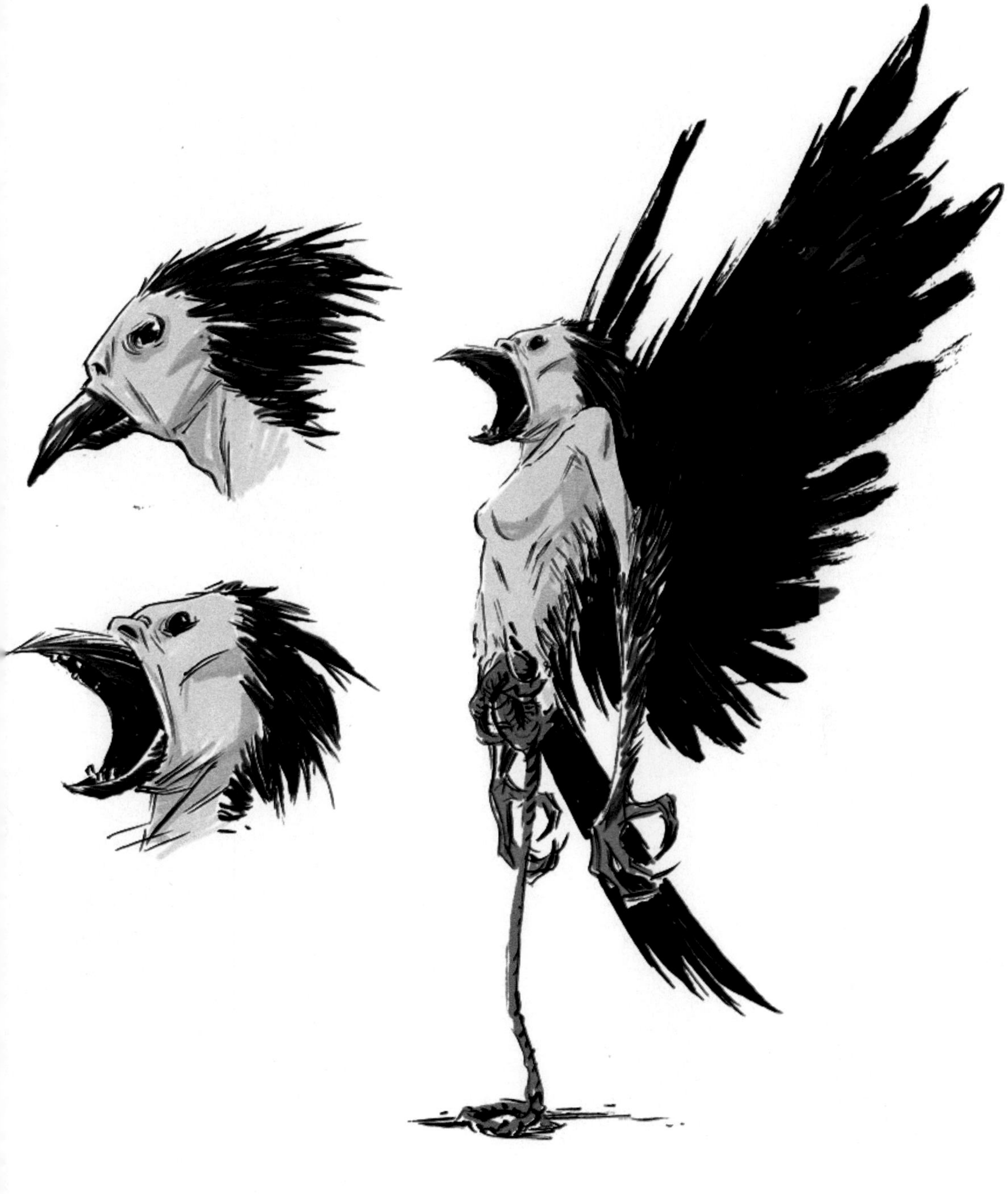

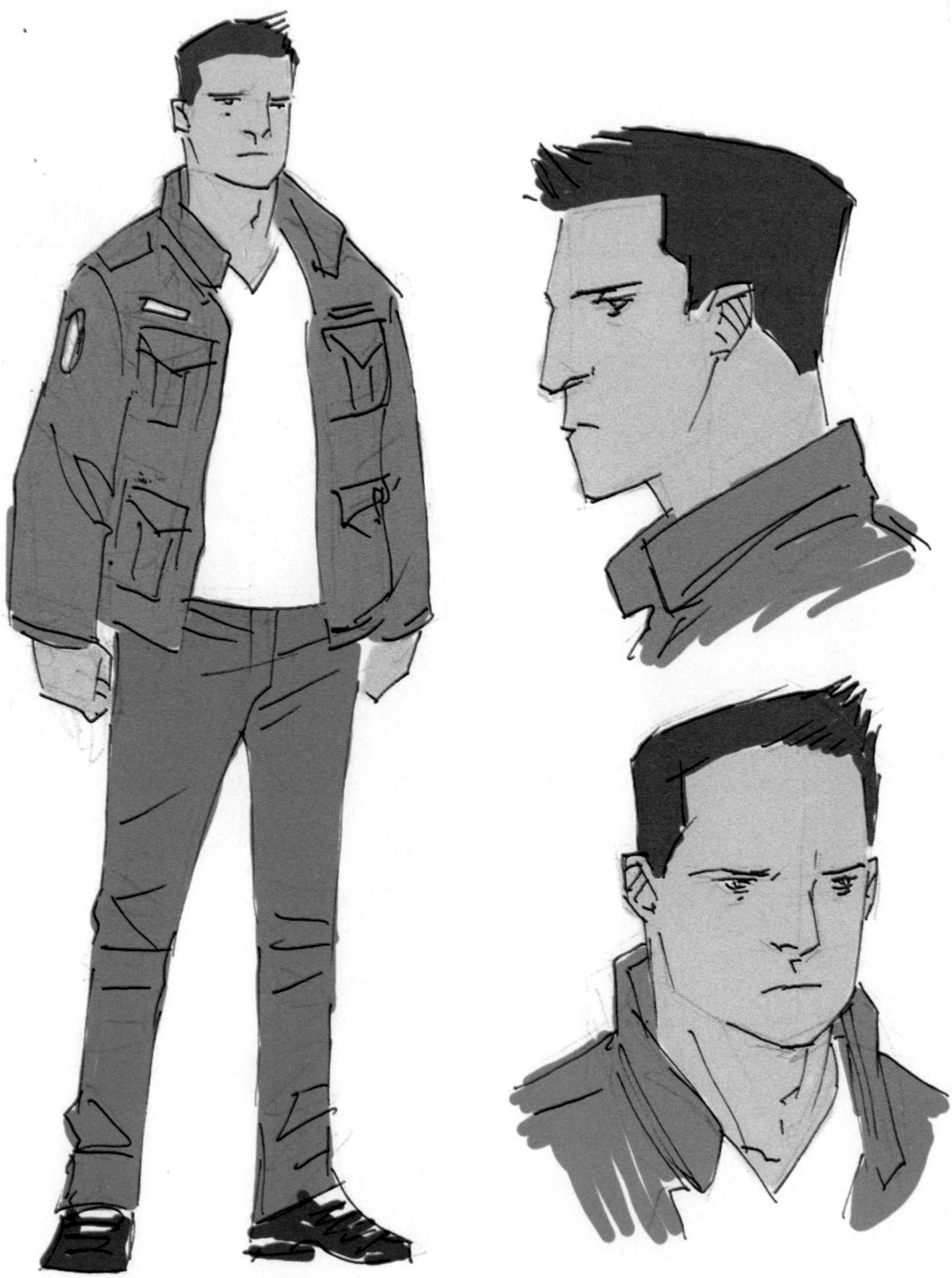

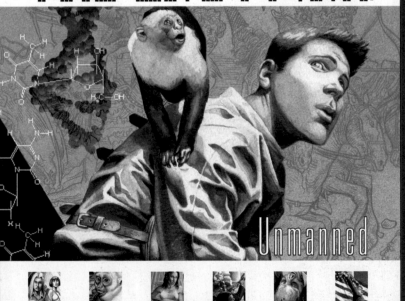

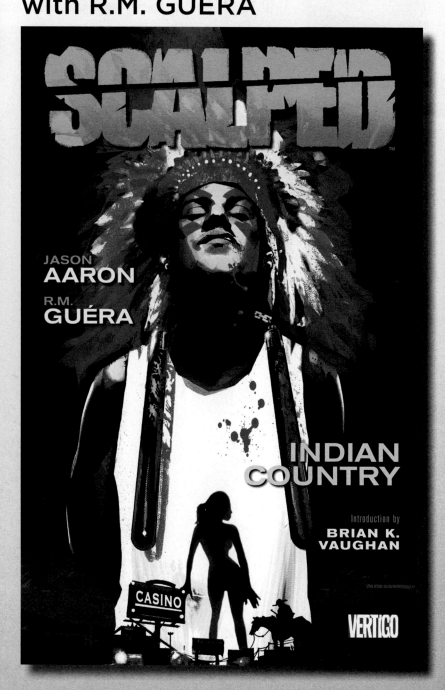